Conscience
and Dividends

THOMAS C. ODEN is Henry Anson Buttz Professor of Theology and Ethics at the Drew University Theological and Graduate Schools, Madison, New Jersey. He holds the Ph.D. from Yale University. Among his many other books are *Radical Obedience: The Ethics of Rudolf Bultmann*, *Beyond Revolution*, *Guilt Free*, and *Agenda for Theology*.

MARTIN E. MARTY is the Fairfax M. Cone Distinguished Service Professor of the History of Modern Christianity at the University of Chicago and associate editor of *The Christian Century*.

Conscience and Dividends

Churches and the Multinationals

Thomas C. Oden

Foreword by Martin E. Marty

Ethics and Public Policy Center
Washington, D.C.

Library of Congress Cataloging in Publication Data
Oden, Thomas C.
   Conscience and dividends.

   Bibliography: p.
   Includes index.
   1.   International business enterprises—Developing countries—Moral and ethical aspects.   I.   Title.
HD2932.035   1985   261.8′5   85-1581
ISBN 0-89633-089-3
ISBN 0-89633-090-7 (pbk.)

$15 cloth, $9 paper

*To Paul Hardin, Thomas W. Ogletree, Bard Thompson,
James E. Kirby, James M. Ault, J. Daniel Joyce,
Stephen F. England, and Merriman Cuninggim,
leaders of universities I have served
whose friendship and support have given me
the courage to dissent.*

Contents

(Continued on next page)

Foreword

By Martin E. Marty

THIS IS A STUDY of two sprawling and consequential multinational realities—business corporations and churches. Each wields vast power, and each has a multiple impact on social, economic, and political life in America and abroad. Everyone knows that the wealth of corporations is great, but few realize that the U.S. churches alone have total assets of some $200 billion. The potential for conflict or accommodation between the two dynamic institutions is great.

In recent years the emphasis has been on conflict. Through stockholder resolutions, meetings with corporate executives, boycotts, divestment of stock, and other means, the church-led corporate-responsibility movement has sought to persuade corporations to alter their policies, particularly in the Third World. Professor Oden here examines the origin, goals, accomplishments, and flaws of this movement. I congratulate him for tackling this complex and sensitive issue. It took more than a little courage.

The various audiences to which this book is addressed will, I believe, appreciate if not always agree with the author's judicious mixture of commitment, moral reasoning, and hard-headed factual analysis. The book will doubtless be read most avidly by mainline Protestants involved in the corporate-responsibility movement. A second audience will be corporate leaders whose duty it is to assess criticism from religious and other activists. A third group of readers are business executives who are practicing church members and can therefore be influential in both agencies under examination here. Fourth are the moral philosophers and theologians with a professional interest in these questions. In addition to these four specific audiences, the millions of church members who own stock are also potential readers.

Veterans of the corporate-responsibility conflicts can skim over some parts of the book. The question "who speaks for the church?" has been addressed repeatedly since Paul Ramsey's book by that name was published in 1967; Oden's discussion of it will be familiar territory to some readers. Moreover, Oden admits he is discussing a movement that is less radical and less potent than it was a decade ago and has indeed undergone some self-correction. Occasionally he throws in a pejorative term that does not advance his argument. The negative connotations of "Machiavelli," for example, do not strengthen his positive sentences about the new mood of chastened corporate-responsibility leaders.

Oden acknowledges that the corporate-responsibility movement has a legitimate mission and is changing, but he insists that further reform is essential if it is to be true to its highest goals. This position may make both church activists and business leaders uncomfortable.

He points out that the church itself as an agent of power is in an ambiguous position when it speaks out against corporate power and influence. After all, American churches own more than $20 billion in securities. He does not expect them to sit passively on the sidelines as corporations use that wealth in ways that the church activists believe have harmful social consequences. He criticizes chiefly mainline Protestant leaders who attack corporations, but he notes that the New Christian Right can play the same game. When it advocates boycotting products advertised on TV programs it does not like, the Christian Right is saying that corporations are not beyond the scope of moral censure.

Oden has the momentum and *Zeitgeist* in America with him. The opinion polls he cites show that most church members are unaware of the corporate-responsibility movement and when they find out about it do not like it or most of its stands. The romance has gone out of the movement that supported "simple living" in societies called underdeveloped. Given a chance the world's poor seem eager to live with the mixed benefits of technology that come with the corporations rather than with the less mixed blight of short and mean lives, unending drudgery, unnecessary pain and suffering, untreated disease. Oden seems to believe there are benighted pockets of the romantic Third World view in the movement, but there is abundant evidence that very few indeed still insist that a socialist revolution bears much promise for the poor or repressed.

If Oden is taking advantage of a new and, to him, better moment, the question is how he and his kith and camp can translate serious analysis and criticism into responsible behavior. Here is where the real value of this book lies. Oden successfully demonstrates that leadership of the movement is very often (a) unrepresentative, (b) ungrounded in the theological traditions it aspires to represent, and (c) inaccurate in many of its empirical assessments and its use of data. He provides just enough clues to what representation, grounding, and accuracy would look like to give constructive direction to newcomers on the corporate-responsibility scene and fresh motive, one hopes, for veterans to change their ways without losing their vocation.

There is no evidence that Oden thinks economic or political ideologues at the other end of the spectrum from the corporate-responsibility leaders will bring in the kingdom, find utopia, or transcend the limits inherent in politics. He knows and shows that decisions must be made, even if they are compromising, partial, and subject to later revision. For that reason it would be a pity if he were neglected by those he criticizes. And it would be a delight if he were to draw new people into informed participation in the complex and consequential world of multinational enterprise.

This study deserves serious attention in the corporate and ecclesiastical board rooms as well as in the business enterprises and churches of Main Street America. The issues of conscience are as much to the point as the issues of dividend. So they will remain.

Preface

THE TITLE WORDS *conscience* and *dividends* point to two broad communities of discourse: ethics and enterprise, deliberate moral awareness and the practical activities of business management. They also point to two communities that sometimes come into stressful conflict: churches and corporations. Our arena of concern is the sensitive point at which church advocacy and global enterprise meet and at times collide.[1]

The five chapters of this book deal with five basic areas of inquiry:

1. *Definition:* What is the corporate-responsibility movement?

2. *Early history:* How did the movement develop in its formative period?

3. *Recent history:* How has the movement matured, and what are its current tendencies?

4. *Evaluation:* What is the fundamental intention of the movement, how adequate are its theological roots and moral understandings, and how effective has it been?

5. *Recommendations:* How can the movement increase its effectiveness?

My purpose is not to challenge the right of religious groups to influence corporations, but to improve the quality and democratic grounding of that influence. It is not to question whether churches as shareholders have a right to seek political change, but to improve the process by which consent is given for such activity. It is not to diminish the social witness of the churches, but to improve the quality of participation by churches. It is not to provide an apology for corporate power, but to search out firmer ground for church groups that seek to address corporate power with moral concerns. It is not to defend democratic capitalism uncritically, but to try to help it work better and more efficiently. It is not to constrict the free expression of Christian social conscience, but to seek a fuller expression of it.

We rightly have high expectations of those who speak to society on behalf of the church. We want them to declare the great Western religious and moral imperatives in public places with historical awareness, factual accuracy, compassion for all, and understanding of those with whom they may disagree. Among these moral imperatives are: truth-telling, respect for persons, care for the poor and defenseless, social tranquility and stability, order and continuity, the protection of basic human freedoms, and the curbing of unjust political and economic power.[2] The prevailing expectation is that groups representing Christian churches publicly will gather facts accurately, think rigorously about moral principles, plant their roots deeply in historic religious wisdom, make prudent applications to existing situations, and acquire a realistic grasp of political necessities. When they do not do so, we must ask why.

Since 1970, numerous American church advocates have been deeply involved in the critique of corporate power, especially transnational corporate power. We will ask whether they have got their facts straight, whether they have been deeply rooted in Christian Scripture and tradition, whether they have reasoned ethically in a way that is useful to policy-making, whether they have had an appropriate historical perspective on contemporary problems and a realistic awareness of political realities, and whether their activities have been effective.[3]

Organized religion has a significant—though difficult to define—role in political and economic affairs. Church agencies make highly visible public pronouncements, appear to represent vast constituencies (though their views may or may not in fact be representative), at times take strongly confrontational actions, and publish extensive research studies intended to influence legislative, administrative, and economic decisions. These public statements and actions need careful scrutiny, always by the church itself and at times by the society. If occasionally some church leaders, whether of the left or the right, speak as if they were the sole custodians of Western religious values, then it is fitting to examine the degree to which they manifest those values in their words and actions.

Twelve Areas of Interest

The output of church agencies, like that of all other bureaucracies, is vast. I have examined periodicals, books, testimony, articles, pamphlets, church documents, news releases, and correspondence. All this is documented in notes. In this research I focused on twelve areas:

1. Scientific public opinion polls about how people in general and church people in particular perceive the morality of corporate activity.

2. The voting and appointive procedures by which local congregations choose representatives to speak on their behalf about the church's responsibility in and for society, particularly with respect to corporate power.

3. Legislative procedures by which representatives of the laity and clergy draw up general mandates of social policy to guide church boards and agencies; the mandates themselves; and the way the mandates become variously interpreted.

4. The complex ways in which denominational agencies pool their resources for cooperative efforts, including the interflowing of staff and intricate modes of channeling funds through special task forces and research groups.

5. The level of surveillance exercised by authorizing and funding agencies to maintain quality in research, strategic planning, action, and publication.

6. The levels of accountability in ecumenical structures that provide services to denominational boards and agencies.

7. The important influence of American missionaries resident abroad, or former missionaries with extensive international contacts, who bring various international perspectives to the evaluation of what might otherwise seem to be domestic issues of corporate policy and social accountability.

8. The sometimes subtle, diffuse, hard-to-determine strand of socialist or quasi-Marxist economic analysis and historical interpretation that weaves in and out of the corporate-responsibility movement, often accompanied by earnest disclaimers.

9. The rhetoric of blame and the function of guilt in the American political conscience, and how these can be used to manipulate some audiences.

10. The role of individual conscience in the public activities of the church-agency representative, and the extent to which such a person is accountable both to a constituency and to his or her own conscience.

11. The influence of reporting by the communications media in the conflict between the churches and the multinationals, and the extent to which the media have been prone to distort one side or the other.

12. The decision-making processes of corporate boards, managers,

and stockholders as they assess claims and demands made by persons representing church constituencies.

Each of these twelve areas has been an important locus for gathering data in this project. We need to examine them all if we are to see the entire complex picture.

Where the Problems Lie

Much of the work of the corporate-responsibility movement has been done by mission boards and agencies of Protestant churches. Most of what these boards and agencies do is caring, responsible, and important, and merits the confidence of church members and of society. A small proportion, however, has raised such serious questions of accountability that it has hampered the laity's confidence in the larger mission effort. One ancillary, longer-range purpose of this study is to help restore confidence in the churches' homeland and worldwide mission and the agencies serving it, so that their funding can be adequate and firmly grounded. The only way that such a restoration of confidence can occur, however, is through a tough-minded, astringent cleanup of those parts of the system that do not meet the highest standards.

The debate over corporate responsibility abounds with rhetorical ploys intended to persuade the public that corporate activity is either wonderfully uncorrupted or irredeemably exploitative. Some critics say that the very engine that moves the system—the profit motive—is intrinsically evil, and that by its nature big business is socially destructive. It is not unusual for those who hold these views to imply, further, that socialist or quasi-socialist philosophy and practice are liberating and are on the side of the inevitable historical progress toward social justice.

On the other side, some corporate supporters view the enterprise uncritically, failing to see that corporations tend to rationalize their acquisitiveness under the guise of altruism or idealism. These advocates may view any questioning of corporate activity as subversive of the free-market system or even unpatriotic. Responsible criticism tries to find a sensible path between the two extreme positions.

This is not primarily an economic study of multinational corporations. It is an empirical and ethical evaluation of the adequacy and effectiveness of church statements and actions toward multinationals. The churches must be willing to subject their own views to the kind of searching criticism to which they have subjected the corporations. The Presbyterian Task Force on Transnational Corporations (1983) correctly called upon the church to be "willing to examine its own character and behavior" by the "same rigorous criteria it applies to the economic transnational corporation":

> Jesus spoke of those who could clearly discern the speck in their brother's eye but were blind to the splinter in their own. They were called hypocrites, in that day as well as this, and no defect of character is more infuriating to those who are on the receiving end of advice from sources unwilling to acknowledge imperfections.[4]

Among the charges against the corporate-responsibility movement that we shall examine are that facts have been skewed to fit ideological presuppositions; that historical developments have been ignored or misunderstood; that political prudence has been badly lacking; that Scripture and tradition have largely been ignored; that religious and ethical imperatives have been misconceived or publicly misrepresented; and that the movement has tended to respond paranoically to its critics.

I am grateful for searching critical responses to this study from Thomas W. Ogletree, Paul Hardin, Donald G. Jones, John Ollom, James O'Kane, Howard Schomer, Finis Crutchfield, Timothy H. Smith, Gerald Anderson, Ernest W. Lefever, E. Stephen Hunt, Carol Griffith, and Tal Oden.

"Miss Dugan, will you send someone in here
who can distinguish right from wrong?"

The Challenge of the Multinationals

THE MULTINATIONAL CORPORATION has been defined by Isaiah Frank as "a company that operates in several foreign countries through affiliates that are subject to some degree of central control":

> The parent company's influence may be exercised in a wide variety of ways, including control over such strategic aspects of the affiliate's operations as pricing policies, choice of technology, appointment of key personnel, and determination of markets. The United Nations tends to favor the term *transnational* rather than *multinational* on the grounds that the former is more descriptive of the concept of a parent firm based in one country with operating affiliates in a number of foreign countries. The term *multinational* would then denote a company owned by several nationalities, whether or not it had affiliates in other countries. Actually, the preference for *transnational* is not merely technical; it also rests on the belief that the term more accurately reflects the quality of "domination" in the parent-subsidiary relationship in contrast with the implication of co-equality in *multinational*.[1]

The three terms transnational corporation (TNC), transnational business (TNB), and multinational corporation (MNC) are generally used interchangeably. MNC will be the preferred term in this study.

According to a 1981 World Council of Churches consultation, multinational corporations generally have two things in common: "Individually, they are centers of decision—and therefore of power—that operate in more than one country and that plan investment, production, marketing, finance, and prices on a transnational scale; collectively, they are the main agent of transnationalization of the development model characteristic of the industrialized West."[2]

The search for an adequate definition of the multinational corporation sometimes leads to technical criteria. One source defines the MNC as a corporation (1) with operations in six or more countries, (2) with at least 15 per cent of its assets, sales, or labor force resident abroad, (3) having an annual gross income of at least $100 million, and (4) frequently involved in high-technology industry.[3] Elsewhere one may find the MNC more loosely defined as "any firm which performs its main operations, either manufacture or the provision of service, in at least two countries."[4]

Misconceptions About Multinationals

Two widely held misconceptions about multinationals need to be corrected. The first is that they are only Western. In fact, some MNCs are based in socialist countries. According to a United Church of Christ report, "not all such enterprises are privately owned stock companies":

> There are cooperatives of state-owned enterprises, particularly in the centrally planned socialist economies, which carry on transnational business very much like that of the transnational companies in the liberal democratic societies of Western Europe, Australia, Japan, and North America. And there are private companies which are heavily supported by their home governments.[5]

Among developed market economies listed by the *United Nations Statistical Yearbook* as being centrally planned are Bulgaria, China, Czechoslovakia, the German Democratic Republic, Hungary, Poland, Romania, and the U.S.S.R.[6] In the business they do, these governments often function analogously to, and in competition with, MNCs.

The second misconception is that multinationals are primarily U.S. corporations. Surprisingly, among the world's 500 largest industrial corporations in 1979, more than half (281) were based in countries other than the United States. Japan had 71, the U.K. 51, Germany 37, France 27, and Canada 19. Other countries that had at least five such corporations include Switzerland, Italy, Sweden, Belgium, Spain, the Netherlands, and South Korea. South Africa had three, and Australia, Austria, India, and Turkey each had two. Even some countries that are usually considered less developed or a part of the "Third World" were listed as the country of origin for at least one of the world's 500 largest corporations: Argentina, Brazil, Chile, Mexico, the Netherlands Antilles, the Philippines, Taiwan, Venezuela, Zaire, and Zambia.[7]

The principal reasons why firms take the risks of entering into foreign operations are: to reduce production costs, to use available labor, to develop natural resources in a given locality, to increase the company's share of the market, to improve distribution and marketing of goods and service, to enhance technological development, and eventually to increase profits and dividends.[8] An *Economic Primer* produced in 1980 by the United Methodist Church Women's Division argued that such goals "serve only the interests of the multinational firm"[9] and inevitably stand in tension with the economic and social goals of the host country—"to increase national income, eliminate unemployment, achieve a balance between imports and exports, and improve income distribution."[10] Accordingly, "the repatriation of profits made in the host country by the multinational firm reduces the host country's national income and retards its capital formation."[11] "Repatriation of profits" means "the transferring of a multinational firm's after-tax earnings (or profits) made in a host country to its home country or where it is headquartered."[12] The impression is sometimes engendered by critics of multinational enterprise that MNCs only take money out of a country, that they provide no wages, resources, plants, technology, standards of production, or expertise to the host country.

How MNCs Can Aid Development

Other observers believe that the multinationals have a constructive contribution to make to world development and that they are a part of a new economic internationalism. Even though church corporate-responsibility advocates think of themselves as true *internationalists,* their initiatives almost always tend to reinforce *nationalism:* they support state power against the new international consciousness being fostered in part by the spread of technological expertise and economic development and expressed in part through transnational enterprise. The church activists seem often to prefer revolutionary rhetoric about exploitation to the process of technological diffusion and democratic change that is gradually taking place in many parts of the globe.[13] They are inclined to associate moral guilt with the new technological internationalism, to deplore computer abuses, technological intrusions, ecological imbalances, mass marketing, advertising misrepresentations, and in general what they regard as technological imperialism. Thus in an indirect way the church activists come off looking quite conservative, in that they seek to conserve the values of older configurations of state power while resisting technological innovation and the cooperative internationalism of free trade.

Less developed states are in great need of capital, and multinationals can help to meet this need both indirectly and directly. Over 85 per cent of the development funds for the Third World now comes from the United States and Western Europe; a much smaller proportion comes from the U.S.S.R., Saudi Arabia, and others. But where do the Western governments get these funds? Not from their own productivity, for governments do not create wealth. Governments get wealth by taxing enterprises that create wealth.

MNCs can also provide capital to LDCs directly. According to Father Theodore M. Hesburgh:

> Most governments—and especially most Third World govern-ments—do not have much flexibility in raising or providing capital, and in directing it toward specific tasks. But multinational corpora-tions do have this flexibility. . . . If a multinational does see a potential for a project in a Third World country, it can direct hundreds of millions of dollars, if need be, into making that project a reality.[14]

MNCs can further contribute to development in the Third World by lending a note of sober realism to an ideologically charged discussion. Church leaders and moralists have been notoriously ineffective in the area of economics, in large part because they have been tempted to stand back from morally complex situations and apply to them simple or absolute norms. Governments, too, can be unrealistic about eco-nomics. Since their money is earned for them by others, they are less attuned to the limits of its use. Governments that stay in power by votes may try to get the votes they need by making promises they cannot keep. As the momentum of voter demand rises, so may the level of government promises. Behind the promises lies the hope that someone else will somehow be creating the wealth that the government can tax to finance its promises.

Businesses cannot live as governments live, because they do not have the luxury of taxing. Their leaders make choices without the benefit of a safe haven. A company cannot make a profit unless its managers realistically assess markets, resources, labor, competitors' strengths, and the like. If the managers make too many miscalcula-tions, the company cannot survive.

This education in realism that business leaders undergo can be very useful in the attempt to relieve poverty and enhance social justice and peace in the Third World. The LDCs desperately need hard facts about what they can do—what crops to plant, what industries to develop, what resources to market. Especially in countries where protracted ideological clashes have intensified the economic difficulties—e.g., Lebanon, Northern Ireland, Ethiopia, the Sudan, Cambodia, Namibia, Iran, Iraq—business realism is urgently needed for economic development and societal renewal.

Father Hesburgh argues that "multinationals have understood interdependence better than any other entity in the world":

> They have certainly learned how to transfer funds; sometimes people say they do it too well and avoid all kinds of taxes. They have certainly learned how to transfer people to work across cultures. They have learned how to transfer technology in meaningful—and sometimes unmeaningful—ways. They have learned how to communicate across a whole world with a multitude of languages and cultures. They have learned to work with many different political systems, and in many cases they have learned to do so without being immoral about it, without resorting to bribery, and without necessarily changing their own standards and values. . . . If we are to achieve this goal of global development, I suggest that we need to employ the full capabilities of multinationals.[15]

There are about 150 nations in the world, and about three times that many multinational corporations. As some states are inordinately aggressive in creating troubles for others while others are responsible partners in the international community, so some corporations act badly and some act responsibly.

Yet multinationals have resources that can be used to help less developed countries reduce poverty, enhance the quality of life for their people, maintain peace, insure social stability, and promote viable development. They should be encouraged to do this.

CHAPTER ONE

The Corporate–
Responsibility Network

THIS EXAMINATION of the corporate-responsibility movement
will be limited as follows:

1. The focus will be more on Protestant than on Catholic forms of
corporate activism, though we will survey the Catholic forms and show
how they mesh with Protestant initiatives.

2. Primary attention will be paid to North American churches.
Since the subject is the churches' responses to multinational enterprise,
however, we will often speak of matters in other countries, such as
South Africa, Korea, and Chile, and of international church bodies,
such as the World Council of Churches, whose actions in this area
affect American church responses.

3. The focus will be more on the mainline churches associated with
the National Council of Churches than on the conservative evangelicals
(who deserve quite separate treatment), though we will occasionally
show how evangelicals relate to the corporate-responsibility movement.

4. The study will deal with church responses to multinational corporations, not to corporations in general.

5. The focus will be upon official church documents and public
actions by church agencies that confront or address multinationals, not
upon individual opinions on business ethics or corporate morality.

Michael J. Francis and Cecilia G. Manrique have summarized the
key points of current debate on multinational corporations (MNCs):

Do MNCs raise or lower less-developed countries' employment
levels and skills? Do high levels of MNC technology lead to high
levels of employment and development in LDCs (less-developed
countries)? Luxury goods or basic consumer goods? What is the role
of MNC advertising and LDC free choice? Can and should LDCs

7

control MNC operations, or is a free enterprise system desirable? Does MNC transfer of technology benefit the host country? Should the relationship of MNC to LDC be a matter of governmental concern? Do MNCs compete responsibly? Are LDC codes, international codes, or internal MNC codes desirable? Do MNCs export or import capital? What is the impact of MNC operations on balancing payments problems in LDCs?[1]

These important questions are largely beyond the range of our inquiry, though some of them will weave in and out of it. The primary task of this study is not to debate such issues but to see what the churches have said about them.

FINANCIAL POWER OF CHURCHES AND CORPORATIONS

The following facts about churches and corporations will show the magnitude of the financial power on both sides:

• According to Donald G. Jones, the total wealth of all churches in the United States, including real estate and portfolio investments, was estimated in 1982 at $200 billion.[2]

• This exceeded the combined assets of the four largest U.S. industrial corporations: Exxon, $62 billion; GM, $45 billion; IBM, $37 billion; and Mobil, $35 billion—a total of $179 billion.[3]

• According to David Vogel, the churches are second only to the federal government in monies received and distributed annually.[4]

• Howard Schomer wrote in 1979 that the total annual income of U.S. churches was at that time more than $20 billion, of which 80 per cent was in voluntary contributions by 110 million members (approximately half the population), guided by 400,000 full-time ministerial leaders.[5] The average annual voluntary contribution per church member is approximately $150.[6]

• More than one million buildings in the United States house religious activities; the real estate value of this has been estimated at $110 billion. Since the church membership figure is about 110 million, the churches own approximately $1,000 worth of real estate per member.[7]

• The nation's 360,000 Protestant churches hold approximately $22 billion in securities. About 5 per cent of the churches' annual income is from the earnings of endowment funds.[8] The Episcopal Church alone owns approximately $1 billion in corporate securities.[9] The United Methodist Pension Fund assets were reported in 1983 as nearly $1.5

billion.[10] Agencies associated with the National Council of Churches' Interfaith Center on Corporate Responsibility have over $7 billion in investments.[11]

• Although cumulative church assets are huge, they are far less than cumulative assets of major multinational corporations. If the aggregate value of all church real estate, endowments, and other assets may be roughly estimated at $200 billion, that is still less than the combined assets of the seven largest U.S. oil corporations (Exxon, Mobil, Texaco, Standard Oil of Indiana, Standard Oil of California, Gulf Oil, and Atlantic Richfield).[12]

• Sales of the twelve largest MNCs amounted to $144 billion in one year—a figure far exceeding the total national income that year of the world's thirty-five poorest countries with their estimated one billion inhabitants.[13] "Over forty of the largest economic entities in the world are multinational corporations, not countries," according to Theodore M. Hesburgh.[14]

These figures leave no doubt that we are dealing with vast aggregates of financial power when we are thinking about the churches and the multinationals.

CHURCH-MEMBER ATTITUDES TOWARD CORPORATIONS

Church leaders must be given latitude to provide creative directions for their constituencies that go beyond popular demands or current attitudes. Yet it would be a sad misjudgment if church leaders failed to listen to what the polls reveal about constituency opinions. This has become a particularly urgent need in the area of corporate responsibility. If church CR (corporate-responsibility) advocates present themselves to corporations as representatives of their denominational constituencies, then we must find out whether American church members are indeed being fairly represented.

There are two major studies on church-member attitudes toward corporations, one done in 1976 and the other in 1981-82; both were conducted by the United Presbyterian Church, which in 1983 merged with the Presbyterian Church in the U.S. to form the Presbyterian Church (U.S.A.). It is a strongly probable hypothesis, though subject to further inquiry, that the Presbyterian data have broad relevance for the half dozen other Protestant denominations most deeply involved in corporate-responsibility activism (United Church of Christ, Episcopal, United Methodist, American Baptist, Lutheran Church in America, and Christian Church–Disciples of Christ), because their demographic and laity profiles are basically similar. This could not be said of other churches that are members of the National Council of Churches (NCC) but have remained relatively inactive in the CR movement, such as black Baptist and black Methodist churches and the nine Orthodox NCC member churches from various ethnic traditions.

In assessing support for church stockholder activism, we are interested primarily in the views of lay church members. Church CR advocates do not claim to represent the views of clergy in particular but rather those of denominational constituencies in general.

As early as March 1976, the United Presbyterian Church's Committee on Mission Responsibility Through Investment (MRTI) sought "an objective assessment of the views of Presbyterians on a number of issues related to investments."[15] There were 1,267 church-member responses to the survey, a return of 84 per cent of the 1,503 questionnaires sent.

When asked who should monitor business practices, 64 per cent designated the federal government; 66 per cent, state government; 66 per cent, local government; 65 per cent, consumer groups; and 60 per cent, the businesses themselves, by self-regulation; only 32 per cent cited church groups.[16] There was little enthusiasm, then, for church groups' surveillance over business practices.

Members were asked: "To what extent would each of the following components be important to you as you make your decisions regarding investments?" The components and the percentage that called them "very important" were: stability and security of one's investment, 78 per cent; company profits, 64; return on one's investment, 63; company's products, 52; company's health and safety record, 39; ecology, 29; company's involvement in campaign financing, 20; company's advertising policies, 16; policies on women and minorities, 13; and company's activities in underdeveloped countries, 10.[17] These figures seem to suggest, not that Presbyterian laity are callous and insensitive, but that they want profits and security from their investments and hope that these major purposes of investments can be balanced with other social goods. To the question "how important is the advice of church agencies" in making investment decisions, a slender 8 per cent answered "very important."[18]

When asked, "To what extent should the church be concerned with each of the following business activities?" the percentage who answered "to a great extent" were: environmental issues, 28 per cent; minority employment practices, 18; effects of multinational corporations in underdeveloped countries, 17; military production, 10; and political campaigns, 8.[19]

The results of a more detailed questionnaire commissioned by the 1979 Presbyterian General Assembly and carried out by a Task Force on Transnational Corporations were published in 1983. There were 695 respondents, 51 per cent of 1,360 in the sample. Respondents included "members," "elders" (lay church leaders), and "pastors" (clergy). Each group was polled and reported separately. The results of this research bear heavily upon the conclusions of this study. Among the most important are:

1. *Attitudes Toward Corporations*

Approximately one in five church members "works for or is retired from a transnational corporation." In some synods the ratio is as high as one in three.[20]

"Majorities of every sample [members, elders, and clergy] clearly agree" that "American corporations are usually welcomed in the less developed countries because of jobs, capital, and technology they bring."[21]

Less than one-fifth (19 per cent) "of members believe that American corporations exploit the resources of other countries unfairly."[22]

"Relatively few of the members and elders (about 20 per cent) say that transnational corporations foster inequity among Americans."[23] A majority of members believe that multinational corporations "help underdeveloped countries," "serve American society well," and "create a better future for the world."[24]

Less than half of the church members think MNCs are inordinately "secretive," or that they "manipulate governments."[25]

"Thirty-nine per cent of members believe that corporations are overly regulated by government."[26]

2. *Church Investment Policies*

"At least two-thirds of the members and elders would probably invest in a corporation with a strong commitment to nuclear power generation (as would more than one-half of the pastors)."[27]

"Almost six of every ten members and elders would probably invest in a corporation that had successfully fought off unionization."[28]

After many years of active church teaching against doing business in South Africa, two out of five members "would probably or definitely invest in a corporation doing business in South Africa."[29]

3. *Monitoring Corporations*

The finding of the Presbyterian task force most relevant to our study is that only about one-third of the members "believe it appropriate for a congregation" or "a higher judicatory" (some agency or board of a synod or of the general church) to engage in "stockholder actions."[30] The single strategy to which the corporate-responsibility movement has given most of its energies over two decades, proxy challenges, apparently has the support of only a third of the Presbyterians surveyed.

"Even smaller groups of members and elders (less than one-third) and slightly less than half of the pastors think it is appropriate for congregations to encourage boycotts, etc. or to participate in demonstrations or other highly visible public actions."[31]

"Approximately six of every ten respondents rate the work of the judicatories in encouraging change in the activities of transnational corporations" as being "of little or no use, with clergy respondents being only slightly more positive than lay persons."[32]

"A bare majority (55 per cent) agreed" that investment should be used "as a means of seeking changes in corporate policies."[33]

"Nine out of every ten laypersons and eight of every ten clergy respondents" rate "the efforts of executives within a corporation" as being "very effective or somewhat effective" in bringing about constructive change in a corporation.[34]

A very small percentage of laity (6-7 per cent) think the churches should be engaged in "attempting to create test cases for court action."[35]

"The widest base of support exists for encouraging corporate executives in the congregation to appeal to other corporate executives to change corporate policies"; almost half considered this an appropriate action.[36]

Yet less than half (41 per cent) of members deem it appropriate for "judicatory executives to make personal appeals to corporate executives."[37]

4. *Effectiveness of Education*

Have sustained attempts by corporate-responsibility committees been successful in educating local church members in this area? "Only one-fourth or less of the members and elders report having heard the relationship between faith and activities of transnational corporations mentioned" in sermons or church schools.[38]

"Ninety-one per cent of members said that neither transnational corporations nor the church's response to their policies and practices have been an issue in their congregation in the last several years."[39]

One-fifth of the members had at some time participated in a boycott campaign.[40] But only 2 per cent had taken part in a public protest against a company.[41]

Fifty-one per cent of members believe that "concern about transnational corporations has created tension" in the church.[42] "Members were equally divided between those who believe, at least to some extent, that the church should be involved with TNC concerns and those who believe only to a slight extent or not at all that the church should be so involved."[43]

The data point to an important difference between clergy and laity, said the report: church professionals are "oriented to focus primarily on the just distribution of wealth, while most of the laity are occupied with the enormously difficult tasks related to its production."[44] This has created (or intensified) tension between clergy and laity over the question of Christian responsibility toward multinational corporations.[45]

INTERFAITH CENTER ON CORPORATE RESPONSIBILITY

Central to the CR network is the Interfaith Center on Corporate Responsibility (ICCR), a coalition of twenty-two Protestant denominational boards and agencies and twenty-two Catholic religious communities, archidioceses, and coalitions (the latter including some 170 Roman Catholic orders and dioceses).[46] (These are 1982 figures.) The ICCR serves in "a central information, research, and technical assistance capacity" and "as an arena in which these groups coordinate strategy and activity on corporate-responsibility issues."[47] It has seven subgroups focused on militarism, international health, international justice, energy and environment, domestic equality, community reinvestment, and systemic analysis.

Formed in 1974, the ICCR grew out of a merger between the Corporate Information Center, a research arm of the National Council of Churches, and the Interfaith Committee on Social Responsibility in Investments. The ICCR is considered a "sponsor-related movement" of the National Council of Churches. The ICCR describes itself as "an organization of church and religious institutional investors concerned about the social impact of corporations and the application of social criteria to investments."[48] Its member agencies "agree that as investors in companies they are also part owners and therefore have the right and obligation to monitor social responsibility of corporations and act where necessary to prevent or correct corporate policies or practices causing social injury."[49]

The work of the ICCR was described in the 1983 Presbyterian Task Force report in this way:

> The ICCR style of operation is not generally well understood. "ICCR" owns no stock, files no shareholder resolutions, and takes no positions. It is literally an arena for coordinating strategies ecumenically and not an ecumenical vehicle acting on behalf of its supporters. Group members send representatives to ICCR working groups to pool issue, concern, and action intentions. On the basis of the agreements reached there, the ICCR staff does research and drafts shareholder resolutions on the matters selected and assists in arranging delegations to discuss or negotiate with management, in the solicitation of proxy support for resolutions or the coordination of presentations at annual meetings of shareholders.[50]

The income of the ICCR derives principally from annual contributions from the constituency-supported budgets of member agencies. The annual minimum for voting membership on the governing board is $1,000 ($1,500 for coalitions). The 1982 budget was $478,839; of this, $326,967 came from member agencies, $45,000 from foundations, and the rest from individual gifts, subscriptions, sales, and other sources.[51]

Each ICCR member agency may name up to four representatives to the ICCR governing board. On the full-time staff as of July 1, 1983, eight persons had leadership roles: Timothy Smith, executive director; Dara Gardner Demmings, Valerie Heinonen, Leah Margulies, Keith Rolland, Edward Baer, and Carol Somplatsky-Jarman, program associates; and Diane Bratcher, manager of publications and budget. (Timothy Smith will be a frequently encountered figure in this account of the CR movement. To distinguish him from a church historian with the same name, I will refer to the ICCR head as T. H. Smith.)

PROTESTANT PARTICIPANTS IN THE NETWORK

A description of one ICCR member agency may serve as a useful example of how the members and related groups intermesh. This description refers to the pre-merger United Presbyterian Church in the U.S.A.; the information is generally true for the new Presbyterian Church (U.S.A.) also, though some names have changed.

The principal Presbyterian agency for corporate-responsibility activities is MRTI—Mission Responsibility Through Investment, a subcommittee of the General Assembly Mission Council (GAMC). MRTI's recommendations "must be submitted to and approved by the GAMC before they can be acted on, unless the GAMC has specifically delegated authority to act."[52] However, MRTI's membership is made up primarily from the pool of Presbyterian agency representatives already in residence at the Interchurch Center, the New York City building that houses the NCC and many denominational agencies. "Membership comes from the GAMC; Board of Pensions; United Presbyterian Foundation; Program and Support Agencies; and the Councils on Church and Race, Women and the Church, Church and Society, and Discipleship and Worship."[53] Therefore anyone who is not already a bureaucratic insider is hardly likely to be appointed to the corporate-responsibility agency.

The 1983 Presbyterian Task Force report commented tactfully on MRTI:

> Something over 100 resolutions are now filed annually in the ICCR context, and MRTI makes a formal recommendation on each of them for the guidance of the church's investment-holding agencies. The number involved and the complexity of some of the resolutions is a considerable call on the limited capacities of the MRTI system. The nature of the ICCR system and the absence of any accountable relationship between ICCR and MRTI create other difficulties in the operation of this substantial strategy.[54]

Investment committees of denominational agencies function according to guidelines that differ somewhat among the denominations but on the whole are quite similar.[55] Major statements on investment criteria and theological rationales have been developed by the United Church of Christ,[56] the (former) United Presbyterian Church,[57] the United Methodist Church,[58] and other bodies.[59] Typical of these is the Presbyterian assertion that "church investment is an instrument of mission and includes theological, social, and ethical considerations," and that "it is appropriate that the church's own determination of how social problems should be resolved should guide institutions within the church in reviewing their investment policies."[60]

The corporate-responsibility network extends throughout various agencies of NCC denominations. For example, among the Presbyterians: "Though the activity of MRTI is the most clearly focused and visible point of the church-TNC [transnational corporation] institutional intersection, the programmatic activity and relationships of the Program Agency constitute the predominant continuing avenue where programs and issues affecting the role and interests of TNC's are addressed." So the work is "not carried on in a clearly focused location—office, department, or division. Such activity is very widely spread in the agency, occurring in the work of nearly every division, and often in many departments of the same division."[61]

Among the Protestant ICCR member agencies are:

• Church of the Brethren Pension Board (1451 Dundee Ave., Elgin, Ill. 60120).

• American Baptist Churches in the U.S.A. (Valley Forge, Pa. 19481).

• Committee on Social Responsibility in Investments of the Executive Council of the Episcopal Church (815 Second Avenue, New York, N.Y. 10017).

The most influential Protestant member agencies, however, are located in one building, the Interchurch Center (475 Riverside Drive, New York, N.Y. 10115). Among these are:

• General Board of Global Ministries of the United Methodist Church.

• Church Women United.

• Reformed Church in America.

• Mission Responsibility Through Investment committee of the Presbyterian Church (U.S.A.), General Assembly Mission Council.

Twice as many NCC member bodies have chosen not to participate formally in the ICCR as have chosen to participate: only eleven of the thirty-two NCC constituent bodies are active members. Among the NCC members that are not members are: the Moravian Church in America, National Baptist Convention of America, African Methodist

Episcopal (AME) Church, AME Zion Church, Christian Methodist Episcopal Church, Armenian Church of America, Hungarian Reformed Church in America, and all the Orthodox bodies (Antiochian, Coptic, Greek, Russian, Serbian, Syrian, and Ukrainian).

The church traditions most engergetically involved in the CR movement are those that were most active in the "social gospel" movement during the first half of the twentieth century: United Church of Christ, United Methodists, United Presbyterians, Christian Church (Disciples of Christ), Episcopalians, and American Baptists. Participating somewhat less are the Lutherans of some synods, the Friends, the Reformed Church in America, and the Church of the Brethren. Some ICCR members are not members of the NCC; an example is the Unitarian Universalists, who do not assent to the NCC confession. Among NCC constituent bodies, the one with the most extensive representation in the ICCR is the United Methodist Church; four of its agencies (the Church and Society board and three divisions of the Global Ministries board: National, Women's, and World) offer financial support, expertise, and technical assistance to the ICCR, and it therefore is entitled to sixteen representatives on the ICCR governing board.[62]

Numerous Protestant bodies play no part whatever in the corporate-responsibility network. Among Lutherans there is no participation by the Missouri Synod (2.6 million members) and several other large synods. Many Presbyterian and Reformed church bodies, such as the Cumberland Presbyterians, Orthodox Presbyterians, and Christian Reformed, do not participate. In the Wesleyan family (United Methodist, Wesleyan, Free Methodist, African Methodist Episcopal [AME], AME Zion, Christian Methodist Episcopal, Salvation Army, Primitive Methodist, and Nazarene), only the United Methodist Church has participated extensively. There has been little involvement by Baptist bodies, except for the American Baptist Churches in the U.S.A.; few black Baptists have given the movement support, and there has been virtually none from America's largest Protestant denomination, the Southern Baptists (14 million members). The interest of the vast number of Pentecostal church congregations has been nil. Among other non-participants: Adventists, Churches of God, and Reformed Episcopal. The point here is that church corporate-responsibility spokesmen should not imply, as they sometimes have done, that they speak *generally* for American Protestant church constituencies.

CATHOLIC PARTICIPANTS IN THE NETWORK

Roman Catholic participants in the ICCR coalition are somewhat more scattered across the church, with most of the activity coming from study and action groups attached to orders, local congregations, and some diocesan staffs. These local Catholic members are also regionally defined, mainly in the belt of industrial cities stretching from Milwaukee to Washington, D.C. Very little Catholic corporate-responsibility activity occurs in the Sun Belt or Far West. Roman Catholic research and action groups are organized into loose regional coalitions and are fed information by the ICCR.[63]

Catholic involvement began early in 1973 when representatives of various groups were called together in Chicago by the National Federation of Priests Councils to explore options for action in the corporate arena. Father Joseph O'Rourke of the New York Jesuit province led in the formation of the National Catholic Coalition for Responsible Investment (NCCRI). In 1974 Capuchin Father Michael Crosby was named coordinator of NCCRI's regional groups.[64] Sister Regina Murphy of the Sisters of Charity of St. Vincent de Paul of New York was the first Catholic to chair the ICCR governing board.

Women religious (i.e., women belonging to religious orders) have taken the lead in Catholic corporate activism. They have initiated three times as many actions as men religious. One reason for this is that the Leadership Conference of Women Religious has stressed corporate-responsibility activity and has sought to get congregations to join ICCR regional coalitions.

In 1982 the ICCR listed 170 (sometimes reported as 180 or 200) Roman Catholic organizations as members. These organizations consist of religious orders, provinces of orders, or congregations within provinces, as well as archdioceses and dioceses. Usually several of these groups join in coalitions, but sometimes they hold individual memberships in the ICCR. Among the thirty-three archdioceses in the U.S. Catholic Church, only two have formally become ICCR members: Baltimore, led by Archbishop William D. Borders, and Milwaukee, led by Archbishop Rembert G. Weakland. Of the 149 dioceses, only four are members: Albany, New York, led by Bishop Howard J. Hubbard; Providence, Rhode Island, led by Bishop Louis E. Gelineau; Richmond, Virginia, led by Bishop Walter F. Sullivan; and Rockford, Illinois, led by Bishop Arthur J. O'Neill.

Religious orders, especially coalitions of local congregations of religious, make up the bulk of the Catholic corporate-responsibility network. Seldom do all segments of a religious order join; most orders are only sporadically involved through the activity of a few local congregations, or indirectly through a regional coalition. The Dominican fathers and women religious provide an example. Of the five Dominican provinces in the United States, the Province of St. Albert the Great (Chicago) is the only ICCR member. Among Dominican sisters, only eight of the thirty-six congregations and provincial houses belong to ICCR coalitions: St. Catharine of Siena (St. Catharine, Kentucky); The Most Holy Rosary (Sinisawa, Wisconsin); The Holy Cross (Amityville, New York); St. Catherine of Siena (Racine, Wisconsin); The Most Holy Rosary (Adrian, Michigan); The Immaculate Conception (Ossining, New York); The Sacred Heart of Jesus (Caldwell, New Jersey); and The Immaculate Heart of Mary (Akron, Ohio). The majority of male and female Dominicans have no association with the ICCR or the corporate-responsibility movement, and this situation is typical of other Catholic orders.

In addition to the Dominicans, the religious orders with relatively more activists in the CR movement are the Franciscan Fathers and Sisters, Holy Cross Brothers, Jesuits, Religious of the Sacred Heart, School Sisters of Notre Dame, Sisters of Charity, Sisters of Mercy, and Sisters of St. Joseph. As with the Dominicans, the segments of these orders that are ICCR members are congregations, provinces, and local groups of religious attached to diocesan operations. Less active, but holding membership in some numbers, are elements of the Benedictine Sisters, Capuchins, Sisters of Notre Dame de Namur, Sisters of Providence, and Ursuline Sisters. In addition, some segments of other Catholic religious orders are now or have been in some way involved, even if minimally, in corporate-responsibility activities. Among them are Adorers of the Blood of Christ, Augustinians, Carmelite Sisters, Glenmary Fathers, Immaculate Heart of Mary Sisters, Marist Fathers, Maryknoll Fathers and Sisters, Passionists, Premonstratensian Fathers, Presentation Sisters, Sulpician Fathers, Vincentian Fathers, and Xaverian Brothers.

Such a lengthy list appears impressive, particularly to those not familiar with the structure of the Catholic Church and the relative independence of its religious orders. In fact, however, the total number of corporate-responsibility activists is a very small percentage of Catholic religious, and a minuscule percentage of all American Catholics. The list is long because each Catholic member group is listed separately, even when it is a local or regional sub-unit of a larger organization. Separate listing emphasizes that each Catholic group has joined the network independently in its capacity as interested stockowner, not as a representative of the church or of an order, a procedure required by canon law. Most Franciscans, Dominicans, or Sisters of St. Joseph, for example, may know nothing about ICCR or the corporate-shareholder activities of some of their activist brothers and sisters.

Unfortunately, this does not deter the press from reporting (or the network from implying) that the ICCR unambiguously represents 170 Roman Catholic organizations. The impression repeatedly gained from the literature is that the ICCR was organized so as to be broadly representative of Roman Catholic opinion. A more accurate summary is that ICCR supplies research information and strategic coaching to many small groups of activist Catholic clergy and religious. These groups do not officially or unofficially represent Catholic opinion on corporate responsibility.

Catholic activity is not confined to the ICCR. Other Catholic social-action agencies have dealt with corporate issues, though their primary activities are not in that area. The most important of these is Network, a coalition with some 5,000 members. Most of the members are nuns, and the rest are priests, brothers, and laity. Network lobbies Congress and publishes ratings of the voting records of House and Senate members, primarily on issues that affect the poor, affirmative action, ERA, and disarmament. While it is not directly a part of the corporate-responsibility movement, Network is generally sympathetic with CR aims, and some of its members are involved in the CR movement. Also not part of the ICCR network but occasionally sympathetic or connected are many social-action staff members of archdioceses and dioceses, activist laity and parishes, and the social-action staffs of the United States Catholic Conference and the National Conference of Catholic Bishops. Together the members of these groups may outnumber Protestant corporate-responsibility activists.[65]

The Protestant and Catholic groups mentioned in this chapter make up the primary corporate-responsibility network. The more extensive secondary network is surveyed in appendix A, and appendix B lists twenty of the most influential CR leaders.

CHAPTER TWO

Encounter With the Multinationals: 1966-75

BY THE LATE 1960s the church activists' interest in multinational corporations was established. By 1970 it had turned into stockholder activism, which grew steadily more intense. The confrontational strategy peaked in the mid-seventies. Credibility of the movement hinged on the assumption that church advocates had constituency support and were duly authorized to speak, but by the late seventies this assumption had become a point of contention. Moderate church officials began to seek correctives for representational abuses, imprudent judgments, and excesses that had occurred earlier in the decade.

By 1980 a major reversal was in the making, both in American political life and in the political life of churches. New forms of political activism appeared among conservative evangelicals, and liberal church bureaucracies began to retrench. In the eighties, voices have increasingly called for clearer representational accountability and stricter surveillance of church boards and agencies whose activities have been at odds with substantial sectors of constituency opinion.

The latest and most thoroughgoing and theologically sound of these voices is the Presbyterian Task Force on Transnational Corporations. Its 1983 report—the single most important document of the movement—calls for a major redirection of corporate-responsibility activity away from a narrow focus upon stockholder proxy challenges, and toward more accurate constituency representation, a more balanced interpretation of corporate contributions to constructive social change, and more stress on the role of vocation in corporate ethics.

In this chapter we will examine the first half of the history of the corporate-responsibility movement, from its beginnings to the apex of

21

its influence in the mid-1970s. This early history will be divided into three periods: the early period of experimentation up to 1970, early stockholder actions of 1970-72, and the accelerating momentum of the movement to 1975. At the end of the chapter we will examine two initiatives that were typical of the corporate-responsibility movement at its peak, the southern Africa and Del Monte cases.

EARLY EXPERIMENTATION: TO 1970

Since the nineteenth century American churches have sought and had significant influence on business activity and corporate behavior. Evangelists like Charles Finney, Phoebe Palmer, Asa Mahan, D. L. Moody, and Billy Graham have addressed business leaders and economic power brokers with philanthropic challenges and moral claims.[1] Social-gospel leaders like Walter Rauschenbusch, Washington Gladden, Sherwood Eddy, and the young Reinhold Niebuhr tried to deal with systemic problems of poverty and the need for social change, and in doing so solicited support from enlightened business leaders. The tactic of the boycott, or selective patronage campaign, had been used by numerous Protestant denominations for decades before the birth of the corporate-responsibility movement. The issues of earlier boycotts included tobacco, liquor, gambling, prostitution, pornography, sabbath-breaking, child-labor practices, and racial injustices.[2]

Corporate responsibility is not an idea that social activists invented in the sixties. As early as 1952 the Methodist Discipline contained a pungent paragraph instructing the Council of World Service and Finance to "review the investment policies of each World Service agency with respect to permanent funds, and . . . require that Christian as well as sound economic principles in the handling of the investment funds be observed."[3] The 1964 Methodist Discipline went considerably further to state sharply that "the principle of diversification of investments shall be observed in order to obtain proper geographical and class distribution of investment commitments."[4]

In 1963 the National Council of Churches proposed that equity ownership in corporations might be used as leverage to influence their social conduct.[5] At that time the NCC asked member churches to review their investments and to "remove such investments from enterprises which cannot be persuaded to cease and desist from practicing racial discrimination."[6] Three years later (1966) the NCC's General Board more explicitly asserted that corporations "must accept accountability for the impact of their decisions on the whole society."[7] These are the beginnings of the so-called social audit of corporate decision-making by church groups.[8]

Kodak, Alinsky, and the Confrontational Model

The churches directly confronted corporate power in a steadily emerging pattern of shareholder actions. A decisive encounter occurred in 1967, when a labor dispute developed in Rochester, New York, between Eastman Kodak and its minority employees who belonged to an organization called FIGHT (Freedom-Integration-God-Honor-Today). The leader of FIGHT was Saul Alinsky, whom one writer has called the "middle-aged deus ex machina of American slum agitation."[9]

Kodak had already complied with the equal-opportunity provisions of the 1964 Civil Rights Act, had actively supported the United Negro College Fund, and had publicly cooperated with the Plan for Progress developed by President Kennedy's Commission on Equal Opportunity. FIGHT demanded that Kodak hire 600 minority-group members, who were to be selected by FIGHT. Kodak replied that it could not "enter into an agreement exclusively with any organization to recruit candidates for employment and still be fair to the thousands of people who apply on their own initiative or are referred by others."[10]

Alinsky then hit upon a novel strategy: confront the company publicly at its annual shareholders' meeting, to be held in April (1967) in Flemington, New Jersey. FIGHT bought ten shares of Kodak stock and immediately sent 700 letters to ministers and civil-rights advocates encouraging anyone with Kodak stock to attend to protest company policy. Approximately 40,000 shares were withheld from voting as a symbolic protest against the company's hiring practices. Thus began a tactic that would become one of the most important nongovernmental mechanisms to protest corporate policies over the next decade.[11]

Alinsky reminisced about the action in his 1971 book *Rules for Radicals*:

> Like any new political program, the proxy tactic was not the result of reason and logic—it was part accident, part necessity, part response to reaction, and part imagination, and each part affected the other.

The proxy idea first came up as a way to gain entrance to the annual stockholders' meeting for harassment and publicity.

On this oddly turned trajectory, Alinsky "set sail into the sea of churches":

I couldn't help noting the irony that churches, having sold their spiritual birthright in exchange for donations of stock, could now go straight again by giving their proxies to the poor.[12]

Building Upon the Model

Kodak did in time increase its hiring of minority workers. The FIGHT confrontation became an important model and inspiration for subsequent shareowner actions. Church social-action groups everywhere began to consider the enticing possibility that they might influence massive international corporate decisions by exercising their proxy rights in public shareholders' meetings even with a very small number of proxy votes or constituency support. Church activists soon began to speak as if stockholder proxy activity could empower David to slay the Goliath of corporate power.

By the end of 1967 several mainline Protestant denominations had begun studies of how church action groups could use this tactic. Standing committees of numerous boards and agencies were asked to provide information for church investors and decision-makers. This pattern would in time lead to intensive research into the specific policies of these multinational corporations.

A central axiom of the early corporate-responsibility movement was articulated by the Sixth General Synod of the United Church of Christ in 1967. This "equal consideration maxim" held that "social values and social justice ought to be given consideration together with security and yield in the investment of funds held by religious organizations."[13]

The 180th General Assembly (1968) of the United Presbyterian Church in the U.S.A. candidly faced up to a dilemma of church investment. In a statement on "Investments in Housing and Business," it asked the church to direct "that 30 per cent of their funds invested, and available for investment, which are subject to no limitations on investment by the donor or by applicable statute or contractual provision, be made available for investment in housing and business in low- and middle-income areas, some of which may offer a low return and a higher than normal risk." This resolution was accompanied by an unusual request for legal release from normal obligations associated with investments: "The authorization and instruction concerns investments of a kind that are not subject to the ordinary rule of prudent investment by trustees, for it is stated that some . . . may offer a lower return and a higher than normal risk." Therefore the resolution asked "that the General Assembly hold them [the trustees] harmless from any losses on investments that they or any of them state are made" to fulfill this directive. Since "normal risk" is assumed in an investment, when "higher than normal risk" is taken, the purpose of the investment changes significantly, and this the General Assembly wished to make clear.

Thus the churches began in the late sixties to refine their understanding of the potential tension between the traditional pattern of using prudent and reliably productive investments to support their activities, and the newer strategy of using investments to affect corporate decisions. This tension would remain a moral dilemma in the ensuing decade.[14]

The Fourth Assembly of the World Council of Churches at Uppsala, Sweden, in 1968 began to raise the South Africa question in connection with multinational investments. The assembly declared that "racism is linked with economic and political exploitation. The churches . . . should also withdraw investments from institutions that perpetuate racism."[15] In February 1969 the Finance Committee of the WCC directed its investment managers that no resources were to be invested "in concerns which are primarily or wholly engaged in (a) production or handling of armaments; or (b) activities in or trade with South Africa or Rhodesia."[16]

Radicalization in the Late Sixties

The principal study by a political scientist of the significant change in the National Council of Churches' political orientation during the late sixties was made by Henry J. Pratt: *The Liberalization of American Protestantism: A Case Study in Complex Organizations* (1972).[17] His study supports the view that the radicalization of social activism resulted in a decrease in constituency support in the ecumenical movement. "The NCC's self-conscious and activist political stance is a recent development in the sixty-year life of the organization," comments Pratt.[18] "Whereas prior to the 1950s staff had been predominantly recruited from among clergymen, now they were drawn from these liberally inclined seminarians bent on a bureaucratic career."[19]

Of pre-sixties NCC social policy, Pratt says: "Despite the secession of several smaller and more pietistic bodies, the organization continued to enjoy substantial backing from its constituents, including many conservative churchmen who found much to approve of in its stands, even though they objected to certain policies."[20] "In general, . . . the NCC treated highly controversial questions with caution and softened the old reformist zeal in an effort to define itself as protector of the status and good name of the main line of Protestant and Orthodox churches."[21]

Pratt further argues in this 1972 study that because of the "backlash effect council leaders may be obliged to modify the extent and intensity of their involvement in national political struggles so as to take account of the changing balance of forces among constituents."[22] "The claim that the council does not accurately reflect the views of its constituents on major social and political issues is widely pervasive among conservatives."[23] "One reason why dissenting opinion could be contained" during the late sixties, says Pratt, was that "the dissidents, instead of being concentrated in one or a few member bodies, the defection of any one of which would have proved highly embarrassing, were scattered about among a number of denominational bodies."[24]

Some critics have claimed that the term "corporate responsibility" is essentially "the rubric under which the radical anti-war and civil-rights activism of the 1960s shifted its focus to American business, one of the remaining symbols of 'capitalistic imperialism.'" "Rather than trying to make business better, the movement is trying to replace business with an 'alternative system,'" commented one critic in 1978. "The 'alternative system' the movement is working towards is, of course, socialism. . . . The goal is to alienate business and to make it more vulnerable to political control."[25] Although there is a body of evidence to support this view, the CR movement is sufficiently pluralistic that the opposite view can also be argued, that the movement has been from the outset fundamentally committed to sustaining and improving the free-market system. In due course we will examine evidence for both claims.

JSAC Grant to NACLA

In 1969 the North American Congress on Latin America (NACLA), a strident anti-capitalist group of self-described socialists, received a grant through the Joint Strategy and Action Committee (JSAC), an ecumenical coalition of home mission agencies (American Baptist, United Presbyterian, United Methodist, Episcopal, Presbyterian U.S. ["Southern"], United Church of Christ, and others) with offices at the Interchurch Center in New York. Through the JSAC system, according to a description in the *Yearbook of American and Canadian Churches,* agencies collaborate on issues, develop strategy options, screen project requests, and work on joint actions.[26]

Critics argue that the JSAC grant and other denominational grants to NACLA display unmistakable evidence of an early and long-sustained mingling of experienced, self-defined socialist ideologues with corporate-responsibility activists. Apparently the mission-agency bureaucrats considered NACLA a legitimate "data-gathering" resource for research support. But what sort of data was this anti-capitalist group gathering?

NACLA was made up of self-styled revolutionary activists who had only recently branched out from Students for a Democratic Society (SDS) to try to use ecumenical church agencies in the crusade for radical social change. The SDS Radical Education Project had candidly stated that a major purpose of NACLA was "maintaining contacts between radical student, church, and academic groups in this hemisphere."[27] NACLA was cited in 1974 by the Committee on Internal Security of the U.S. House of Representatives as being led by persons who "not only favor revolutionary change in Latin America, but also take a revolutionary position toward their own society."[28]

The CR movement was engaged in political and economic research for the churches. But some important questions about its operation did not get the attention they deserved until much later. Through what ideological sieve were the facts being filtered before they were reported back to the churches? If church agencies were going to farm out research to independent non-church groups, did they not have an obligation to know whether such groups had biases that might color their findings? Weren't the church agencies also under obligation to know and take into account the opinion, tolerance, and conscience of their constituencies? Had such questions been raised earlier, the CR movement might not have suffered the increasing loss of constituency that was to become its gravest problem.

During the early decades of the modern ecumenical movement, the spirit of Christian unity was manifested brilliantly by leaders such as Wilhelm Visser t' Hooft, Martin Dibelius, Henry Knox Sherrill, Anders Nygren, D. T. Niles, John Baillie, J. H. Oldham, Martin Niemöller, M. M. Thomas, Richard Niebuhr, Robert Calhoun, and Georges Florovsky. Leadership was then rooted accountably in democratic constituencies.[29] While critical of the flaws of both Communism and capitalism, these leaders were deeply committed to key Western ethical imperatives, such as respect for persons, justice, individual freedom, and the rule of law.

By the mid-sixties, however, centrist leaders like William C. Martin and Edwin T. Dahlberg had yielded to more intense, determined, ideological types with less concern about democratically representing their constituencies, less empathy toward those who saw things differently, and less patience in working through complex differences.[30] (An interesting 1965 exchange between a congressman and an NCC spokesman on the question of NCC representativeness appears as appendix C.) Leaders such as William P. Thompson, Robert McAfee Brown, Richard Schaull, and T. H. Smith put more emphasis upon "prophetic witness," direct action, and active confrontation of "power structures."

A 'Fundamentalism of the Left'

By the late sixties, ecumenism was being invaded by what came to be called "liberation theology." Gustavo Gutiérrez, a principal liberation theologian, later reflected on the spirit at work in that period:

About 1966, biblical reflection appeared which was named and published as a theology of revolution (it contained a chapter, which turned out to be the tree that hid the forest, on the "theology of violence"). First elaborated by non–Latin American theologians, it was taken out of context, found resonance in a certain German theology, and eventually reached Latin America. . . . Its merit lies in the commencement to destroy the image of a faith tied to an unjust social order, but it risks paying the high price of becoming a "Christian revolutionary ideology". . . . Its theological insufficiency also shines through when it presents itself as a simple ad hoc revolutionary treatise, not exempt from a certain fundamentalism of some biblical texts, particularly from the Old Testament.[31]

This "fundamentalism of the left" was soon to spread like a prairie fire. By the late sixties most observers would agree that a sizable part of ecumenical leadership—whose headquarters is New York's Interchurch Center at 475 Riverside Drive—and many of the working cadres that supported it with research had become overwhelmingly leftist in political orientation, and were often willing to use church organizations to further political interests that could hardly be called consensual—i.e, based upon a consensus of both leaders and their constituency. Consensus, admittedly, is not the central interest of the prophet. Yet the true prophet must bring the addressed community along with his prophetic vision.

The ecumenical leadership elsewhere in the country embraced a far greater diversity of opinion. Since the mid-1960s, Presbyterian synod leaders and United Methodist bishops and Disciples of Christ executives in Pittsburgh, St. Louis, Atlanta, and Seattle have been far more deeply rooted in processes of democratic representation than the enclaves of 475 Riverside Drive. Top ecumenical activists, however, learned during this period to use the pluralism of the churches as a means of bureaucratic defense. When under fire, the activists could always point to some persons on their boards who presumably represented centrist constituency views.

1966: A Landmark Event

The World Council of Churches' 1966 Geneva Conference on Church and Society was a landmark event in the radicalization of ecumenical social-action leadership (see the Afterword for a personal view of this process). Thereafter, as Pratt's excellent study indicated, the core of ecumenical leadership increasingly took on the appearance of leaders without a flock, of self-styled prophets who believed their mission was to provide church support for radical social causes. Their initiatives were often salted heavily with the rhetoric of romantic socialism. These latter-day ecumenical leaders seemed determined to embody the stereotypes that had led early critics to dismiss ecumenism as theologically unsound. This is why more centrist ecumenists such as myself were forced to back away, not from our ecumenical commitment, but from this distorted form of it.

EARLY SHAREOWNER ACTIONS, 1970-72

In 1970 Ralph Nader's newly founded Project on Corporate Responsibility succeeded in getting two resolutions included in the General Motors proxy statement.[32] His bold stockholder action was noted with keen interest by church advocates.

That same year a group of Puerto Rican Episcopalians appealed to U.S. Episcopalians to help them study and oppose strip-mining on the island. Fourteen representatives of six denominational investors who held over $7 million in stock of the companies involved, Kennecott and American Metal Climax, held hearings in San Juan on the long-term and immediate environmental impact of the plan. Allegations of collusion between the government and mining operators were made public. The companies were asked to halt mining operations until rigorous requirements were met, and mining operations were delayed.[33]

By April 1970 the United Methodist General Conference had adopted legislation that encouraged the church's boards and agencies to invest in "corporations that make a positive contribution toward the realization of goals outlined in the Social Principles of our Church."[34] Although it is doubtful that the General Conference intended such an extensive result, this language left the door open for the boards to interpret any phrase of the Social Principles as a duly mandated ground for specific stockholder initiatives and proxy activism.

In October 1970 the Executive Council of the United Church of Christ adopted "guidelines for investment policy" that were to influence subsequent denominational and ecumenical policy statements:

> The General Synod has established priority concern for racial justice, poverty and economic justice, peace and world development, and the environment. The General Synod suggests that the social impact to be promoted by the use of investments be similar to, or at least consistent with, the social impact promoted by church programs.[35]

The San Francisco Presbytery submitted an overture to the 1970 United Presbyterian General Assembly requesting that the church develop guidelines by which its investment practices could "best express the whole Church's commitment to its mission in the world and its ethical teachings." (The text of this overture is in appendix D, part 1.)

The selection of issues in the early seventies fell into a pattern that would continue throughout the decade. Four interrelated arenas of activist concern were summarized in a 1970 United Church of Christ report, "Investing Church Funds for Maximum Social Impact": the environment, disarmament, equal opportunity, and poverty and economic development. These concerns were to reappear as church stockholder objectives in many subsequent documents.

Research and action groups, recognizing the need to feed information to one another, developed a network of publications, shared values, and reinforced opinions.[36] The CR movement began to take on a surprisingly homogeneous look, partly because the core leadership of the network learned to keep a firm in-group consensus by controlling the flow of facts, ideas, and tactics. It learned to choose only those issues most publicly damaging to media-sensitive corporations, and to keep skeptical centrists out of its decision-making.

Some CR activists had already written off the capitalist system as intrinsically evil and unreformable. Others thought that minor reforms were possible but that only systemic or revolutionary changes could make any significant difference. Still others took the free-market system for granted but wished to make it more fair. The last of these three positions is seldom articulated in the earlier literature. One is more likely to find the view stated in the National Council of Churches' 1973 "Corporate Action Guide":

> The danger of movements like Corporate Responsibility has been in leading people to believe that the problem of corporate power in our time could be resolved by token reforms, whether by increasing quotas for minority hiring or by democratizing shareholder regulations. Such campaigns are waged on corporate territory, according to corporate rules. As such, they legitimize the values and structures of the corporate system.[37]

CR Activity in 1971

The February 1971 issue of the *Grapevine*, published by the ecumenical Joint Strategy and Action Committee (JSAC), listed these strategies that were under consideration: petition, divestiture, incentive investments, proxy actions, stockholder class-action suits, and combined actions. The rhetoric that supported these practical strategies tended to reflect a highly jaundiced view of free enterprise:

> Increasing numbers of people, within and outside the church, are of the opinion that the above described actions are realistic options for the church, but only limited steps toward improvement of the social

order. Their concern, based upon past performance and historical analysis of capitalism, is that it is basically an exploitative system, even if reformed.[38]

The 1971 General Assembly of the United Presbyterian Church in the U.S.A. stated the crucial principle that "church investment is an instrument of mission."[39] The Assembly tried to solve the prudence/service dilemma by adopting this careful statement:

Like its other functions, investment must also be a part of the church's mission. Church investment policy involves not only sound economic but also theological considerations. Its central goal should match effective investment management with imaginative and efficient allocation of resources to programs that contribute positively to a Christian concept of humanity's spiritual and material wellbeing.[40]

The statement went on to affirm "ethical criteria and guidelines for church investors in the pursuit of peace, racial justice, economic and social justice, and in the establishment of environmental responsibility and women's rights." Although this statement asked boards to ensure that "ethical criteria" were applied to these areas, it did not specify what those criteria might be or what scriptural or theological basis they should have.[41]

In 1971 the National Council of Churches set up a Corporate Information Center (CIC) in New York City with a staff of five under the direction of Frank White. Its purpose was to disseminate information on the social consequences of corporate decisions, and to serve as a clearinghouse for information on corporate activities, ethical investing, and shareholder actions.[42] The CIC's major areas were: social profiles of corporations, alternative investment possibilities, government policies on corporate activities, current challenges of corporate actions, and church economic research.

It did not take long for the CIC to become the subject of considerable controversy. Its 1971 booklet called *Corporate Responsibility and Religious Institutions* showed how deeply "implicated" church groups themselves were in corporate investments.[43] In the same year the CIC made a thorough analysis of church portfolios entitled "Church Investments, Technological Warfare, and the Military-Industrial Complex." It documented the equity positions of ten major Protestant denominations in corporations that had extensive military contracts. The NCC's own portfolio included stock in twenty-nine of the sixty largest defense contractors. Among the fifteen CIC "social profiles" (i.e., an attempt at an audit of the social responsibilities of a corporation) was one that was to gain immediate attention: "Gulf Oil—Portuguese Ally in Angola."[44]

In early 1971 the Episcopal Church became the first major denomination to file, as a national church body, a shareowner resolution with a corporation. It asked General Motors to cease all operations in the Republic of South Africa immediately.[45] T. H. Smith, then at the United Church of Christ's Council for Social Action and later the ICCR director, reflected the strident mood of the movement when he stated that "General Motors is a mirror of the Fascist South African society."[46]

In April 1971 the United Presbyterian Task Force on Southern Africa, led by attorney Josiah Beeman, petitioned the stockholders of Gulf Oil at their annual meeting to cease operations in Portuguese Africa. Although the petition was overwhelmingly defeated, it did not fail to cause a ruckus.[47]

In May 1971, two proxy challenges to Honeywell were defeated. Corporate-responsibility activists had asked the company to add two new board members with expertise in ecology and economic conversion (i.e., from defense to "peace" products).

During this time the North American Congress on Latin America (NACLA) continued to receive funding from JSAC, which described NACLA as a source for "publishing heretofore hidden statistical data on church investments."[48] Some observers may argue that benign quasi-Marxists had influence at this time on only the fringes of the NCC, but in fact JSAC represented the key leadership of domestic missionary efforts in mainstream Protestantism, including the United Church of Christ, United Presbyterian, United Methodist, American Baptist, and Episcopal missionary agencies.

Already some cautious criticisms of CR activism were beginning to be heard, particularly on the grounds that the church activists suffered from an "unfamiliarity with the workings of big business" and that "many doubted their competence to analyze the morality of American corporations."[49] But the overriding hope of the activists was that a creative new form of Christian social action had been devised,[50] and that investing could be a powerful means of social action.[51]

The Cuba Resource Center

Another "research group" that supplied the churches with data and support studies on corporate activity and investment policy in Latin America in the early seventies was the Cuba Resource Center (CRC). In January 1972 the CRC newsletter stated that one of the center's major purposes was to "expose and combat Church complicity with and support of U.S. imperialism in Latin America, with Cuba as historical background."[52]

The Cuba Resource Center was founded by Castro sympathizers in 1971 as a "solidarity organization" that invariably argued the case of the Communist government in Cuba in an effort to influence U.S. policy. It sponsored a number of pro-Cuban "socialism expositions," offering posters of Fidel as an "excellent memento." It sought to sustain and increase contacts between NCC leaders and liberal Cuban church functionaries who have unremittingly taken the Cuban regime's political line. These functionaries have gained control of the Cuban Protestant church but are quietly scorned by many persecuted Cuban Christians who have been deprived of their civil rights.

During the early seventies the CRC was receiving grants channeled through various boards and mission agencies of the Presbyterian, United Methodist, American Baptist, and other Protestant bodies. The CRC was at this time benignly regarded as a legitimate part of a data-gathering "research network" that sought to expose injustices being perpetrated by multinational corporations against exploited workers in Latin America.[53]

CR Activity in 1972

In 1972 a group of eighty Catholic and Protestant missionaries in Chile wrote and distributed to U.S. church leaders a letter on the adverse impact of transnational corporations on Chile and other South American countries. It proclaimed that "the radical Gospel of Jesus Christ stands opposed to a capitalist world."[54] Salvador Allende, Marxist president of Chile, speaking before the United Nations that year, declared:

> In July [1972] the world was shocked to learn the details of a new plan of action which ITT itself presented to the United States government, a plan aimed at overthrowing my government within a period of six months. . . . Its objectives included strangling the

economy, diplomatic sabotage, sowing panic among the population, and fomenting social disorder. . . . Before the conscience of the world I accuse ITT of attempting to bring about civil war in my country, the greatest possible source of disintegration of a country. This is what we call imperialistic intervention.[55]

In response, the United Nations set up a Commission on Transnational Corporations to investigate international standards of accounting of transnationals and agreements between TNCs and governments. Following a resolution by the U.N. Economic and Social Council in July 1972, the U.N. secretary general appointed a "group of eminent persons" to study the impact of multinationals on the developing world.

Although many anti-corporate advocates were urging strong measures for international control of MNCs, the less developed countries themselves were divided about what was needed. No agreement was possible on what sort of international convention or apparatus should be created or whether, if created, such a thing could be effective. Dow Chemical's chief executive, Carl A. Gerstacker,[56] argued that "the multinational companies would welcome standard international rules to work by, together with a code of international standards governing their proper treatment by host nations—some internationally approved method of governing the relationships between the nation-states and the MNCs and settling their disputes in an impartial court."[57]

Two main targets of shareowner resolutions sponsored by church groups in 1972 were multinationals dealing heavily in military contracts and multinationals with dealings in South Africa.[58] The United Church of Christ sponsored a shareowner resolution at the annual meeting of Mobil Oil Corporation requesting disclosure of the company's operations in South Africa.[59] Bishop John E. Hines of the Episcopal Church announced that the newly formed Church Project on U.S. Investments in Southern Africa would launch a major campaign against several multinationals.[60]

At its Utrecht meeting in 1972, the Central Committee of the World Council of Churches asserted that "the effect of foreign investments in Southern Africa is to strengthen the white minority regimes in their oppression of the majority."[61] Although that view was challenged by critics as a potential abandonment of one of the few effective elements of leverage on the South African regime, the WCC firmly took the position of absolute and immediate withdrawal. It urged "all member

churches, Christian agencies, and individual Christians outside Southern Africa to use all their influence, including stockholder action and
disinvestment, to press corporations to withdraw investments from and
cease trading with these countries."[62]

In 1972 the General Board of the Church of the Brethren, a 200,000-
member "historic peace church," adopted the view that "it is right to
expect the General Board to know the heritage of faith and the nature of
life sufficiently to apply Christian ethics to its participation in the
economic life of today's world. . . . It is also clear that the demands of
justice should be met as fully as possible in the investment program of
the Board." In March 1972 the church took what the *New York Times*
reported as "the first action of its kind by a United States denomination
. . . to sell its stock in all corporations that produce defense or weap-
ons-related products."[63]

In 1972 the United Church of Christ, the United Methodist Council
on Corporate Review, and Clergy and Laity Concerned (an ecumenical
group formed in 1965 to mobilize opposition to U.S. intervention in
Vietnam) presented shareowner resolutions to the Honeywell Corporation again calling for a disclosure of all defense contracts and for the
establishment of a committee on "economic conversion" to peacetime
products. Clergy and Laity Concerned presented shareowner resolutions to ITT and Exxon, requesting disclosure of type and dollar
amount of defense contracts. An NCC shareowner resolution asked GE
about military contracts and the possibilities of "economic conversion" to peacetime products. The American Baptists sold their stock in
United Aircraft because of the company's substantial involvement in
military production and its refusal to discuss conversion to non-military products. The Puerto Rico Industrial Mission questioned the
intention of Westinghouse in its plan to construct a nuclear power plant
in Puerto Rico.[64]

IBM became the target of several church actions early in the decade,
partly because many church groups owned IBM stock. It continues to
be a prime target of such actions. One of the most widely reported
efforts was a vote by the faculty and students of Union Theological
Seminary recommending immediate and complete divestiture of all
IBM stocks because of the company's U.S. defense contracts and its
operations in South Africa. When the seminary board rejected the
recommendation, fifty students walked out of the graduation cere-

mony. The Society of Friends in Philadelphia also took on IBM, attending the 1972 IBM shareowners' meetings to protest the production of guidance systems for air attacks in Southeast Asia.[65]

Meanwhile the Communist press was exploiting church idealism for its own purposes.[66] The *Daily World* reveled in reporting impassioned outcries from the churches that in its view were evidence of "a growing thrust against corporations that profit from war." Such actions, said the *Daily World,* "take the form of boycotts of these firms' consumer products and of protests at their headquarters, and during board of directors' meetings." It offered a list of such companies: "ATT, Chrysler, DuPont, Ford, GE, GM, General Telephone and Electronics, General Tire, Goodyear, Honeywell, IBM, ITT, Kodak, Litton, Magnavox, RCA, Singer, Sperry Rand, Teledyne, Westinghouse, and Zenith."[67] The church activists were not motivated by the same moral energies that shaped the *Daily World,* but the CR movement made no noticeable effort to defend itself against the charge that it was being blatantly used by cynical propagandists.

MOMENTUM DEVELOPS, 1973-75

By 1973 the General Assembly Mission Council of the United Presbyterian Church had discovered a vast new battlefield—Alaska. It had circumspectly purchased $150,000 in municipal bonds in a remote area of northern Alaska precisely where major international oil companies (Mobil, Exxon, British Petroleum, Amoco, Amerada Hess) were doing oil exploration and development and beginning to build the Alaska pipeline. The purpose was to provide step-by-step resistance to energy multinationals in their presumed intention to have their way with the Alaskan wilderness. By now the church advocates were gaining confidence that they could take on any corporate management anywhere and go toe to toe with it in the courts and proxy fights. However, the oil companies won a court injunction that prevented the Alaskan borough from taxing them.[68]

In March 1973, the NCC Governing Board stated the principle of "equal consideration" in its "Guidelines for Mission Investment":

These guidelines are being promulgated in recognition of the fact that, in addition to safety, marketability and yield factors, social values should be given at least equal consideration in investing NCC funds and in exercising its rights as a shareholder. Some of the current social criteria concerns to be considered by the investment decision-makers of the NCC include: environment, employment policies, military involvements, foreign investments, and consumerism and marketing.[69]

The issues list was familiar. But it was left to the investment advisors to decide how "social criteria" such as "environment" or "marketing" might be understood and applied.

Subtle evidence was emerging that a conflict had developed between NCC leaders who were attempting to heal divisions and those who were more aggressively committed to confrontational strategies. The confrontationists won, and they exercised hegemony for the rest of the decade. In much of the NCC literature of this period the "advocates of social change" and the "powerful instrumentalities threatened by that change" were portrayed as adversaries.[70] The assumption seemed to be that change as such would inevitably be good, and that all or most forces of social continuity were on the side of exploitation.

In November 1973 the Council on Finance and Administration of the United Methodist Church again echoed these four by now familiar "investment guidelines":

. . . concern for persons; concern for justice and self-development of peoples; concern for human culture; concern for the quality of human life. The Church's concerns which relate most directly to investment guidelines are environment, housing, consumerism, employment practices, and military endeavors involving domestic as well as multinational enterprises.[71]

As a "theological rationale," the document appealed only to the generalized notion of "man as a creature of God, capable of humanizing the world as radically witnessed by the Christ of the New Testament."[72]

In November 1973, *Esquire* magazine announced the winners of its First Annual Corporate Social Responsibility Advertising Awards, saluting "that vanguard of farsighted companies who have demonstrated a high degree of social consciousness in addressing themselves to the pressing problems that confront society."[73] The premise that corporations could attend to society's problems to the neglect of stockholder interests was promptly challenged by some critics. *Fortune*'s William Rukeyser argued that the corporate executives were coming "perilously close to thievery" if they applied stockholder earnings "willy-nilly to causes in which the executives personally happen to believe" but which may not be in accord with their fiduciary responsibility to represent their stockholders' financial interests.[74]

By 1973 the NCC's Corporate Information Center (CIC), along with its working group, the Interfaith Committee on Social Responsibility in Investment (ICSRI), had begun publishing a newsletter, *The Corporate Examiner,* and coordinating shareowner campaigns to influence corporate business decisions. Among the extensive initiatives of this period were: (1) The United Church of Christ Council for Christian Social Action attempted to carry out a nationwide boycott against Gulf Oil. To protest Gulf operations in Angola, church members were asked not to buy any Gulf products, and the Gulf Boycott Coalition unsuccessfully urged persons to turn in Gulf credit cards.[75] (2) In 1973 the NCC commissioned a study by the CIC on the impact of transnational corporations on economic oppression and underdevelopment in the Philippines. Part of this study was turned over to the North American Congress on Latin America (NACLA), the strident anti-capitalist group mentioned earlier in this chapter.[76] (3) In August 1973 the American Baptist Churches in the U.S.A. sold their 21,000 shares in United Aircraft Corporation stock after the company had shown its "unwillingness to discuss conversion to non-military production."[77]

CR Activity in 1974

By 1974, church activity on multinationals had significantly increased. Representatives of ten Catholic orders and colleges had formed the National Catholic Coalition for Responsible Investment in 1973. This group merged with the Corporate Information Center in 1974 to become the Interfaith Committee on Social Responsibility, which soon became the Interfaith Center on Corporate Responsibility (ICCR). The ICCR (which we looked at in chapter one) described itself in 1977 as a coalition that "through the decisions of its Board and services of a permanent staff . . . acts as a clearinghouse and resource center for the independent actions of its member religious organizations."[78] Four task forces were designated: (1) transnational corporations; (2) equal employment opportunity, and woman and corporations; (3) military production and sales; (4) eco-justice, agribusiness, energy. All four task forces provided their client organizations with a monthly fund of investigative research on selected multinational targets.

The most frequent targets were ITT, Exxon, Mobil, IBM, GM, and Gulf + Western, because many of the ICCR member agencies' pension and mission boards held extensive stock in these companies. Ironically, those corporations whose profitability was such that church investors were originally attracted to invest in them became the companies most frequently subjected to stockholder challenges and scorn because of their presumably ill-gotten profits.

Even though one of the stated purposes of the ICCR has been to "facilitate an exchange of views," most of the views "exchanged" internally among researchers and advocates have reflected the same cast of mind.[79] There is little evidence that articulate free-market proponents who could have challenged the anti-free-market bias of most CR documents were ever invited in at the research level.

The key initiatives of this period included:

• The Project on Corporate Responsibility filed a lawsuit against ITT in 1974 to gain disclosure of documents dealing with the Chilean government, and the NCC wrote an open letter to ITT protesting its interference in Chile's political affairs.

• The Project on Corporate Responsibility filed a suit against Gulf Oil to require the company to pay back company funds given to political campaigns of government officials in countries where they operated.

• Rockwell International, Boeing, and General Electric remained prime targets of initiatives by the American Friends Service Committee and by Clergy and Laity Concerned because of their defense contracts.

• The United Church [of Christ] Board for World Ministries appeared at the annual meeting of the Southern Company to protest the company's policy of importing coal from South Africa.

• The NCC sponsored public hearings on IBM's influence in South Africa. A debate ensued over whether IBM should discontinue all or part of its company operations in a nation that practiced apartheid.[80]

CR Activity in 1975

Among major actions during 1975, probably the apex of shareholder confrontations,[81] were:

• The United Church of Christ presented a resolution to Control

Data requesting disclosure of its personnel policies in South Korea. The church's Committee on Human Rights in Asia charged that Control Data had distorted portions of a report to stockholders on wage scales in Korea, and that Motorola had refused to provide information on working conditions in its Korean operations.[82] (A later shareholder resolution printed as appendix E has to do with the closing of Control Data's South Korean plant.)

• Fourteen Protestant and Catholic groups holding nearly $9 million in IBM shares presented a shareholders' resolution to end sales of IBM computers to southern Africa. Open letters were published and "dialogue sessions" were held with the IBM chairman prior to the annual meeting.[83]

• The Sisters of Divine Providence petitioned Tenneco concerning disclosure of land ownership in developing countries.

• In an open letter to Chrysler, Ford, and General Motors, the northern California branch of ICCR questioned the three companies' influence on the reorganization of Chile's automobile industry. In August 1975 fifteen Protestant and Catholic mission-agency executives signed a letter to GM chairman Thomas A. Murphy arguing that it would be immoral to build cars in Chile because of the violations in human rights that had occurred since the Pinochet government came to power by overthrowing President Salvador Allende.[84]

• In 1975 the ICCR issued a hard-hitting report on Gulf + Western's operations in the Dominican Republic. It charged collusion between G + W and the Balaguer government to fix a de facto maximum wage: "Since the State Sugar Council pays cane cutters about $1.45 per ton, G + W argues that it must follow suit as a guest of the country." It charged collusion also between the union leaders of the major union, Sindicato Libre, and the government, and suggested naïveté on the part of union workers who "seem quite pleased with what they call the philanthropic approach of G + W management."[85]

On July 21, 1975, the ICCR held the first of several "dialogue meetings" guided by "dialogue facilitators" with G + W executives. The company was then given written questions to answer. In August a church team made an eight-day visit to the Dominican Republic. Early in September the ICCR filed a disclosure resolution for inclusion in the G + W December annual meeting. The SEC ruled against G + W's claim that the resolution should be excluded from proxy materials.

Among the information that the resolution asked the company to disclose about its operations in the Dominican Republic was: "A list of land held, leased, and in direct contractual arrangement; other assets; operating income and revenues from sugar, molasses, and furfural [a liquid used in the manufacture of plastics] . . . a chart listing functional job categories and number of employees in each category, along with average wage in that category. . . . Evaluate whether wages paid . . . are sufficient to cover basic living costs. . . . Summarize the history of the company's policy toward unions. . . . State whether or not any payments, gifts, or any other gratuities or advantages have been offered or paid to union leaders. If so, list them with amount, date, and reason for each. . . . State whether or not any contributions, concessions, gratuities, stipends, gifts, use of the company's facilities, influence, or personnel have been given to Dominican public officials and/or political candidates. . . . List amount of taxes . . . and effective tax rate on operating income." In requesting "a full review" the resolution stated: "While it is true that sugar products bring much-needed foreign exchange to the Dominican Republic, the poor are receiving a smaller portion of the income each year."[86]

G + W management responded that it was "more saddened than upset" by "the hostile attitude conveyed . . . in the resolution":

> G + W believes that while the resolution appears to elicit information, it could create the erroneous impression that our role in the Dominican Republic is not a constructive one. That, in our opinion, is not so. . . . We are proud of our record in Latin America.[87]

Although the resolution received only 4.1 per cent of the shareholder vote, that was enough to allow resubmission the following year.

In sum, the corporate-responsibility movement reached its peak of influence and vitality in the mid-seventies. The mood tended to be angry, confident, and confrontational. What the corporations at first regarded as a mild nuisance had become a serious matter of shareholder meeting strategy, public relations, and an inward examination of conscience.

THE SOUTHERN AFRICA DEBATE

Throughout the early seventies the CR movement began calling for companies to withdraw all investments from South Africa. Both corporations and the church advocates declared their abhorrence of that country's apartheid system. Opionions differed, however, regarding which strategies for change in South Africa would be most likely to produce increased social and political justice.

In 1973 a World Council of Churches publication called *Time to Withdraw* took a strong initiative that was followed by most American CR advocates. It urged all investors in any company doing business in South Africa either to sell their stock or to work to get the company to withdraw. The theological basis was stated in this way:

> The Holy Spirit convinces us of sin regnant in the structure of our society, impels us to seek a just society and not to be afraid of judging the powerful forces of evil in the world which God has already condemned in Christ. None of our societies are free from sin, nor can any of our nations claim that we have achieved justice. But today we find a blatant form of sin and injustice in Southern Africa, where a white minority, many of them our brethren in Christ, is oppressing a black majority.[88]

So it became established theologically in the minds of advocates that, even though all nations sin, the quality and dimension of systemic evil in South Africa was so much greater than in, say, the Soviet Union or Cambodia or Libya that an absolute form of resistance was demanded. Corporations, it was argued, had been guilty of direct complicity in racism for profit: "The main inducement to British and U.S. companies to invest in South Africa is the exceptionally high rate of profit made possible by the system of cheap forced labor." [89]

Rejected: Economic Progress, Gradual Reform

Two policy alternatives were unequivocally rejected by ecumenical advocates. The first was increased involvement and more investment by Western companies with a commitment to democracy so as to increase their potential influence within South Africa, in the hope that the economic growth thus stimulated would improve economic conditions for blacks. This "growth theory" was sharply rejected on the grounds that "an influx of blacks to the cities reinforces the electorate's fears and brings on greater repression."[90] The more fundamental reason, however, was that the church advocates did not believe that black incomes would increase as jobs increased with new capital initiatives.

Also rejected was the argument for company-influenced reform, in which corporations would offer special training for blacks and use a portion of profits for the benefit of the black community. This was

rejected on the grounds that "there is no method of policing improvements."[91] T. H. Smith argued against reform measures on the grounds
that most liberal industrialists "do not ask for an abolition of
apartheid": "By pressing for certain limited economic reforms but not
for deep-rooted change, liberal industrialists will be able to . . . put a
face to the rest of the world that their intentions are honorable."[92]
Smith argued that the goal must be "to alter that power relationship"
between the white ruling minority and the black majority. Yet some
critics observed that if reform measures were altogether rejected, the
only alternative was violent (and at this stage almost certainly unsuccessful) revolution, an option clearly rejected by most South African
black church leaders.

The WCC's *Time to Withdraw* was regarded by some critics as a
cynical turn away from the reforming democratic and liberal tradition
of evolutionary change and toward a tacit approval of terrorism and
revolutionary tactics, and thus as a betrayal of liberal ecumenism.
Some saw it as a prime case in point of the "fundamentalism of the
left." Later the Presbyterian TNC Task Force would correctly observe
that "the church's own effectiveness is weakened by the implicit
withdrawal from the area of economic activity that seems condemned."[93]

Rejecting economic progress and gradual reform as ways of increasing justice for blacks in southern Africa, the ecumenical movement
committed itself to a position of absolute and immediate disengage-
ment. American churches were urged to withdraw their investments in
all companies doing business in southern Africa (South Africa,
Namibia, Zimbabwe, Angola, and Mozambique) and in Guinea-Bissau
(which until it achieved independence in 1974 was struggling to overthrow its Portuguese rulers) and to bring "pressure upon governments
and corporations to withdraw their support from racist regimes." The
churches were urged also to support "voices of African resistance" that
called for economic isolation of southern Africa and for black nationalist revolution.[94]

Several initiatives that began in the early seventies have continued
into the early eighties.[95] Utility companies importing coal from South
Africa were petitioned to cease trade immediately. International banks
were urged to cancel all loans and agreements with businesses in South

Africa. Divestment of GM stock was advocated because GM was selling vehicles to the South African military. Kennecott was critized for increasing the wealth of the regime through mining profits. Holiday Inn was boycotted because it was thought to reinforce apartheid. Union Carbide's chrome operation was regarded as an implicit affirmation of apartheid. Texaco and Standard Oil were petitioned to halt all planned expansions in South Africa.

Some Gains for South African Blacks

These measures may have had some positive effect, though it is difficult to say which of the constructive changes that occurred in South Africa did so because of church initiatives and which did so in spite of them. Corporations have increased their awareness of South African racial policies. Personnel practices have been improved. Wage scales have risen. Blacks have increasingly found their way into managerial positions in some companies. If the companies had taken the advice of the church activists and pulled out altogether, it is arguable that personnel policies would have proved less tractable, fewer blacks would be in managerial positions, and living conditions would not have improved.

The question remains as to whether the continued presence of foreign corporations in South Africa is an absolute moral evil, where unmitigated indignation and the support of violent change are the principal moral responses, or whether a continued corporate presence has had a constructive effect. If unequivocal resistance is required and the ends justify virtually any means available, including terrorism and violent revolution on behalf of greater justice, then the arguments of church activists would have more compelling force.

The absolute moral certainty of withdrawalism left little room for relative moral judgments or incremental progress. But the facts speak otherwise. Urban blacks in South Africa have a higher standard of living than blacks anywhere else on the continent. The 1980 per capita income of blacks in the Johannesburg area (primarily Soweto) was $1,048, twice that of oil-rich Nigeria ($750) and more than twice that of Ghana ($420) and Senegal ($330). Even black South Africans living in the Homelands had a per capita income ($334) higher than that of Mozambique ($220), Malawi ($200), and Kenya ($196 in 1981).[96]

Deficiencies of Moral Absolutism

The CR strategists called for an absolute and immediate end to injustice without asking how it was to be achieved or what the costs would be to the current black victims of injustice. Although later self-corrective alternatives were to develop, at this mid-seventies stage the church activists had given up all hope of positive corporate influence on the economic and political system. They showed little interest in the interrelated and complex historical forces that influenced the economic circumstances of South African blacks, and little patience with peaceful methods of dealing with entrenched injustices.

In the name of democracy and justice, the church absolutists may have inadvertently helped bring about a number of one-party states in Africa that deny their people free elections and freedom of the press and show only minimal sensitivity to human rights. "Their preoccupation with racism in South Africa tends to destroy one system with little prospect of establishing a satisfactory alternative," says Edward Norman:

> Some, indeed, are themselves guilty of a sort of unconscious racism in their attitudes to the rest of Africa, by implying that the political structures about which they become so passionately exclusive in the western context, are somehow less to be insisted upon when it comes to independent black people.[97]

It is as paternalistic to imply that blacks cannot handle incremental democracy as it is to rationalize totalitarianism as a necessary stage of African economic development.

Certain developments among American black thinkers in the early 1970s influenced corporate-responsibility activism. Among them were the rejection of racial integration, the preference for militant black nationalism, the attraction to Marxist historical analysis and revolutionary tactics, and the espousal of a racially exclusive black state. While ecumenical activists rightly resisted the idea of the racially exclusive white state, some saw the racially exclusive black state as the answer to all the problems of blacks. Accordingly, any search for less than absolute and complete change, for dialogue, for incremental changes toward some form of democratic self-government, was considered a hypocritical betrayal and branded as racism.

Happily, the CR advocates moved beyond this period of rhetorical simplism and moral absolutism. By 1977 a more moderate, ameliorative, and constructively incremental approach would emerge.[98]

DEL MONTE: A CASE STUDY IN RHETORIC

The Del Monte case is typical of the strident rhetoric that pervaded much of the church/multinational conflict during the mid-seventies. In September 1977, members of a northern California task force of the Interfaith Center on Corporate Responsibility took a shareholder initiative to the Del Monte annual meeting in San Francisco to protest "Del Monte's bribes and land and labor practices" in the Philippines.[99] The resolution called on Del Monte to provide full disclosure of its employment practices and to appoint a committee with representatives for consumer affairs, agricultural economics, labor, and the Filipino community. "Resolutions were orderly and politely discussed, and then overwhelmingly defeated, as expected," commented a newspaper reporter. "More important to the vanquished, however, was a chance to air their grievances."[100]

A year earlier, in September 1976, the North American Congress on Latin America (NACLA) had published "Del Monte: Bitter Fruits," written by Patricia Flynn and Roger Burbach, as a section of its *Latin America and Empire Report*. This Del Monte report became an integral part of the ICCR's *Agribusiness Manual* (1978), prepared by its Eco-Justice Task Force.[101] Since the *Agribusiness Manual* containing the Del Monte report was still being sent out to corporate-responsibility study groups as late as 1984, when other ICCR publications had become defunct, it seems reasonable to assume that the report was still considered an accurate indication of ICCR positions.

Good Words and Bad Words

The Del Monte report has the appearance of objective journalism, but it is strongly rhetorical throughout. Certain terms are regularly used in a pejorative, negative way, and certain others in an affirmative, positive way. Among the "bad" words are: agribusiness, agri-imperialism, bulldozer, capitalist, centralization, class domination, colonialism, concentration of wealth, conservative, corporations, expansion, exploitable labor, financing of vigilantes, forces of capitalism, ideology of cooperation, labor exploitation, modern capitalist agriculture, monopolized land, monopoly capital, multinationals, multinational manipulation of world markets, new local bourgeoisie as a buffer class for multinationals, nouveau riche, premium pricing, profit, reactionary, repression of labor militancy, safety of U.S. investments, sales techniques, sell-out union, stockades for striking workers, subsistence wages, super-profits, upper-class pawns, U.S.-sponsored counter-revolution, vast plantation systems.

"Good" words, terms that usually have positive connotations, include: analysis of the forces of monoply capital, aspirations of peoples, development policy, an ideology of anti-corporate class interest, labor militancy, left-wing unions, liberation support groups, Moro National Liberation Front, outspoken and militant workers, the people's struggle, progressive land reforms, progressive unionism, socialist revolution, Third World solidarity.

Some Arguments in the ICCR Manual

This juxtaposition of positive and negative terms conveys something of the rhetorical tendency of the Del Monte report. The following quotations from the manual will suggest some of its political assumptions and arguments:

• "Del Monte and the banana multinationals . . . will certainly be a major obstacle to the socialist revolution necessary to meet people's needs in the Third World."[102]

• "Del Monte is one of the agribusiness corporations that have integrated the industrialized and Third World countries into a global system of production and distribution that responds to the forces of capitalism rather than to the people's needs."[103]

• "The multinationals, because they control the marketing and distribution system, are always able to reap the lion's share of the profit and manipulate reform measures to their own advantage as long as the basic structure of trade is not changed. Finally, whatever economic benefits producer countries do obtain are not likely to benefit the majority of people, but rather the ruling class groups that control the government."[104]

• "To further control its labor force, Del Monte relies on the union itself. . . . [The union] may oppose the company on bread-and-butter issues, but promotes an ideology of cooperation and common interest with the company, rather than one of anti-corporate class interest."[105]

• "As long as multinational firms like Del Monte play a decisive role in Mexican agriculture, there can be no real solution to hunger and underdevelopment: for these companies depend on and reinforce an economic system that is in direct conflict with the real needs of the Mexican people."[106]

• "This Report . . . analyzes the forces of monopoly capital that have shaped the company."[107]

'Along Socialist Lines'

The same writers state in another NACLA publication that "it is only in societies organized along socialist lines—where production and distribution is organized by the principle of social equality rather than private profit—that the possibility of ending hunger exists. China is a dramatic example."[108] So these corporate-responsibility researchers applaud Communist China as a country that exhibits social equality, and believe that the only way to end hunger is "along socialist lines."

There can be no doubt that Del Monte had permitted abuses that made some of these charges plausible. But our interest here is in the historical frame of reference, the moral assumptions, and the rhetorical form in which the ICCR pressed these charges and commended them to the churches.

An ICCR representative admitted that "Del Monte wages are almost always above the minimum," and that "it is commonly held that Del Monte is one of the 'better' places to work in developing countries." Yet the complaint persisted that the benefits offered by the company were insufficient to supply basic necessities. What benefits were provided? "Housing, schools, hospitals, stores, and recreational facilities"—but unfortunately, the ICCR official said, "Del Monte's benefits do not include food or clothing."[109] Worst of all, "the worker and family become wholly dependent upon the corporation for providing their livelihood."[110] A churchgoer in Dubuque might be very surprised to find such views expressed by a church group that identifies itself (on the cover of the report) as "an affiliated body of the National Council of Churches."[111] He might also think, in a period of economic recession, that a job with Del Monte sounds rather good.

When ICCR officials appear before corporate executives, they wish to present an impression that they represent the opinions of millions of lay persons in constituent denominations—a united front of 170 Protestant and Catholic organizations.[112] Yet when they seek to commend their own actions back to grass-roots lay constituencies, they provoke amusement or anger more often than agreement. The conversation ends, the pocketbook closes. The gulf that developed between the views of church activists and those of their supposed constituencies created a crisis of credibility in ecumenical social ethics in the mid-seventies that remains largely unresolved.[113]

CHAPTER THREE

The Movement Since 1976

THE CHURCHES' CONFRONTATIONAL STRATEGY reached its peak of influence in the mid-seventies. By the time of the Carter administration, 1976-80, several self-corrective trends had emerged. A moderate and centrist critique began to take shape. Tactics were diversified. A pocketbook revolution in which church members refused to give money for some of the more controversial social activist agencies necessitated a painful retrenchment. Ameliorative codes like the Sullivan Principles were developed. The conservative evangelical presence in American political life was increasingly challenging the National Council of Churches' claim to represent the center of American church opinion.

This moderating trend was reflected in the report of the United Presbyterian Task Force on Transnational Corporations. Writing in 1983 but looking back to the mid-seventies, the task force made a perceptive summary of earlier and later phases of the denomination's corporate-responsibility (CR) activity that is applicable to the movement as a whole:

> The church's approach to the TNC has not been as effective as it could have been in recent years, in spite of a number of genuine achievements and general demonstrations of usefulness. In part, the diminished effectiveness has resulted from the normal process of maturation. There have been errors along the way—errors flowing from precipitate action, miscalculation of potential impact, or lack of experience. MRTI [Mission Responsibility Through Investment, the denomination's corporate-responsibility committee] has learned from these mistakes and steadily improved its procedure and refined its tactics. In contrast to the early days of the corporate-responsibility movement, an often confrontational style has become less "self-righteous," more open to negotiation. Issues are not so often cast as "black and white," partly due to the efforts of management more

aware of public image, but also due to church efforts at compromise in order to achieve mutually acceptable solutions.[1]

This moderation took place slowly, over half a decade, and not without tension with continuing volatile elements in the movement.[2] By the early eighties, the more moderate approach had become strong enough to challenge the older, angrier version of corporate activism.[3] By early 1984 there was a widely felt need for a thorough re-evaluation of goals and tactics.

MATURATION AND MODERATION: 1976-80

That CR advocates were beginning to have a noticeable effect on Roman Catholic decision-making became evident in October 1976 when the U.S. Catholic bishops, commending the NCC-related Interfaith Center on Corporate Responsibility, urged that "all Catholics and Catholic institutions review their purchases and investments, applying . . . ethical criteria suggested in the guidelines published by such groups as . . . the National Council of Churches."[4] Although Catholic CR research was to take on a distinctive quality of its own, at this point the bishops appeared to have confidence in Protestant research. Catholic voices later had a positive effect on Protestant activism.

In 1976, fifteen Protestant and Catholic church bodies holding 50,433 shares of GM stock jointly presented a resolution proposing that GM's "present and future operations in Chile" be "contingent upon that government's commitment to honor basic workers' rights throughout the auto industry."[5] Curiously, after years of protest against the multinationals' power to influence governments, now the church activists were seeking to persuade a corporation to influence a foreign government's internal affairs. It is interesting to imagine how American workers and managers might respond if religious groups in Iran, Saudi Arabia, or Syria attempted to influence the restructuring of the American automobile or banking industry by exerting pressure on U.S. corporations through moral suasion or stock ownership.

Among the chief targets of actions concerning South Africa during this period were IBM, ITT, Mobil, General Motors, Kennecott, and Citibank. The United Church of Christ presented resolutions to Union Carbide against importing chrome from Rhodesia, and to Texaco and Standard Oil of California against expanding their South African interests; it also resubmitted its resolution to the Southern Company opposing the importing of South African coal. The Board of Social Action of the Disciples of Christ presented resolutions to Kennecott seeking an end to its mining operations in South Africa, and to ITT against its sale of high-tech products to the South African government. The United Methodist Women's Division joined the Atonement Friars and the Sisters of Charity in requesting data from Goodyear and Phelps Dodge on their employee policies in South Africa.[6] In 1977 the ICCR sent representatives to a U.N. seminar in Havana, Cuba, at which delegates from twenty-five countries discussed ways of influencing transnationals to withdraw all operations from South Africa.

The CR movement's interest in the influence of transnationals on agribusiness and food products intensified during 1976. An investment task force of the Sisters of the Precious Blood of Cincinnati sued Bristol-Myers over alleged misstatements regarding sales of infant formula, and presented shareowners' resolutions requesting data on sales, promotion, and nutritional value. An unsuccessful effort was made to require the company to call a special stockholders' meeting to consider the ethics of promoting the sale of infant formula in the Third World.[7] At about the same time the Sisters of Charity of St. Elizabeth presented shareholders' resolutions to Nabisco and Kraftco resisting the sale of processed foods in developing countries. General Foods entered into a negotiation with the Sisters of Charity, the Ursuline Sisters, and the Sisters of Loretto on the same matter. The Sisters of St. Francis presented a shareowners' resolution to Cook Industries requesting disclosure of data relating to charges that the company had misrepresented facts in grain shipments to developing countries. The ICCR protested Coca Cola's alleged attempt to prevent unionization of Guatemala, but later commended the company's settlement with the United Farm Workers.[8]

Gulf + Western in the Dominican Republic

On September 14, 1976, the Division of Overseas Ministries of the National Council of Churches sponsored a public hearing into the role in the Dominican Republic of Gulf + Western, which had $200 million in assets there and was the largest private landholder. The company declined to participate on the grounds that the event was organized not for inquiry but largely for the media.[9] "The conference was conducted like a congressional hearing," said a report in *A.D. Magazine*. "A panel of persons received testimony from a diverse set of witnesses, further examined the witnesses, and then made an assessment of their findings. . . . Twenty panelists from fifteen religious bodies heard testimony and asked questions of a broad cross-section of witnesses, including labor leaders and university specialists." The conclusions "indicated a significant negative influence by the company on the economy and politics of the Dominican Republic," according to the *A.D.* report.[10]

In September 1976 another shareholders' resolution was jointly resubmitted to Gulf + Western by the National Council of Churches, the Maryland Jesuit Province, and the Adrian, Michigan, Dominican Sisters. It requested lists of political contributions in the Dominican Republic and lobbyists hired to "affect legislation, regulations, sales, or the public image of G + W or its subsidiaries' operations in the Dominican Republic."[11]

G + W fought back, charging that the church action groups were using hearings, annual meetings, and proxy statements essentially as a way of getting press coverage that would stimulate public opposition to the corporation. The company felt it had been assumed guilty by the media without evidence. The use of media coverage of anti-corporate events has, in fact, been a part of CR strategy. The ICCR's handbook for church CR committees states that "a main concern of all strategies should be to exploit the vulnerability of MNCs regarding their public image."[12]

The 1976 G + W resolution created intense conflict among some shareholders and a fair amount of ill will toward church advocates; yet it managed to garner nearly 6.5 per cent of the shareholders' votes, enough for reconsideration at the subsequent meeting. The following year, in October 1977, the weary litigants finally reached an agreement. The ICCR member agencies agreed to withdraw their shareowners' resolution, and the company agreed to make a disclosure statement.[13]

South Africa: The Sullivan Code

One of the most constructive developments of the late seventies was the formulation of the "Sullivan Principles," a code of conduct for corporations with operations in South Africa. This code was evidence that the earlier absolutist and confrontational tactics used by the CR movement were slowly giving way to greater realism and prudence.

The Reverend Leon Sullivan, a highly respected civil-rights activist, was the pastor of Zion Baptist Church in Philadelphia and a member of the board of General Motors. He became convinced that as long as companies were operating in South Africa, they should at least work toward equal employment opportunities and try to improve the working and living conditions of blacks through company initiatives.

In March 1977 the top management of twelve U.S. corporations endorsed these six principles: (1) nonsegregation of eating, comfort, and work facilities; (2) equal and fair employment practices, and the right of black workers to form their own unions; (3) equal pay for comparable work; (4) programs to train blacks and other non-white workers for supervisory, administrative, clerical, and technical jobs; (5) more blacks and non-whites in management and supervisory positions; and (6) improvements in housing, transportation, schooling, recreation, and health care for employees.[14] By early 1984, 127 U.S. companies had signed the Sullivan code. This is a prime example of the value of a longer-range constructive incrementalism, earlier rejected by the WCC (*Time to Withdraw*) for not challenging the basic system.[15]

Continuing the Pressure to Withdraw

While this constructive, reformist approach was developing, the pressure for withdrawal from South Africa continued. For some time, ICCR leadership remained unimpressed with reformist efforts. "Many of the signatories of the [Sullivan] principles act in ways that directly assist and strengthen the power of South Africa's white rulers,"[16] stated T. H. Smith. United Methodist, United Presbyterian, and American Baptist groups continued to protest the presence in South Africa of companies such as Ford, GE, GM, Goodyear, and Texaco, asking for total or partial withdrawal of their operations. The United Church of Christ Board for World Ministries sought to convince Mobil to cease all oil sales in Rhodesia and to make a full response to shareowner charges that it had flagrantly violated diplomatic and economic sanctions in southern Africa for over a decade.[17] A United Presbyterian task force petitioned Citibank, Morgan Guaranty, Hanover Trust, First National of Chicago, and other international banks to terminate all loans to firms in South Africa. The New York State Council of

Churches sponsored a symposium on General Electric's corporate practices in South Africa, and on the feasibility and morality of withdrawal of U.S. business operations from South Africa.[18] The Episcopal Church joined the United Church of Christ in petitioning General Motors to discontinue its subsidiary operations in Namibia. Episcopal Church and Reformed Church task forces petitioned Kennecott, Phelps-Dodge, and Union Carbide not to expand any company operations in South Africa.[19]

Other 1977 Issues

Among other initiatives taken in 1977: The United Methodists asked General Motors to account for its labor-relations policies in Chile. The United Christian Missionary Society (Christian Church–Disciples of Christ) petitioned ITT for information on political contributions in Chile. The NCC protested the sale of computers by IBM in Latin America "where such equipment may facilitate repression."[20]

The ethics of MNC political contributions to foreign governments had become a subject of debate within the CR movement. Protests of alleged company practices were lodged by the United Church of Christ, Religious Sisters of Mercy, Passionists, and Capuchins. Shareowners' resolutions were directed to Tenneco and United Brands. The Sisters of Loretto sought to stop Gulf Oil from making such contributions in South Korea.[21]

Church activists continued their work on agribusiness issues during 1977. The United Church of Christ and the United Christian Missionary Society confronted Castle and Cooke on labor-relations issues in Hawaii and several developing countries. Unitarian activists petitioned Union Carbide for data on marketing procedures for pesticides abroad. The Sisters of Providence petitioned Coca Cola to terminate its Guatemalan franchise unless its relations with labor could be improved. Warner-Lambert was asked to supply information on differences in its drug labeling and pricing in the United States and Latin America. The Sisters of St. Joseph, the Adrian Dominicans, and others challenged the infant-formula marketing practices of Borden, Abbott Laboratories, and American Home Products. The Sisters of the Precious Blood continued their litigation with Bristol-Myers over infant-formula sales, appealing their case to a higher court. The Dominican

Fathers petitioned United Brands for data on its land holdings and labor practices in thirteen Third World countries.[22]

A Report From Cuba

Some lay churchmen were becoming increasingly uneasy about the one-sided anti-capitalist rhetoric they heard coming from church sources.[23] An event in June 1977 that heightened their concern was the visit to Cuba made by an ecumenical group of Christian leaders. After ten days there the visitors felt moved to defend the Cuban record in a "Report From Cuba." This report, signed by Robert McAfee Brown, B. Davie Napier, and other prominent ecumenical leaders, said in part: "There is a significant difference between situations where people are imprisoned for opposing regimes designed to perpetuate inequities (as in Chile and Brazil, for example) and situations where people are imprisoned for opposing regimes designed to remove inequities (as in Cuba)."[24] So two distinct standards were to be applied to human-rights violations: one in Communist countries like Cuba where the regimes were thought to be sincerely seeking "to remove inequities," and the other in free-market countries such as Chile and Brazil where regimes were "designed to perpetuate inequities." Both the empirical basis and the morality of such a statement appalled many lay churchmembers.

The NCC was later to point out that "more than 120 resolutions on human rights have been passed by the governing board in its 32-year history."[25] Not one, however, criticized Cuba for its human-rights violations, despite the severe reprimands these had received from such independent groups as Amnesty International and Freedom House.

The CR movement intensified its encouragement of media events and publicity unfavorable to corporate enterprise in 1977. It devised a detailed strategy for media influence. Local CR activist groups received model news releases and were coached on how to get radio and TV coverage.[26] "Encourage TV news coverage on activists by sending written notice of action-filled events, followed by telephone contact the day before the event," said one ICCR guideline.[27] Such events might include: "The announcement of the beginning of a major public campaign like a letter campaign, a boycott, or a law suit. The revelation of new, surprising, or controversial data about a company's affairs. A demonstration of concern such as liturgical commemorations, sym-

bolic actions, dramatizations, pickets. A critical statement by a prominent figure directed at a corporation or corporate practice. The dramatic
presentation, at a press conference or public forum, of a 'human
interest' story about an individual or group victimized by a company."[28]

There was apparently no thought that a corporation might do something meriting *favorable* publicity, such as creating jobs, or expanding
workers' benefits, or bringing needed technology to underdeveloped
countries. Clearly, the primary effort was to discredit private corporate
enterprises.[29] That is what the phrase "corporate responsibility action"
came to mean to many of its leading exponents in the seventies, and it
is in part what caused the slowly developing negative response to the
movement.

Caveats Articulated

In 1978 six Lutheran lay leaders, all corporate executives, stated that
if church bodies were going to "propose action in corporate ethics,"
then "laymen of the church with related practical experience should be
called upon to act in a consultative and participative manner." They
cautioned that "social ministries must be determined carefully and
adopted universally by congregations, lest they detract from that key
responsibility ['the preaching of the Gospel'], or lest they be infiltrated
by positions of individuals who espouse political and economic doc-
trines" contrary to prudent Christian judgment.[30]

Searching questions were being raised in 1978 about the support
given to the Marxist-backed Patriotic Front of Zimbabwe from the
World Council of Churches' Special Fund to Combat Racism.[31] The
Patriotic Front was an armed revolutionary group that had killed missionaries and other innocent people, black and white. The WCC
support for the Front and for other groups involved in armed struggle
(the Zimbabwe African National Union and the Zimbabwe African
People's Union, headed by Robert Mugabe and Joshua Nkomo)[32] was a
slap in the face of those who were seeking reform instead of revolution.
Prominent among the latter was United Methodist Bishop Abel
Muzorewa, a nationalist leader whose application for aid the Fund
turned down. The Salvation Army, a long-time member of the ecumenical community, whose missionaries had suffered at the hands of
the revolutionaries, withdrew from the WCC in 1978 to protest its
moral and financial support of the Patriotic Front of Zimbabwe.

The deep discontent that many lay persons at that time felt toward the church bureaucracy's apparent lack of interest in democratic values was expressed in 1978 in an anonymous letter from a member of a United Methodist local board to a church officer. The letter, which was widely copied and circulated, said in part:

> We are concerned about the direction in which the board bureaucracy is clearly moving and believe that the only voice we now have is through the withholding of funds. (The Board of Global Ministries itself frequently practices the withholding of funds in its effort to achieve social goals.) . . . We question the probity of the General Board of Global Ministries and do not feel that they handle the funds we supply in a responsible manner. . . . An event that finally triggered our response was the article . . . praising Cuban Marxism. [The author] compares John Wesley's Aldersgate power with Fidel Castro's power for revolution and expresses a preference for Castro. He is open in his denunciation of the United States, capitalism, private enterprise, American foreign policy, and the church's traditional evangelism. [The author remains] on full pay from the Board of Global Ministries.[33]

A statement on corporate responsibility made by the United Church of Christ Boards in 1979 was a harbinger of the turn toward a more moderate, less ideologically biased view. "The business system as it exists today" has "evolved in an endeavor to meet the needs and aspirations of human kind," the statement said. It affirmed the principle often stated by free-market advocates, that if a corporation does not serve some societal interest, "its business will decline and ultimately it will perish."[34] (Excerpts from this report are in appendix D, part 2.)

The confrontational tactics that had remained largely unquestioned in the middle to late seventies were now encountering serious scrutiny. The Cuba Resource Center (described on page 34), for example, was forced to reorganize in 1979; it disclaimed its religious affiliation and was largely shut off from church support. The church press toned down its references to the Center. By October 1980 the United Methodist Communications news service was describing it as an organization that sought "to provide religious communication with an accurate description of the Cuban revolution" and to "counter U.S. and church policies which contribute to injustice with respect to Cuba and Latin America." As late as 1983, however, some church organizations, such as the United Methodist Women's Division, were apparently still giving small grants to the CRC successor organization.[35]

In the "Easter Declaration" of April 1979, "A Call for Renewal of the Board of Global Ministries of the United Methodist Church," the Ad Hoc Lay Study Committee on General Conference stated openly what many lay leaders had been feeling:

> The social stands of the Board reflect the narrow elitism of a mission hierarchy which acts upon its own understanding of world needs while flagrantly disregarding the opinions and experience of the broader constituency of the church. We object to the propensity of Board publications to extol the transformations in socialist societies while ignoring the accompanying privations of Christian nationals. . . . We decry the use of church agencies by humanist social activists as institutional and financial power bases to promote movements which make no creditable pretense of Christian theological motivation. . . . The Board expended thousands of dollars to fly scores of staff members to the 1972 and 1976 General Conferences in Atlanta and Portland to lobby for the sanctioning and funding of its programs.

The declaration protested the result of the quota systems for the Board of Global Ministries, which, in trying to increase minority representation, had "restricted the representation of other groups whose presence is both just and in the best interest of the board." It called for legislation that would "prevent the use of funds by general boards and agencies for unauthorized purposes" and give local churches "the opportunity to designate part of their World Service apportionment to specific projects which reflect their interests and inspire their confidence."[36]

By 1979 one could observe among CR advocates a turn away from the volatile rhetoric of liberation theology and a turn toward a less emotional, more pragmatic, non-theological, sometimes Machiavellian approach. The guarded conclusion of an extensive ICCR study of Gulf + Western published in 1979 stated:

> We have attempted to avoid the debate over the general merits of capitalism as opposed to socialism, of the profit motive as opposed to government planning, and of liberation theology as opposed to more conventional interpretations of religious belief. Such debates are often used to divert discussion from the real issues.[37]

The report was filled with economic analyses of G + W's worldwide sugar operations, including its policy on worker benefits and its alleged collusion with governments and ruling elites. Ironically, some observers were relieved to find that the ICCR had ceased trying to make feeble theological justifications based on liberation theology, though profound theological and moral reflection was still greatly needed in the economic sphere.[38]

REVERSAL OF THE MOMENTUM: 1980-

There are two reasons why the start of the eighties was a turning point in the corporate-responsibility movement: (1) the sudden emergence of conservative evangelical Protestants on the public-policy scene with an unexpectedly stunning force; and (2) the increased criticism by both clergy and laity of a church bureaucratic maze that had failed to demonstrate accountability to its constituency.

A 1982 Burson-Marsteller report entitled *Church, State, and Corporation* identifies 1980 as the turning point in the dialogue between churches and corporations. Ecumenical advocates were astonished to find that suddenly they had to share the field of Christian public policy activity with what the report called "the much more visible conservative evangelist-led Christian Right." Though it is "avowedly friendly to business and supported by many corporate leaders," said the report, "the Christian Right demonstrated in a threatened 1981 television boycott that it was not averse to involvement in business operations."[39]

The Rise of the Christian Right

Evangelical preachers and leaders have long attempted to exercise influence on moral standards and, to some degree, indirectly upon public policy. In 1980, however, conservative TV preachers like Pat Robertson, Jerry Falwell, and James Robison were "responsible for an entirely new development," said Burson-Marsteller—"the recruitment of hundreds of thousands of their followers into a potent force in support of conservative political candidates."[40] Conservative evangelicals were able to make a difference in the election of senators and congressmen they preferred and even in the defeat of some they most disliked. They were able to take key leadership roles in some state party organizations and influence many others.

Key groups in the Christian Right are the Moral Majority, the Religious Roundtable, the Christian Voice, and the National Christian Action Coalition. They are loosely associated with other conservative groups such as the Conservative Caucus, the Committee for a Free Congress, the American Security Council, the American Conservative Union, and the National Conservative Political Action Committee, differing from them not primarily in policy preferences but rather in their constituencies. The Christian Right aims at motivating political action on the part of individual believers, usually through television, radio, and mail campaigns.

Broadcasting preachers, mostly evangelicals, own some 35 TV and more than 1,300 radio stations. Four-fifths of the religious broadcasting in America is thought to be fundamentalist or conservative evangelical, with an estimated weekly listening audience of 100 million. There is nothing approaching that among liberal Protestant groups. The Moral Majority claimed a membership of four million in 1981 and an affiliation with 100,000 clergy. Said Calvin Thomas, Moral Majority vice president for communications: "We know we were responsible for 2.4 million first-time voters in 1980."[41] They were credited by many observers with providing a significant measure of the electoral victory of Ronald Reagan that year.

The Christian Right believes that a strong national defense is the best deterrent to war. Therefore it provides implicit (but not active) opposition to the attempts by liberal church activists to influence corporate policy against accepting military contracts. In other ways it provides a countervailing viewpoint to some of the key views of the corporate-responsibility movement. The Christian Right supports equal rights for women but does not think the Equal Rights Amendment is the way to achieve them. It strongly supports the state of Israel on biblical-eschatological grounds. It is pro-traditional-family, pro-life, and pro-decent-literature (that is, opposed to legitimizing homosexuality, to abortion, and to pornography). But the boardrooms and stockholder meetings have yet to hear significantly from the Christian Right, inasmuch as it has not turned to stockowner resolutions as a key tactic.[42] If it does, it is likely to have far more influence because of its firmer grass-roots support and its leaders' experience in broadcast media.

Increased Resistance From the Churches

The other major development in the early eighties has been the growing willingness of Protestant clergy and laity to resist entrenched bureaucratic activists. A case in point: Among the denominations that support the corporate-responsibility movement, none is more crucial than the United Methodist Church. A turning point came in April 1980, when David Jessup issued an unpretentious mimeographed statement called "Preliminary Inquiry Regarding Financial Contributions to Outside Political Groups by Boards and Agencies of the United Methodist Church, 1977-1979."

Jessup is an employee of the AFL-CIO and former Peace Corps worker in Peru who had participated in the civil-rights and farm-worker movements in California. He became interested in investigating United Methodist financial contributions to political groups, he says, when his children brought home some "Sunday-school appeals for wheat shipments to the government of Vietnam, and the controversy over Methodist support for the Patriotic Front in Zimbabwe became public."

Jessup's research was done on the largest member church of the NCC, and the one that has made the largest financial contributions to the corporate-responsibility movement. In his examination of church connections to organizations dealing with Cuba and Latin America, he concluded that "judging from their financial contributions, statements, and actions, several agencies of the Methodist Church seem to be favoring the totalitarian option" rather than the democratic option. Among the organizations supported by church groups were the North American Congress on Latin America (NACLA), "which attempts to publicize the futility of democratic reforms in Latin America and the need for revolutionary change"; the Cuba Resource Center (CRC), whose primary purpose appears to be "the promotion of the virtues of Cuban society and of Castro's attempts to export his revolution to other parts of the world with Soviet backing"; and the Washington Office on Latin America (WOLA), which "regularly condemns human-rights violations in all Latin American dictatorships except Cuba and blames the United States for most of the difficulties." (Excerpts from Jessup's report are printed in appendix F.)

In September 1980, the NCC Executive Committee, distressed about the increasing influence of the Christian Right and about charges by Jerry Falwell, declared: "Christians may not agree on all political decisions but they are enjoined not to hold one another in contempt, for all stand before God's tribunal."[43] This appeal to moderation is itself evidence of a modest shift of mood. Meanwhile business writers were beginning to offer more overt resistance to the CR movement than it had faced before.[44]

Standard socialist clichés on capitalist avarice continued to appear in CR literature.[45] The 1980 *Economic Primer* published by the United Methodist Women's Division stated that "even the poorest of socialist countries have excellent reputations for providing their entire populations with such things as good quality education and health care," and that "socialist countries are usually evenhanded in the allocation of their productive resources."[46] In this literature, "profitability" is a pejorative term, and socialism is commended precisely because it supposedly avoids the dictates of profit-making: "In socialist countries a more balanced program of investment can be followed because investment decisions are not dictated by considerations of profitability."[47]

Is it reasonable to fear that socialism may involve a loss of personal freedom? "Capitalism hardly guarantees democracy," the *Economic Primer* reports. "After all, fascism has a capitalist economic base." In one of the CR movement's prize understatements, the document guardedly admits that "those countries which have been able to go the farthest in developing a socialist economy are probably not the most open politically."[48]

Actions by the Right

Two controversies in 1981 revealed the kind of leverage the Christian Right was able to exert upon corporate decisions. In August the Moral Majority made a inquiry into the Upjohn Company's development of a product (15-methyl prostgladin F2 methyl ester suppository) to cause abortion in the early stage of pregnancy. The Moral Majority feared that this might "herald the day of an abortion in every medicine cabinet."[49] It did not take the now familiar route of stockholder proxy challenges. Its "preliminary inquiry" did, however, elicit considerable anxiety among Upjohn executives, who feared that the issue might damage the company's reputation or cause tighter restrictions upon the development of the suppository.

The second controversy had to do with network television programming that was considered morally offensive. The Coalition for Better Television was formed by Methodist minister Donald Wildmon of Tupelo, Mississippi, who was the head of the National Federation for Decency. Under the sponsorship of the Coalition and of Jerry Falwell's

Moral Majority, 4,500 volunteers monitored network programs from February through April 1981 and kept "scorecards." In addition, half a million questionnaires were distributed to members of approximately 500 supporting groups, asking them to evaluate the levels of sex, violence, and profanity in prime-time programming. A boycott was planned for the sponsors of the shows with the worst ratings.

By mid-June, Procter and Gamble, television's largest advertiser, announced that it was refusing to sponsor shows with excessive sex, violence, and profanity, and that it had withdrawn from sponsorship of some fifty shows for that season (they were not named). On June 29 the Coalition victoriously called off its boycott. The Knights of Columbus, a Catholic fraternal order with 1.4 million members, also became active at about the same time in monitoring television programming, also using the threat of boycott.

An NCC Response

By 1981 the Christian Right had become a presence that the NCC could no longer avoid. On April 22 the NCC put forth a response to the New Right in which it castigated the Right for having "a flagrant intentional disrespect for pluralism at all levels."[50] The point is strikingly similar to the charge so often leveled against the NCC, that its social-activist elitism has not been sufficiently sensitive to the actual pluralism of the churches.

The NCC's self-analysis in this response, belated though it was, was essentially correct. It recognized that the Right was affecting the NCC because "our liberal identification separates us from the 'main' stream." It acknowledged that some NCC tactics are "not now working," one being "too many pronouncements and resolutions that have no follow-through or interpretation at grass-roots."[51] At last there was some recognition that the sheer number of social issues addressed was too much for the thinned-down bureaucracy to handle and still maintain contact with ordinary church supporters.

What should be done? The NCC memo rightly stated the need "to define who is or ought to be our constituency," "to develop a grass-roots strategy," and to "develop a pastoral response to people, not just to structures."[52]

During this time of the dissolution of the ecumenical consensus, ecumenical leaders had made few attempts to enter into dialogue with those whose viewpoint differed substantially from theirs. In 1982, however, a long-awaited debate on "The Relationship of Christianity and Democracy" was held at the Interchurch Center in New York. Two critics of the NCC, Lutheran pastor Richard J. Neuhaus and United Methodist evangelist Ed Robb, Jr., debated two NCC defenders—its president, James Armstrong, a United Methodist bishop, and Arie Brouwer, general secretary of the Reformed Church in America.

Neuhaus pled for active engagement of the church in social change but castigated the NCC for having lost and betrayed both the liberal vision and the ecumenical task. The pattern of the NCC's political agenda "betrays the liberal enterprise of evangelical Christianity," reflecting "a perverse liberalism that thinks it is being prophetic when in fact it is indulging in nostalgia and negativism":

> The meaning of prophecy is debased when it is equated with calls for a return to the failed policies of the past, and that is the gravamen of the message to the churches from the Governing Board. The meaning of prophecy is debased when identified with revolutionary fantasies for the future. Leadership that offers only failure or fantasy gives Christian social action a bad name. By its reactionary posture toward political changes in the actual world, the National Council becomes the mirror image of the forces that it calls reactionary. By its depressingly predictable partisanship, the National Council reinforces the stereotypes on which its opponents prosper. Thus the National Council, rather than the Moral Majority, may turn out to be the Reagan administration's best friend in the world of religion.
>
> The liberal tradition protests anti-intellectualism in all its forms. But in recent years we witness a pattern of leadership which appeals to emotions in order to mobilize, rather than to reason in order to understand. . . . If it lacks the courage to undertake the harder tasks of Christian unity, the National Council will justly be dismissed as a regressive and defensive enclave, an institution that has become the enemy of the ecumenical movement.[53]

Armstrong and Brouwer's defense of the NCC hinged on the church's responsibility to the poor and the assumption that leadership agencies of the church are called to lead the church, not follow it.

The Record in South Africa

In 1982, 107 firms that did business in South Africa and had signed the 1977 Sullivan Principles were reviewed by the designated monitoring agency, Arthur D. Little, Inc. Thirty-two were "making good progress," thirty-eight were "making progress," and thirty-seven "need to become more active," according to the report.[54] All but one had desegregated eating, comfort, and work facilities and had established common medical, pension, and insurance plans for all races. Although the proportion of blacks in supervisory positions had dropped because of "weaker economic times," it was found that "black employees are receiving higher average pay increases than whites," "the proportion of blacks participating in training programs has continued to increase," and corporate "contributions for community development have doubled since last year."[55] This record of achievement lends strong support to the idea that corporations can best serve the cause of social justice in South Africa not by withdrawing immediately, as most leading CR advocates have recommended, but by undertaking and encouraging reforms.

Meanwhile, how successful had the hundreds of stockholder resolutions calling for immediate withdrawal of all investments from South Africa been? Howard Schomer reported in 1983:

> No home government of any international corporation has adopted policies requiring such withdrawal. Not more than 3 per cent to 5 per cent of the shares of any corporation have been voted in favor of any shareholder proposal calling for such disinvestment. . . . The only case on record of the withdrawal of a significant foreign business asset from South Africa is the sale by Chrysler in early 1983 of the last 25 per cent of its stake in Sigma . . . [which was done] purely for business reasons.[56]

Widening the Controversy

Early in 1983, the controversy over ecumenical social action was brought to a vast audience through a magazine article and a television show. A January *Reader's Digest* article, "Do You Know Where Your Church Offerings Go?" by Rael Jean Isaac, suggested that leadership in the liberal social-action establishment was unrepresentative, and a CBS-TV "60 Minutes" show on January 23 inquired into controversial stewardship of ecumenical funds by social activists. (An excerpt from the TV report appears as appendix G.) Public debate about NCC accountability to its constituency intensified. Commented *Time* magazine:

> From their shared New York City headquarters, the "God Box" to insiders, the accused Protestant agencies have fought back with a barrage of publicity, defensive polemics, and at least 36,000 explan-

atory packets sent to local church leaders. NCC General Secretary Claire Randall admits no serious mistakes in the council's political judgments.

Time pointed to these "core questions" of the controversy:

What is the political line of secular groups that receive Protestant funding? Do the churches take enough responsibility for the political activities of these groups? Have in-house church programs and pronouncements shown a leftist pattern?[57]

The *United Methodist Reporter* of April 1983 devoted a major supplement to "the most extensive and intensive investigative effort in our paper's history," focused on accountability in the NCC. It reported that "the NCC has devoted at least four times more effort to addressing abuses by dictatorial rightist regimes (such as South Korea) than to those by dictatorial leftist regimes (such as Vietnam). And when the NCC did respond to repression of persons living under governments with Marxist leaders, it did so with much less intensity."[58]

Yet in August 1983, when the World Council of Churches met in Vancouver, British Columbia, for its Sixth Assembly, the repudiation of moderate voices by ecumenical leaders continued: "This system ['the world market system as a whole'] and TNC's operation within it are incompatible with our vision of a just, participatory, and sustainable society."[59] The view persists among WCC leaders that transnational corporations offer no promise for less developed countries but rather merely "render dependent the southern economies,"[60] "exploit the land,"[61] and provide threats to "cultural identities through colonial and neo-colonial structures."[62] If the Vancouver Assembly is an accurate reflection of what the WCC believes—and surely we must take seriously the documents of its most authoritative organ, the Assembly— its view is that the "world market system" is "incompatible" with the "ecumenical vision."[63]

Finally in 1983, there appeared a long needed report that treated multinational corporations with theological depth and prudent balance. This United Presbyterian report, called "Review of Policies, Strategies, and Programs of the United Presbyterian Church Related to Transnational Corporations," is the best church statement yet made on transnational corporations—their challenge, their promise, and the future of their dialogue with churches. (See appendix H for the conclusions of this report.)

By the time of its publication, the general mood of the church advocates had already become somewhat more realistic, less ideologically biased, less inclined toward simple moral outrage. The report's language was ameliorative, balanced, prudent, conciliatory, and in a deeper sense prophetic. The church's corporate-responsibility activity must now, it said, assume "a stake in the system, a responsibility for it. The church approaches the corporation and its officers as an owner in both the system and the particular institution, not an enemy."[64] "The commitment to reform and improve rather than to destroy and replace rests on the assumption of the basic positive value of essential legitimacy."[65] Legitimacy of what? Responsive democratic capitalism. How different from the polemics of the previous decade.

A Change in the Rules

One more episode in the recent history of the corporate-responsibility movement took place in the Securities and Exchange Commission on August 16, 1983, when SEC rule 14a-8 was significantly changed. As a result, CR activism is subject to new procedural limits that make it more difficult both to submit stockholder resolutions and to resubmit them the following year. Regulations that many corporate executives thought had allowed annual meetings to be turned into "soapboxes for activists"[66] were now abruptly changed.

The revised rule affects church stockholder activism in these decisive ways: (1) Under the old rule a stockholder resolution had to receive 3 per cent of the vote in order to be resubmitted the following year. The new rule raises the percentage to 5. This means that 66 per cent more proxies have to be garnered than were needed previously. (2) The sponsor of a resolution must own at least 1 per cent or $1,000 in market value of stock for no less than one year. (3) The number of words per resolution is limited to 500, far fewer than the CR movement wanted in order to state its cases. (4) A proponent can submit only one resolution per company. (5) If a proposal substantially duplicates one previously submitted, the company can omit it from the proxy statement. And (6) if it "relates to operations which account for less than 5 per cent of the issuer's total assets," the company can omit it.[67]

An extensive list of shareholder resolutions and their sponsors published by the Interfaith Center on Corporate Responsibility in January 1984 appears as appendix I.

RETROSPECT AND PROSPECTS

Chapters two and three have reviewed the major statements and events of the corporate-responsibility movement from its inception to 1985. The periods of development may be summarized thus:

• 1952-1966—occasional generalized church declarations on the social responsibility implied in investment policy.

• 1966-1970—from the Geneva Conference on Church and Society to the first stockholder actions, a period of early statements, preliminary experimentation, and a radical social vision.

• 1970-72—the early stockholder actions, characterized by liberal hegemony in activist groups, with minimal criticism from centrist church persons or from those who resist strong government control over the marketplace.

• 1973-75—an increase of stockholder activism, with a primary focus upon proxy actions, and a refinement of confrontational tactics seeking direct church leverage on corporate decisions.

• 1976-1980—the beginnings of increased moral, theological, and democratic criticism of the CR movement, both from within and from without; a heightened sense of polarization, and calls for improvement of the representational systems by which denominations authorize social-action activities.

• 1980-85—a significant reversal of momentum because of increasing criticism from inside and outside the CR movement, new influences from conservative evangelicals on the political process, and significant changes in SEC rules for stockholder resolutions.

In its brilliant summary review of the CR movement, the Presbyterian TNC Task Force sized up the periods in a similar way:

> The strategies of the seventies were implicitly confrontational. Though the shareholder resolution and the boycott, the main elements of engagement, were often preceded by correspondence, discussion, and negotiation, these activities were usually perceived in both the church and the corporation, we believe, as threshold tactics. That is, they were carried on in an atmosphere heavily overhung by the incipient resolution or the decision to participate in a boycott already in progress by others.[68]
>
> We believe that repetitive use of the shareholder resolution and the ritual confrontation of the annual meeting may often be unnecessary for productive access to the corporation and may well be a block to potentially fruitful dialogue in an increasing number of situations. It

is always an available strategy but ought to become less prominent as the church tests the results its earlier use has produced.[69]

The church's role in the seventies was "solely as a critic of corporate performance";[70] this tended to obscure the presence of many church persons in the transnational corporations, faithful lay persons committed to responsible life within that vocational setting. Now, in the eighties, "the church should seek to be seen as a valuable resource in corporate planning,"[71] not merely as a critic or outsider:

A broader strategy for the years ahead, then, should place more emphasis on communication and dialogue and less on confrontation; should place more energy and emphasis on the vocational witness of its members as the context for institutional engagement; should balance its prophetic criticism with positive appreciation; and should be more anticipatory and less reactive as it defines the issues that will form the substance of its continued approach to transnational corporations.[72]

If the corporate-responsibility movement heeds these wise and needed injunctions, the prospects are indeed bright for its revitalization.

CHAPTER FOUR

Flaws and Achievements

IN THE THREE PREVIOUS CHAPTERS we examined the role of the American churches in the emergence, growth, and decline of the corporate-responsibility (CR) movement. Here we will consider questions of authority, consistency, intention, political and theological underpinning, and effectiveness.

As we have seen, concerned church leaders have taken one of two approaches to corporate values and structures. The *reformist* approach assumes the *legitimacy* of the free market; its goal is to make economic enterprise more beneficial for more persons. The other approach is *immediatist* and absolutist in tone. It tends to assume the fundamental *illegitimacy* of the free-market system. It objects to the system itself—its profits, its capital, its risks, its size, its multinational character, its technological competencies, and its broad range of economic powers. Since these things are intrinsic to the current world economic system, absolutist CR advocates talk of systemic change rather than incremental reforms, and call for an "alternative economic system"[1] (almost always a euphemism for centralized socialist planning), rather than adjustments or changes within the current system.

Throughout the history of the CR movement these two approaches have been in contention. Generally, the harder line characterized the earlier period, a softer line the later years. But both views may be found in the CR literature of any year. In some quarters, such as World Council of Churches staffers in Geneva, proto-Marxist Christian missionaries, NACLA (North American Congress on Latin America) researchers, and some voices on American Protestant mission boards, the weight of opinion still strongly supports radical systemic solutions or vaguely romantic "wholistic alternatives." In denominational documents on corporate responsibility, however, the tendency is largely reformist.

THE CORPORATION: A FORCE FOR GOOD OR FOR EVIL?

Some CR advocates believe large business firms are useful economic instruments that occasionally engage in anti-social behavior and must be brought to task. Others regard corporations, particularly the multinationals, as intrinsically evil, motivated wholly by greed, and hence irredeemably anti-social. Other activists advocate reforming the corporation when their hidden agenda is to destroy it and the market system that makes corporate activity possible.

To ascertain the moral legitimacy of corporations is beyond the scope of this study, but let us review recurring complaints against them. First, everyone acknowledges that the large multinationals have a significant influence at home and abroad. The MNCs are modernizers of the Third World. They can raise the standard of living in Brazil and at the same time cause serious economic and cultural dislocations. They have an impact on the international monetary system and on the tax structure of both their home country and other countries where they operate.

Despite allegations that they are more powerful than countries, MNCs are not beyond the reach of political and democratic controls. They do not have armies. They cannot conscript. They cannot tax. And they are subject to the laws of the host government, whether that be democratic, authoritarian, or totalitarian.

Principal Allegations

A barrage of charges was directed against MNCs by a November 1975 Consultation on Multinationals sponsored by the Christian Conference of Asia: "Foreign-based enterprises create and sustain dependent, anti-democratic elites." "Under the guise of industrial development, the multinational system has intensified the centralized control of technology and has not transferred the technical skills necessary for self-reliant industrialization." "MNCs increasingly bring polluting industries to the Asian countries where less protective regulations [exist]." Corporations allegedly have "widened the gap between rich and poor and increased the dominance of the rich."[2]

Though these results are by no means universal, corporations do indeed share in the sinful self-assertiveness of all human power, including ecclesiastical power. Their behavior falls below the moral ideal. Among the most persistent flaws of American-based multinational corporations, in my view, are: (1) They tend to emphasize short-range planning for quicker results and profits, rather than longer-range planning for more stable markets. (2) There is collusion with tyrannical governments both of the left, as with Hewlett-Packard's deal with the U.S.S.R., and of the right, as with ITT in Chile. (3) There are deep-set patterns of bribery in some countries, and the constant temptation to use economic power to influence political events. (4) There is a much too cozy tie between the military and MNCs, especially those firms involved in weapons, aerospace, oil, and transport industries.

MNC Activity in Developing Countries

Although corporations have made serious mistakes and misjudgments, they also have accomplished many socially useful tasks. They have provided food, clothing, shelter, washing machines, life-saving medicine, grain, soap, and other products and services that enhance the welfare of developing countries. They have created jobs with higher wages than were otherwise available. (A statement of responsibility by one MNC—Johnson and Johnson—appears as appendix J.)

Less developed countries respond to multinationals in widely varying ways.[3] First, there is sometimes an enthusiastic courting of international companies, as in Singapore, Hong Kong, and Taiwan. Second, there are quasi-socialist governments like India that, though they do not really trust or welcome the multinationals, would nonetheless like to have some of the benefits that derive from them; therefore these governments try to attract MNCs selectively and then regulate them inordinately. Third, in socialist-bloc societies virtually all business by Western MNCs is forbidden; that which is permitted because it is perceived as furthering national interest, such as bank loans to Poland or Hewlett-Packard's computer sales to the U.S.S.R., is greatly constricted. Fourth, there is the tragic example of Khomeini's Iran, where religious zeal and the fury of nationalism combine to throw out transnational corporate influence as morally corrupting, and to punish harshly anyone who may have been tainted by it.[4] Regrettably, some CR rhetoric sounds as much like the fourth as any other alternative.

A brief example of what an MNC does in a developing country is instructive. General Electric has been the target of numerous church protests. What does GE actually do in Central America? It produces consumer appliances, electrical components, lamps, power lines, and other products that are useful for economic development. In the Dominican Republic, which for over ten years the church advocacy groups have been describing as repressively dominated by multinational corporations, GE was responsible for the beginning of rural electrification in Laguna de Nisibon in the early 1970s, with the obvious benefits of light, radios, and refrigerators. Power stimulated the growth of industry and commerce.

Less than one-half of one per cent of GE's Mexico work force is American. Compared to European MNCs, North American ones tend to shift leadership to indigenous leaders more quickly.

MNCs have been criticized for accepting kickbacks in Third World countries, but the fact is that they are more likely to resist such practices than the local firms. Reginald H. Jones described GE's experience:

> In some Latin American countries . . . the institutions of graft and kickbacks are so deeply ingrained that it is impossible to do business in accordance with our own policies and principles of attracting business on the merits of our products and prices. This is especially true in construction work. . . . So we have simply closed down our construction businesses in some locations and decided to forgo the business.[5]

Some CR activists charge that U.S. corporations "move in" and "take over" countries. This allegation is sustained neither by facts nor by common sense. The MNC operation would not last long if the host government considered it undesirable or counterproductive. In a spirit of enlightened self-interest, MNCs move in slowly, study the market, and seek opportunities that will be profitable for them and beneficial to the country. A gradually reinforced circle of mutual interest develops. Many governments have local-content laws that require items used in a given country to be manufactured or assembled in that country, thus increasing at-home jobs. So the corporation may over a period of years patiently work out production supply systems. All this runs counter to the stereotype of a quick takeover. As Reginald Jones said about GE:

> Our strategy is basically to learn what nations need and want, what their plans and priorities are, what rules and regulations they have for participating in their local economy, and then be flexible enough and creative enough to match our business strategies to their perceived needs and desires. This is a far cry from the imperial multinational corporations of popular fiction and Marxist caricature.[6]

While the CR caricatures assume that MNCs abroad are exploiting workers with low wages and quick profits, it is more likely that the MNCs are bringing humane U.S. labor and workplace standards to other countries. People employed by MNCs increasingly have a chance to own their homes and means of transportation, to provide their children with better education, and to fight their way out of deep poverty.

In 1976 Gallup conducted a massive international poll on what mankind thinks of itself.[7] This study concluded that the inhabitants of the developing countries want more industry, more technology, more material advantages, by ratios exceeding 20 to 1. They do not reject Western society, as the socialist rhetoric maintains. They do not want to "think small" about their futures. They want a growing GNP and material progress. They hope for a redistribution of wealth, but many of them realize that the best way to achieve this is to create new wealth through initiative, imagination, and hard work, rather than fighting desperately over existing wealth.

ACTIVIST INCONSISTENCIES AND IRONIES

Inconsistencies abound in the corporate-responsibility literature. And several key charges of abuses by multinational corporations can be plausibly turned against the activists themselves.

The first inconsistency is that profit is attacked as evil by those who benefit from the system of profit-making. The Protestant churches have a considerable financial interest in American corporations and their profits. Member agencies of the Interfaith Center on Corporate Responsibility alone invest over $7 billion.[8] Obviously, they want their investments to prosper in order to support mission work, pensions, and other endeavors.

No economic system functions long without productivity or profit. The Chinese commune must show productivity or its managers are in trouble. In socialist economies, profits benefit the political managers, who serve presumably as rational surrogates for everyone else, whereas in free-market economies, profits belong to free individuals and groups, who in turn can spend or reinvest.

A second inconsistency is that church activists criticize MNCs as too "individualistic," failing to recognize that the modern corporation is intrinsically *corporate*. It involves many persons, each making his contribution toward a common goal—investors, inventors, engineers, executives, workers, and salesmen. Modern democratic capitalism grew by corporately shared risk, complex activity, coordinated planning, and the pooling of resources, not by the independent efforts of individuals working alone.

Another inconsistency is that charges of corporate elitism are made by church elites. The activists often criticize the MNCs for their autocratic tendencies, using the stereotype of rugged individualists like Howard Hughes or H. L. Hunt running vast money empires singlehandedly. Or the corporations are said to be managed by small, introverted in-groups. Yet that charge can be turned back upon many church board and agency elites. They tend to be ingrown, homogeneous, and self-perpetuating. Meanwhile they have been losing their constituency, a fatal error in political strategy.

A fourth inconsistency is that the activists appeal to the goodness of humanity and inevitable progress but are quick to use coercion rather than persuasion to gain their own objectives.[9] They frequently complain about secret collusion between corporations and foreign governments, but they do not hesitate to work secretly and collusively when it suits their purpose. They charge the MNCs with financial manipulation, but such manipulation has taken place in their own agencies as well. They make contributions to suspect causes without consulting or informing the church members; often the evidence of radical actions does not come to light until it is too late for democratic review.[10] If church members feel betrayed by such manipulativeness, the activists should not be surprised.[11]

Finally, it is ironic that paternalism flourishes so much among those who claim to be fighting paternalism. One of the most frequent complaints in the CR literature is that MNCs imagine that their values and approach are the answer to everyone else's problems. Yet the radical activist has no hesitation in telling his fellow church leaders from Brazil, Zambia, or Korea, "I am going to take responsibility for you and raise your consciousness about what your country's needs are." The self-styled liberator believes that his Third World colleagues do not and cannot fully understand their own situation. They need an upper-middle-class American to inform them that they are "alienated and oppressed." Such arrogance is bound to backfire.[12]

Two Ironic Cases

Two telling examples illustrate how inconsistently CR values have been pursued: Gulf Oil operations in Angola and the sale of infant formula in Algeria. In their early stockholder actions on Angola, church advocates strongly criticized the collusion between Gulf Oil and the Portuguese government. In 1975 Angola became independent, and with Soviet and Cuban help a socialist dictatorship was established under revolutionary black nationalist auspices. Gulf Oil, considered demonic when it was operating under Portuguese rule, was immediately seen as benign. Did Gulf change? Let us review the story.

During the seventies, church activists sided vigorously with the Marxist-supported black nationalist revolution in Angola. Although Gulf's discovery of oil in Angola led to the creation of thousands of new jobs, Gulf was subjected to constant church-advocacy attacks during the early seventies. Today Angola is ruled by one of the most brutal dictatorships in Africa, surviving only because it has been propped up by a Soviet-backed expeditionary force of some 20,000 Cubans. Gulf continues to operate just as it did before, and is credited with keeping Angola afloat economically. But it is now largely ignored by church activists. Could this be related to the fact that Gulf has befriended a socialist dictatorship? As David Vogel described it:

> The rebels assured Gulf that they had no present intention of expropriating its property; they just wanted to receive the royalty checks that had formerly gone to Lisbon. Gulf's management was more than happy to comply; they had indicated all along that they were indifferent as to who ruled Angola, and now they were able to demonstrate the consistency of their conviction.[13]

Gulf's methods or operations or technology or marketing did not change; only the regime under which it was doing business changed. That was apparently enough to exonerate the company of its earlier sins.[14]

The sale of infant formula in Algeria was another intriguing and ironic case. In 1980 Herman Nickel wrote:

> The [CR] movement's stated goal is the total demarketing of infant formula. In testimony before Congressman Jonathan Bingham's subcommittee on foreign trade last year, Edward Baer, an ICCR staffer, explained what demarketing is supposed to mean by citing socialist Algeria. There the importing and distribution of infant formula are in the hands of a state monopoly, and all brand competition has been

eliminated. What Baer failed to add is that imports of infant formula have risen from 2.5 million half-pound cans in 1976 to 12 million in 1979, and are expected to reach 16 million in 1980. Baer's reply is that the steep rise in infant-formula use in Algeria does not bother him, since it is taking place under government aegis. This reduces the controversy to the absurd but revealing proposition that capitalist infant formula kills babies, but socialist infant formula does not.[15]

In the interests of perspective, it is useful to compare corporate and church behavior. This the Presbyterian Task Force did:

> The entry of transnational corporations undermines the culture and values of other lands? The church has been in this business for centuries, most of the time proudly and self-consciously since it assumed that those traditional customs and values were "bad." Transnational corporations create, sustain, or enhance an indigenous elite and thus contribute to class tension and polarization? Examine the class structure of indigenous churches produced from Protestant mission activity, with its emphasis on education. Labor unions are the ethically preferable way of structuring industrial relations? Why don't the churches organize them among their own employees? Plant closing and abandonment is a socially irresponsible act? The urban landscape in the United States is littered with closed Presbyterian and similar churches. . . . It is . . . highly probable that the insight and experience that Presbyterians have gained working in transnational corporations—in such areas as labor and personnel relations, health and safety, EEO, for instance—could contribute significantly to reform and improvement of the church's corporate practice.[16]

FOR WHOM DO THE ACTIVISTS SPEAK?

Every Christian as a citizen has a right and responsibility to participate in political life. Church bodies and agencies also have a right and obligation to make a social witness, but they have an equal obligation to respect the ethical norms of their tradition and to take into account the views of their members on issues that affect the well-being of all citizens. This raises questions of the relation of individual conscience, Christian norms, and consensus. It also raises the question of the authority to be attributed to the pronouncement or action of a particular church body on a particular issue. In principle these conflicting points of reference can be sorted out rather clearly; in practice they are often confused, and on occasion the activists deliberately foster confusion to gain influence or other objectives.

As we saw in the foregoing chapters, CR activists have often spoken for only a minority of the members. Unfortunately, they tend to use language that implies a broader mandate, to stretch credentials, and to neglect disclaimers.

The Churches as 'Sponsors'

The following quotations from activists reveal their assumptions about those for whom they speak: "Church groups are submitting resolutions. . . ."[17] Stockholder resolutions are "sponsored by more than one hundred Protestant church agencies."[18] "Church shareholders, members of ICCR, filed resolutions with each of three companies involved."[19] Resolutions were "sponsored by the United Presbyterian Church in the U.S.A. and the Sisters of the Presentation."[20] From an open letter by H. William Howard, former president of the National Council of Churches: ICCR activities constitute the "responsible program efforts for seventeen major Protestant denominations."[21] "Churches have generally been responsible for at least two-thirds of the social responsibility shareholder resolutions."[22] Such assertions suggest that the church bodies acting through their duly constituted agencies are proposing the stockholder resolutions. An attorney for the ICCR told the Securities and Exchange Commission: "We are submitting the following comments on behalf of the twenty-two Protestant religious institutions and seventy-eight Roman Catholic religious institutions listed in Appendix A to this letter."[23]

In T. H. Smith's introduction to *Church Proxy Resolutions, 1982*, he described the ICCR as a "coalition of church investors" and as a "coalition of denominations."[24] The unwary reader is likely to assume that the denominations themselves, rather than particular denominational boards and agencies, are the members of this coalition, and that the coalition speaks for all the denominations listed. These denominations "seek to have their social concerns reflected"[25] through the actions of the ICCR, says Smith. "More than 100 church agencies are responsible for filing the various resolutions."[26]

CR advocates are quick to use phrases like "the churches believe" or "the church says," or to speak in "the voice of the church."[27] Who actually is speaking? Often a relatively small cadre who hardly represent democratically expressed influence—who in fact have often systematically ignored constituency opinion and resisted investigation, while fiercely defending their absolute right to speak for others. There is little evidence that the great majority of church members agree with the social-action elite of their denominations. Church bureaucrats are notoriously uneager to take the risk of putting their views up for open discussion and vote.

When the activists come before denominational bodies they admit: "No, we are not speaking *for* you technically and officially; rather we are speaking *to* you." But when they come before corporate board meetings they imply that they speak broadly and prophetically for the church, and for denominations. When pressed with the question "Are you speaking for the church or for the ICCR?," Smith acknowledged, "ICCR is a coalition of church agencies" that "act in their own behalf; ICCR does not speak for them or represent them."[28] Yet elsewhere in ICCR literature there is abundant evidence that the ICCR intends to speak "prophetically" to the corporations on behalf of "the church" generally, and the denominations represented in the coalition in particular.

Deterioration of Democracy in the Churches

The fixed quota system that was sponsored by George McGovern in the Democratic Party and adopted by church groups in the late 1960s has had several regrettable effects as well as some positive ones. Church groups were originally motivated to adopt the quota system because they wanted to get more young people, women, minorities, and lay persons involved in making local and national decisions within the churches. But the actual cost to fairly elected democratic representation has been high in unexpected ways.

The quota system gave the ruling liberal social-action elite a golden opportunity to eliminate conservative and moderate opinion. Centrists, fiscal conservatives, and moderates have tended to be the first ruled out by quotas. The few moderate leaders who remained in these radicalized decision-making bodies often faced a barrage of political invective. Feeling helpless, many dropped out and left the agencies largely in the hands of strident special-interest groups. The various versions of liberation theologians, trend feminists, and gay-rights advocates, plus a few opportunists, at times have virtually had the field to themselves.

Hence, the well-intentioned effort to make the agencies more representative has instead made them less representative. Fair elections were severely curbed by rigid quotas administered by idealists who believe in them and by political realists who know how to manipulate them. The resulting entrenched bureaucracy moved even further away from the possibility of criticism and constituency feedback. This deterioration of democracy has afflicted principally the mainstream Protestant churches. The evangelical and orthodox churches have been largely unaffected.

Thus the CR movement has rejected the spirit of classical liberalism represented by John Stuart Mill, who insisted that every democratic community needs the free competition of ideas to save it from sterility.[29] The CR movement is one of many liberal church bureaucratic subsystems that have carefully protected themselves from this competition. Rather the tendency has been to collect look-alikes and distrust outsiders. (I speak from experience as well as observation: after years of loyal ecumenical commitment, I soon became cast in the role of an outsider when I began asking questions at 475 Riverside Drive.[30])

The Gap Between Principles and Practice

According to the 1983 Presbyterian Task Force, many observers of the corporate-responsibility movement have felt that it "(1) projects a moral judgment of non-legitimacy on the U.S. economic system, the corporation within it, and the managers of it; and (2) takes a uniformly critical stance."[31] Where did these attitudes come from? Did they derive from denominational statements? Speaking of the United Presbyterian Church, the Task Force said it was unable to find "any policy statement of the General Assembly that suggests [such a] sweeping judgment."[32] There is a noticeable gap between the formal mandates passed by general legislative assemblies on broad principles of social concern and the way they are being carried out by CR advocates.

When church activists appeal to the Protestant tradition, they tend to emphasize not its central moral heritage but rather its nineteenth-century democratic tradition of fair representation, tolerance, historical relativism, and cultural pluralism. Yet in practice they have cared too little about these values. They have also turned their backs on the twentieth-century ecumenical vision that binds various Christian traditions together in the pursuit of greater unity and greater effectiveness in this world. They use the beautiful pluralism of Christian historical traditions merely as leverage for tolerance for their own idiosyncratic positions, which depart significantly from the Christological center that holds the varied historical traditions together. When the church advocates are charged with intolerance and lack of empathy, they dogmatically appeal to a very recent brand of liberation ideology as normative for all Christians and unquestionably faithful to the Scriptures, which they seldom quote or otherwise refer to.

This rigidity and lack of enthusiasm for genuine dialogue with those who differ is illustrated by the ecumenists' response to the charges on the CBS-TV "60 Minutes" program that church money was given to revolutionary causes in Central America and elsewhere. The typical reaction was that the sums involved were very small. Indeed, most mission funds of the National Council of Churches and the mainline denominations go to worthy causes; but should not the ecumenical bodies and the churches be accountable for even the small fraction of their money that is used to spread socialist propaganda, undermine economic freedom, or aid violent revolutions? "It's like virginity. You don't lose it in percentages," said Carl F. H. Henry.[33]

Noted *Time* magazine: "It is this willingness to blink at potential excess in the sunny glow of the social gospel that has caused so much trouble for the WCC, and now the NCC. Such blinks disturb Christians who view Marxism as the world's greatest long-term threat to human rights."[34] James Wall, editor of the *Christian Century*, reported that when he asked NCC staffers about potential NCC political extremism, they often supplied answers "filled with romantic revolutionary rhetoric. Mistakes of the left are either not seen or, as one person put it to me, 'We can't afford to indulge in that kind of criticism as long as people are oppressed anywhere in the world.'"[35] This attitude is the root cause of the distortions that necessitated this study.

THE PREFERENCE FOR SOCIALIST VALUES

Democratic capitalism has slowly gained constitutional protection for economic activity, guarding it against political intrusions in which state power pretends to have the moral right to control wages, prices, markets, and market mechanisms. Democratic capitalism allows freedom to persons and groups to gain and use income, to take risks, and to profit or lose from risk-taking.

It is difficult to discern why activist Americans who have benefited from a market system are so prone to scorn it. When wages and prices are open to bargaining, the results are more likely to be both efficient and fair. The market can serve these purposes only when it is relatively free from political control. Yet church-advocacy polemics against MNCs are filled with calls for political control of economic processes.[36]

What do radical critics intend to substitute for the free market? They talk less openly about practical alternatives to the market system, but all the signals point to their hidden agenda—socialist planning, the systematic political control of production and distribution. The operative word is "systematic." They tend to trust power that is vested in political rather than economic entities. They optimistically assume that political control of economic life will in the long run become democratically and constitutionally oriented, even if it may have to go through phases of revolutionary repression. This is a highly dubious assumption, if the experience of the Soviet Union, Eastern Europe, and Cuba is at all instructive. Despite these clear lessons, social planners deny the legitimacy of the market and insist that they have the moral right to plan the economic affairs of others.[37]

Fascination With State Power

The hardline CR advocates want the state to be the principal, or in some cases apparently the sole, economic agent. They often align themselves with those who distrust all independent economic initiative and advocate systematic political regulation of all economic activities.[38]

This fascination with rationalistic control of state power goes back to the French Revolution with its overconfidence in human reason and rational social design, and its faith that central planners knew best what was right for the masses. For these and other reasons, the French Revolution, which was rooted in class conflict, led to a bloody tyranny and became the model for the Marxist-Leninist revolution in Russia.[39]

In sharp contrast, the American Revolution was not a revolution in that rationalistic sense. It did not turn things upside down but was really an act of self-determination by a distant colony that wanted to enjoy the full liberties of the mother country. The abuses of French rationalism have occurred relatively less in the American tradition of democracy and free-market economy because of the greater stress on freedom from state power, and the principle of checks and balances limiting all government powers. Americans instinctively knew what theologian Reinhold Niebuhr frequently articulated—that governments, like all other collectivities, are prone to aggrandizing their power and control. Niebuhr saw a vigorous economy and market system as a healthy counterpoise to excessive government power. Yet church activists have opted more often for the French revolutionary pattern in their assumption that planners and government functionaries know best.

The socialist ideal seeks the overthrow of all existing economic structures not under socialist control, on the presumption that all such structures are corrupted by colonialism, militarism, and racism. The fact that socialist regimes themselves show signs of colonialism, militarism, and racism is overlooked by CR advocates.

Thinking Small—For Others

The same dogmatic rhetoric is addressed to international business enterprise. Much CR literature carries familiar complaints of state socialists against the multinational corporations. They dislike profits. They distrust economic freedom. They dislike bigness, and what they call monopoly. Yet they love monopolies. They love single, cohesive, "rational" economic structures that do not have the freedom and self-correcting mechanisms of the market.

These Western idealists welcome computer technology to manage their mailing lists, communication technology to reinforce their network, and transportation technology to fly them to conferences, but they resist introducing these technologies to developing countries, even to those countries clamoring for them. They encourage Third Worlders to "think small" while they, in the typical American way, think ever bigger.[40]

Frequently CR literature has called for radical income redistributions. But by whom and to whom is the income to be redistributed? How can the planners insure that the supposedly benign "distributors" (presumably bureaucrats like themselves) do not get more than those whom they claim to protect? Do not the elite in every "socialist" scheme get a great deal more in material benefits than the masses?

Freedom in socialist countries is restricted chiefly to the controlling elites, except for the ever-present black-market activities, which oddly enough become a thwarted symbol of justice in a distorted world. Yet it is almost impossible to find in all the corporate-responsibility literature a line of condemnation of the evils and damaged dreams and disillusionments of socialist romanticism.[41]

Worker 'Alienation' Under Capitalism

CR "research" efforts have frequently sought to demonstrate that MNC workers in Guatemala, the Philippines, the Dominican Republic, and other developing countries are alienated from meaning in their work, just as Marxian analysis decrees workers under capitalism are supposed to be.[42] They claim that MNCs intensify this alienation because top management is more distant geographically from the labor force, as well as more acquisitive and more manipulative.

But to what are we to compare the work environment of an enterprise in a developing country? If placed in a socialist environment or centrally planned economy, would that work be intrinsically more "meaningful"? Is a worker better off working for Del Monte in Mexico or for the Cuban government in a Cuban sugar-cane field? Would a worker rather be in unionized mining with Gulf + Western in the Dominican Republic or in a state-controlled coal mine in Poland where striking workers can be shot? The harder-line activists characteristically overlook the deficiencies of socialist practice and focus their criticism doggedly upon the deficiencies of free-market economies. Often they imply—and sometimes they explicitly state—that socialist models are more humane or even "implicitly Christian."[43]

It seems odd that many CR activists are more enthralled by socialist revolutions rooted in class warfare than by peaceful and democratic efforts at incremental change.[44] In Africa they have consistently supported such liberation movements as Frente de Libertação de Mocambique (FRELIMO), Frente Nacional de Libertação de Angola (FNLA), the South-West Africa People's Organization of Namibia (SWAPO), the Pan-Africanist Congress of Azania (PAC), the Zimbabwe Patriotic Liberation Front, and the Africa 2000 Project—all military organizations that have aimed at or achieved violent revolution, with various degrees of Marxist-oriented leadership and Soviet support—rather than grass-roots democratic initiatives such as those led by Abel Muzorewa in Zimbabwe. Muzorewa, a Methodist bishop, showed strength at the polls under internationally observed democratic elections. In November 1983 he was put in prison, where he was kept until September 1984. He has never had significant Western ecumenical support, and yet Muzorewa is one of the few African leaders who have stood the test of free elections.

Reams of church literature on multinationals carry virtually no criticism of Marxist repression. Church activists discover in Marxist categories something akin to the Christian concepts of liberation from bondage or the exodus from Egypt.[45] They say nothing of repression in Marxist Albania, Ethiopia, or Vietnam, but they are eager to speak about repression by the West. The double standard is appallingly disingenuous.

An Antagonism to Capitalism

Multinational corporations are viewed in a 1974 World Council of Churches (WCC) statement as a part of a decaying order. Their aim is "to take advantage of the cheap labor that is available in the host countries and to draw out profits from them, making use of the immense control they exercise over world trade and prices."[46] To some degree, this WCC statement rehearses the standard Marxist stereotype of international capitalist business operations.[47]

A Tanzanian delegate to a WCC commission on development boldly stated: "Ujamaa—Socialism—in the context of Tanzania is both an ideology for development and an ethic of distribution":

> [It] seeks to encourage spontaneous development of co-operative forms of production, through which the farmers and workers would obtain the social and economic advantages of socialist transformation, while the government provides only the costs and necessary inputs mainly for infrastructural development.[48]

The depth of Marxist influence in such rhetoric is very difficult to determine. Of these views Peter Berger rightly observed:

> It is important to note that in this ideology there is a general bias against market economies. I think to call this bias socialist is perhaps too precise. There are sympathies of a vague socialist character, but the overriding spirit is an antagonism to capitalism, to free enterprise, to the market.

"I'm not talking here about the hard Marxist supporters of this ideology," he continued. "I'm talking here about a softer element which really is not Marxist, but is much hazier" in its feeling that "there is something fundamentally wrong with capitalistic economies."[49]

Critics of the CR movement have wondered how deeply its leadership has been indirectly influenced or even directly guided by New Left "graduates" of the late sixties. According to Herman Nickel:

For student radicals of the 1960s, one way to turn the "struggle" into a steady job is to join the issues staff of organizations like the Interfaith Center on Corporate Responsibility, where they have come to occupy some key positions and coordinate and orchestrate those shareholders' resolutions that almost every chief executive of a large American corporation is familiar with by now. To generalize, the resolutions seem designed less to uplift the world's less fortunate people than to indict the business establishment. Much of the data on which the church activists rely is supplied by radical research organizations. . . . For the radicals, the alliance with church groups has many other tangible advantages. It provides a way of conducting political programs behind the shield of tax exemption, and access to a large organizational network. The church activists can gather information from missionaries throughout the world and disseminate propaganda to the memberships of participating churches.[50]

WEALTH AND THE CHRISTIAN ETHIC

Can hard-line church advocacy groups in good conscience accept money directly (contributions) or indirectly (profits on church investments) from corporations? If the corporation is so "evil," would not Christians be corrupted by association with it?

There is a strong Christian tradition for refusing assistance from corrupt sources. The *Apostolic Constitutions* of the fourth century called upon Christians "to avoid corrupt dealers, and not receive their gifts."[51] Further, the classical tradition required recipients of charity to be accountable publicly for everything received and given. The second-century Shepherd of Hermas wrote in the Mandates: "So those who receive will give account to God as to why they took it and for what purpose," adding: "Those who receive something in hypocrisy will be punished."[52] The early church fathers were intent upon avoiding money taken under false colors. Hermas wrote: "If at any time you be forced unwillingly to receive money from any ungodly person, lay it out in wood and coals, that so neither the widow nor the orphan may receive any of it. . . . For it is reasonable that such gifts of the ungodly should be fuel for the fire, not food for the pious."[53] Those who receive "in hypocrisy or through idleness, instead of working and assisting others," according to the *Apostolic Constitutions,* are not innocent, because they have "snatched away the morsel of the needy."[54]

Both the Scriptures and classical teaching warn about the dangers and benefits of wealth. Clement of Alexandria wrote on "Whether a Rich Man Be Saved," and John Chrysostom on "The Vanity of Riches," but they did not regard property or ownership as evil. Much later the great reformers, John Calvin and Martin Luther, recognized the need for creating wealth as well as the imperative for helping the poor. John Wesley balanced acquisition and social responsibility when he said: "Earn all you can, save all you can, and give all you can."[55]

CR Theological Sources

These classical sources apparently hold little interest for those activists who have so often invoked the Christian moral tradition.[56] Instead, they draw almost exclusively from recent secular idealist, rationalist, utopian traditions despite the hunger in the churches for a more classically ecumenical theology.[57] The writers most frequently cited by the activists are Gustavo Gutiérrez, José Míguez-Bonino, Paulo Freire, Harvey Cox, Dorothee Sölle, and Robert McAfee Brown, all proponents of some variety of liberation theology. Movement leaders have not even attended the instruction of the stronger thinkers among liberation theologians such as Juan Luis Segundo, Johannes Metz, Jürgen Moltmann, Letty Russell, Fred Herzog, and John B. Cobb. If asked what classical theology means to them, they might laboriously dredge up names like Paul Tillich, Rudolf Bultmann, and Dietrich Bonhoeffer. But they will speak more luminously of leftist heros like Ernst Bloch, Herbert Marcuse, Ché Guevera, and Ivan Illich. The recent political thought of Pope John Paul II is ignored.

The creation and intensification of a sense of guilt is a central concern of CR theology. It seeks to make Westerners feel guilty about production and profit, to make corporations feel guilty about bigness and technology, to make church members feel guilty about their political impotence, to make the rich feel guilty about their wealth, to make whites feel guilty about their whiteness, to make males feel guilty about the plight of females, and so on.[58] But surprisingly these political appeals are linked intimately with a religious view that elevates individual freedom above law, and that speaks about God's forgiveness and toleration of sin while it revs up its guilt machine.[59] There could be no politics of guilt without a theology of license.[60] This is the deepest dimension of disagreement between classical Christian teaching and the quasi-theological stance of the CR movement.

HAVE THE TACTICS BEEN EFFECTIVE?

Turning from the questions of authority, intention, and philosophy in the CR movement, we must now evaluate effectiveness. Have the strategy and tactics adopted by CR advocates succeeded in modifying the behavior of business corporations? From the beginning CR strategy has been focused on what the investor could do. Charles Powers, prominent early CR advocate, noted four tactics designed to "alter or encourage a corporation": (1) the buying or selling of stock; (2) investor proxy prerogatives; (3) litigation; and (4) informal persuasion.[61] This list has remained a standard conception of CR alternatives for over a decade. Notably absent from the list is the one most important avenue of influence—vocation, the daily presence of millions of church persons who in good conscience work in corporations, believe in their fundamental integrity and usefulness, and have many opportunities to affect corporate life.

According to classical Protestant ethics, the believer can serve God through accountability to his near and far neighbors in and through his vocation.[62] This theme, relevant to the discussion of Christian responsibility in the corporate order, has hardly been mentioned in the vast CR literature. In part the reason may be that the CR movement is simply embarrassed to have many of its own constituency in the camp that it is constantly attacking as immoral. But the neglect of the concept of vocation is due also to the movement's singleminded devotion to the more dramatic strategy of proxy challenges.

This failure of ecumenical imagination is intrinsically linked to one of its chief temptations: it has focused, as one might expect, on power, especially overt expressions of power at the highest levels of financial and governmental clout. This intensive focus has caused the neglect of the presence of committed Christians as workers and managers in corporate organizations.

Divestment, the selling of stock holdings, has not become a popular option among most CR activists, though from the sweeping rhetoric against capitalism that some of them engage in, one might think divestment would be the most consistent or conscionable tactic. The activists learned early on that it is usually more effective to stay within the system. There are, however, some examples of divestment. The United Methodist Church and the NCC withdrew $65 million from Citibank because it participated in a loan to South Africa.[63] United

Presbyterians took the divestment option in the ambiguous case of Duke Power, after an accident at the Brookside Mine in Kentucky, "without having first fully utilized available avenues of discussion and negotiation," said the Presbyterian Task Force Report. "As a result bonds, which in themselves convey no ownership stake or access, were sold precipitately at some loss."[64] In March 1981 thirteen Roman Catholic religious congregations in the Chicago area announced their withdrawal of $1.8 million in stocks and bonds from fifteen nuclear-weapons-related contractors.[65]

In June 1982, the United Presbyterian Church voted to withdraw its investments in twenty-one corporations heavily involved in military contracts:

> It is the policy of the General Assembly of the United Presbyterian Church not to invest in common stocks of corporations: (a) that are among the ten leading military contractors (measured as dollar volume of military contracts in the most recent year); (b) that, among the one hundred leading military contractors, are dependent on military contracts for more than 25 per cent of their sales (measured as the average ratio of military contracts to sales in the most recent three-year period); (c) that make the key nuclear components for nuclear warheads.[66]

Among the more widely used tactics in the movement are stockholder resolutions, dialogue with managers, policy forums, and jawboning attempts to persuade institutional investors to stay away from certain companies. Only occasionally, and with dubious success, have church groups undertaken a selective boycott, as they did in the J. P. Stevens, Gallo, and Nestlé cases.[67]

A significant tactic, according to T. H. Smith, is "network-building."[68] But this tactic tends to take the church groups even further away from their rightful constitutencies. It operates on the assumption that if political-action groups link with other action groups with impressive names, all presuming to represent someone, then they have created a constituency. But linking together a number of paper groups, each of which has little or no constituency, does not create an actual constituency for the "network."

The vacillation of the activists between the tactics of coercion and persuasion reflects a deeper ambivalence over the extent to which they regard corporations and the market system as morally legitimate institutions. The general tendency has been away from persuasion and toward coercive acts, legal threats, and media manipulation. Throughout the 1970s, the activists were testy and ligitious. On the whole they have distrusted corporate leaders, who were assumed to be deceptive, greedy, and anti-social.[69]

Proxy challenges at annual shareholder meetings have been the centerpiece of the CR movement. Church stockholders clearly have a right and at times a responsibility to use their shares to influence management.[70] There have been some successes, but we may ask: at what cost? Certainly this activism has given the churches the reputation for being unnecessarily confrontational and has underscored the disposition of the activists to overclaim the constituency they represent. For example, the shares of a denominational pension fund represent the assets of all persons covered, not just those who believe that the target corporation is misbehaving.

A limited focus on stockholder challenges bespeaks a distrust in the tedious pace of popular democracy and an impatience with the market economy. This mood was sensed in the responses to a Presbyterian questionnaire showing that only about one-third of the members thought it was right for church bodies to initiate stockholder resolutions.[71]

The Choice of Issues

The issues chosen by CR activists reveal their hidden agenda as well as their avowed objectives. Some questions have been persistently addressed, others completely ignored. Dr. S. Prakash Sethi, professor of business and social policy at the University of Texas at Dallas, observed: "Nuclear power plants and apartheid in South Africa consume masses of energy on the part of reformers, while less dramatic but potentially more helpful issues are ignored. Why do not we see many resolutions on product safety, conservation, reduction of brand proliferation, consumer protection, employee rights, or shareholder democracy?"[72]

The 1981 list of ICCR actions against U.S. corporations fell into these categories:

- Agribusiness (Del Monte)
- Biotechnology (General Electric)
- Economic conversion [from military to non-military products] (McDonnell Douglas)
- Foreign military sales (Ford, Textron)

• General energy policies and practices (Mobil)
• Infant formula (Abbott Laboratories, American Home Products, Borden, Bristol-Myers, Carnation)
• Latin American operations (Atlantic Richfield, Bank of America, Chemical Bank, Exxon, Fluor, Occidental Petroleum, Pennwalt)
• Namibian independence (Superior Oil)
• Nuclear energy policies and practices (UNC Resources, Westinghouse)
• Nuclear weapons (AT + T, DuPont, General Telephone and Electronics, Honeywell)
• Pesticide exports (American Cyanamid)
• Policies and practices in developing countries (American Home Products, Continental Illinois Corporation, Upjohn)
• South African operations (Bank of America, Citibank, Control Data, Doyle Dane Bernbach, Dresser Industries, First Union Bancorporation, Hewlett-Packard, IBM, Ingersoll-Rand, Republic National, Sears, Shearson-American Express, Southern Company, Squibb, Wells Fargo, Xerox)
• Toxic and genetic hazards (Bendix, Rockwell International)
• Toxic waste disposal (Occidental Petroleum)[73]

The Controlling Assumptions

The infant-formula issue dramatizes the controlling assumptions of the CR activists. In the earlier phases of the effort, instead of trying to improve the promotion methods of the manufacturers and help them serve mothers in less developed countries more effectively, the church advocacy groups tended to call for "an end to bottle feeding" in the Third World. This would have had the effect of depriving infants living there of a useful source of nutrition. An unstated assumption was that corporations were intrinsically unjust because they were driven only by the evil profit motive. The CR advocates pursued a complicated pattern of legal and strategic actions that revealed a rigidly anti-technological, anti-advertising, anti-profit, and generally anti-corporate mentality.

When Dan Raphael, director of the Human Lactation Center, suggested that infant-formula producers "could help solve the problem by devising cheap but nutritious local weaning foods," his proposal was rejected by some ICCR leaders, in part because it provided a potential solution to a controversy that CR advocates preferred to continue and exploit.[74] Even when companies accepted the WHO (World Health Organization) code designed to eliminate abuses in the sale of formula in developing countries, CR advocates were reluctant to loosen their grip on the dramatic issue.

In 1983 the United Methodist Task Force on Infant Formula finally made a formal request to the denomination's General Conference asking it to declare "'inappropriate' the continued boycott of Nestlé Corporation products by any general agency" of the church. The 1980 Methodist General Conference had declined the requests of two boards (Church and Society, Global Ministry) to commit the whole denomination to the Nestlé boycott. (The 1980 resolution on the infant-formula issue appears as appendix D, part 3.) The task force in 1983 stated that "the time has come for the denomination to act with unity, dropping confrontational strategies and pursuing goals through the task force's dialogue style."[75]

CR Successes

What has the CR movement as a whole achieved? In April 1983, Patricia Wolf, R.S.M., ICCR chairperson, and T. H. Smith reviewed the successes of the movement in an article called "Twelve Years on the Corporate Ballot."[76] A year earlier Howard Schomer had summarized achievements in "ten major issue-areas in church shareholder action."[77] In my view, the positive accomplishments mentioned by these writers include these:

• "From 1973-1976, resolutions that had been filed with Burroughs, Chrysler, Eastman Kodak, Ford, Gillette, International Harvester, IT + T, 3M, Pfizer, Texaco, Weyerhauser, and Xerox were withdrawn when the companies disclosed information requested in the resolutions. Most of the information concerned working conditions (wages, training, benefits) of South African employees. Over thirty companies have made such reports."[78]

• In 1977 churches sponsored shareholder resolutions with some large TV advertisers asking them to "discontinue advertising on shows with 'excessive or gratuitous violence.' A number of companies issued public pledges to that effect, and the shareholder resolutions were withdrawn."[79]

• In 1977 church resolutions challenged Exxon's strip-mining operations. The resolutions were approved by the stockholders.

• In 1978, in response to a request from a group of the Sisters of Loretto, Gulf agreed to adopt a policy that its officers and employees "are hereby directed not to provide or contribute corporate funds to any individual or political party for any political purpose or use in the Republic of Korea."[80] Mobil similarly developed a policy prohibiting foreign political contributions, which "drew heavily on the wording of the church-sponsored shareholder resolution."[81]

• In 1981 the World Health Organization developed the Code of Infant Formula Marketing to reduce the possibility of formula misuse.[82] (The boycott against Nestlé was formally ended in October 1984.)

• In 1982, when Western Air Lines was requested to report to its shareholders about its role in transporting deported Salvadoran exiles back to Salvador, where execution was expected, the company tried unsuccessfully to have the proposal excluded. When the request received 7.5 per cent of the vote, the management agreed to observe this request.[83]

• Goodyear decided to rehire 700 black workers who had been summarily dismissed in South Africa, in part through the influence of some United Presbyterian corporate-responsibility advocates.[84]

• "Many corporations have been effectively pressed to make their boards of directors more representative by the election of highly qualified minority persons, women, and independent outsiders."[85]

• In October 1983, leaders of the agricultural chemical industry announced they had agreed upon advertising guidelines for developing countries that "emphasize proper uses, limits, and hazards as well as benefits" of agricultural chemicals, in part because of pressure from church advocates.[86]

The Cost-Benefit Ratio

These achievements must be assessed against the costs of church activism. In many cases the results were little more than an agreement by companies to disclose various types of information. GM and four other companies agreed in 1974 to disclose employment information; Northrop agreed to disclose details of political contributions; Rockwell International disclosed information on weapons production; and so on. In other cases the "success" noted was nothing more than a hearing or a proposal for a study by the company. Hearings, for example, were held to study the environmental impact of Kennecott and AMAX copper-mining in Puerto Rico; GM promised to study the counseling and retraining of laid-off workers; GE agreed to study the company's involvement in nuclear weapons. Do such results as these actually confirm the claim that "the shareholder resolution process has resulted in some remarkable successes"?[87] There is no evidence that any of these actions has led to the "systemic changes" that much of the CR literature says are required to make the capitalistic system acceptable by Christian norms.

The modest achievements must also be measured against the cost in dollars—over $2 million for the ICCR alone in a twelve-year period (assuming an average budget of $200,000), not to mention the separate budgets of denominational groups engaged in CR activities. The movement has probably spent many tens of millions of dollars of church funds to gain its limited successes. Other costs include the energy that might have been directed to humanitarian activities, and intangible liabilities such as the loss of trust, diminution of respect between business and clergy, and the fostering of a reputation for aggressiveness, cynicism, radicalism, and litigiousness.

THE ECUMENICAL ORDEAL

Prior to the mid-sixties, dialogue in the ecumenical movement was more thorough, language was more constrained, sources were quoted more carefully, those who differed were given a hearing, statements went through numerous drafts, and when the process was over, a consensus emerged that usually was fairly reliable and enjoyed considerable grass-roots support. Not many topics were treated, but those that were had been examined fairly and thoroughly.

These disciplines and constraints have eroded. An inverse ratio now seems to prevail: the poorer the empirical research, and the less thorough the examination of theological and biblical roots, the greater the number of resolutions adopted. As theological reflection becomes less rigorous, the activists feel competent to speak about nearly everything. Literally hundreds of "research documents" have been produced by small cadres who presume to speak for us all. The ecumenical activists display an inordinate confidence in public pronouncements as a means of social change.

The denominations have permitted the activists to take over the store, and the center no longer holds. In place of the profound moral instruction for which their constituent communities and society hunger, mainline churches offer pretentious public actions, prophetic initiatives, and feigned shareowner righteousness about literally hundreds of subjects that dutifully echo the professional lobbies of the American political left.

The activists are determined to alter the course of history immediately and dramatically, without bothering with the disciplines of democratic and peaceful change. They support revolutionary groups with bold names and snappy slogans, but never seem to sense the logical consequences of their support. If they are aware that all socialist states—from the Soviet Union and Poland to Ethiopia—have been miserable failures not only in economic terms but often in the human cost of brutally repressive regimes, they do not mention it.

In the name of "prophetic witness," CR activists have condemned the whole American value system, sometimes without qualification.[88] Is it true that the United States is, as the Reverend William Howard, former president of the NCC, stated it, "a greedy, domineering global aggressor"?[89] Few people seem to be leaving this evil place for socialist utopias. Eldridge Cleaver, who had left, returned as a born-again American patriot. Some CR advocates would rather stay here and enjoy the freedoms and benefits while attacking the system with bitter rhetoric. They are free to do this, but in doing so they cannot expect the blessing of the church members they purportedly serve, and upon whose support they depend.

Where were the member denominations of the NCC and WCC while all this was happening? Clearly, there has been a massive failure of the mainline churches to control and discipline the ecumenical agencies that have presumed to speak on their behalf.

CHAPTER FIVE

Toward a More Effective Witness

THE CORPORATE-RESPONSIBILITY MOVEMENT should not be abandoned but rather reconceived, redirected, strengthened, and better grounded theologically. The lines of reconstruction have already been astutely articulated by the Presbyterian Task Force. Church social-action agencies need an infusion of new leadership that better understands Protestant pluralism, democratic values, and membership opinion. The strategy of shareowner resolutions need not be abandoned but should be balanced with other strategies.

Worldwide corporate enterprise needs the worldwide church as a partner in dialogue to search for ways in which corporations can contribute to Third World development, reduce poverty, and increase the prospects for justice and peace. That dialogue needs to be broadly based rather than limited to a few largely self-perpetuating bureaucratic elites. The churches should give more attention to their nurturing and teaching role and less to coercion and confrontation. They should seriously examine the moral underpinning of economic and political freedom, and recognize that the free market is more just than the state-controlled market.

Every pronouncement or action by a church body should be rooted in that body's theological and ethical traditions. Herein lies its ultimate moral authority. At the same time, the statement or action should be based on a thorough understanding of the facts of the matter being addressed. All the churches that have CR activists also have thousands of lay members who are experts in business, government, or international affairs. This kind of practical knowledge should be brought into the process of deliberation before church bodies act.

This does not mean that all pronouncements and actions must be based on a nose-counting consensus, or that the majority is always right. It does mean that the "prophetic witness" must be attuned to both the transcendent norms and the people for whom the "prophets" speak.

Every CR action has limited authority. The persons responsible for it cannot claim divine sanction for specific words or acts. Therefore, church leaders charged with making investment decisions, for example, should consult their own consciences as well as the policy statement of their denomination. It should be evident but often is not that the denominational investment officer, the layman in Omaha, and the CR activist are all part of the same moral tradition. Each has a conscience, and each has some ideas of how the churches should relate to corporations and to the economy as a whole. Social-action advocates and agencies have a duty both to *speak to* and to *listen to* their members so that the whole Christian community can make a constructive contribution to the public issues that affect them all.

Church officials also have a duty to *speak for* the agency or board they represent as long as they are authorized to do so by the policy of the denomination or ecumenical body concerned; but they should not claim to represent their whole denomination, much less all Protestants or the entire Christian church.

Some Questions for Activists

If the church activists can demand that corporations disclose information about their operations, sometimes including financial data, should not corporations have the right to ask the same of the activists? The answer is yes. The corporate manager has the right and a duty to ask of the church activist who is trying to influence the corporation such questions as these:

• Precisely whom do you represent? Do you come before stockholders with the force of the moral conviction of yourself only, your agency, or your denomination as a whole?

• Have the members of your denomination been consulted about this action?

• Are your views supported by the majority of them?

• If the press quoted you as a spokesman for "the church" or "the churches," or as one who "represents" your denomination, would you deliberately seek to amend or qualify that characterization? Do you actively and publicly disavow the term *representative* or *spokesman*?

• The ICCR *Shareowners' Manual* says that shareholders have a right to information about the corporation: "By law any shareowner may inspect the books and records of the corporation for any proper business purpose. An owner can inspect the company's list of shareholders, for instance, or certain of the company's financial records, or the minutes of meetings of the Board of Directors." Are your church records equally open to inspection? Are all expenditures open to public scrutiny? Will you provide copies of your agency's budget, showing line items for all sources of income and expenses?

• To whom does your agency or working group report? How is its board of directors chosen? What is your term of office?

• Will you provide the names and addresses of current members of your organization who have voted to take this action?

• How do you respond to the conclusions of the 1983 Presbyterian Task Force Report that (a) the quantity of resolutions processed annually by church groups may have surpassed the capacity of those groups "to insure adequate research support" and (b) "the church's witness in economic affairs has frequently suffered from an overemphasis on the negative aspects of corporation and governmental policy"?

The Vocational Approach

The CR movement has been asking how churches are most meaningfully to exercise practical influence on corporate life. Far more important than boycotts, litigation, and stockholder actions, yet only incidentally or occasionally acknowledged, is the presence of large numbers of Christians in transnational corporations.

If one believes, as I do, that corporations despite their imperfections perform legitimate and socially constructive services at home and abroad, one is compelled to conclude that working for a corporation as a janitor or the chief executive officer can be seen as a Christian vocation. At the very least, the morally sensitive employee will seek to avoid involvement in corrupt practices and will bring them to the attention of his superiors. But in positive terms, he can be a force for greater corporate responsibility within the system.

This vocational approach is perhaps the most effective way to ensure the accountability of the corporation or, for that matter, the church, the state, or a university. Constant vigilance, dedication to basic values, and a commitment to renewal from within are probably the best means for keeping any institution true to its purposes and responsive to the needs of a democratic and pluralistic society.

Concluding Observations

To conclude this examination of the corporate-responsibility movement, let us return to the twelve points about church involvement raised in the preface.

1. Polls of church members show they are far more favorably disposed toward multinational corporations than the official church pronouncements. The majority do not regard MNCs as inimical to their own interests or to the cause of peace, freedom, and justice. Nor do they view corporations as intrinsically corrupting.

2. Many church members are dismayed that their views have been overlooked or bypassed in the decision-making process that produces pronouncements and actions with which they disagree. At the same time, they are reluctant to call for accountability.

3. Church bodies have a right and responsibility to address corporate and other social issues, but often this responsibility is distorted because the final decisions are left to social-action bureaucrats who are not fully responsive to the views of their constituency or to the democratic procedures for making decisions. These abuses must be corrected by a reassertion of democratic control all along the line.

4. Denominations that have repeatedly had difficulty in making boards and agencies more accountable have reasonable grounds for dissolving offending agencies or restructuring them, building in more reliable mechanisms to assure accountability.

5. Church funds should not advance state-controlled economic systems but rather should encourage market economies that are compatible with Judeo-Christian ethical norms of respect for human dignity, truth, freedom, justice, order, and the rule of law.

6. Mainstream Protestant churches must reject, as a betrayal of the ecumenical movement, ecumenical agencies that presume to speak for the whole church or a major portion of it but are actually controlled by self-perpetuating bureaucrats whose ties with grass-roots Christians are slight and who have demonstrated a preference for secular solutions.

7. Missionaries and others who provide information and advice from abroad to American churches on social issues must be tested to ascertain the reliability of their sources and their political orientation. Are they more Marxist than Christian in their fundamental assumptions? If so, their credentials must be questioned and their advice taken with more than a grain of salt.

8. Persons whose historical and moral assumptions have been decisively determined by Marxist ideology must be told in no uncertain terms not to foist these assumptions off on the churches as Christian.

9. The serious Christian conscience must be attentive to real guilt for actual social injustice without permitting itself to be manipulated by those who would cynically use guilt as an instrument of political strategy.

10. Freedom of conscience must be steadfastly protected both in the church and in society as a whole. Delegated church representatives must remember that it is unjust and unfair to represent the consciences of others without consulting them.

11. Each church member is primarily accountable to God and his conscience nurtured by Scripture and tradition. Those who make a social witness in word or deed should not become inordinately concerned with the response of the press. They should resist the temptation to manipulate the media by selecting partial and self-serving facts or by promoting stories primarily because they are dramatic or sensational.

12. In the attempt to improve corporate behavior, the social activism dramatized in shareholder action is less effective than the vocational approach. Christians working within corporations have many opportunities—as workers or managers—to improve the quality and sensitivity of corporate operations at home and abroad.

A Personal Afterword

WHEN I ARRIVED in Geneva in 1966 to attend the World Council of Churches' World Conference on Church and Society, I had high expectations that the conference would be as important to me as the WCC's 1954 Evanston Assembly had been. For over fifteen years I had been actively involved in ecumenical activity, primarily in the Inter-Seminary Movement, first as a student and then as a professional advisor. I had happily labored in ecumenical vineyards with full confidence in ecumenical leadership. I had written and edited books, articles, and study guides for the Student Christian Movement. I had conscientiously been involved in making denominational campus organizations more ecumenical (which of course I did not realize would later be seen as a dubious achievement). I had planned and guided numerous ecumenical conferences and events. So as I came to Geneva I felt myself a loyal participant in the modern ecumenical tradition, with Albert Outler and Richard Niebuhr my chief mentors.

But at Geneva I quickly realized that I was swimming in a very different ecumenical stream. It was a blatantly politicized and media-hyped event, reeking with romantic idealism, mixed with unusually high levels of resentment and outrage. This high-decibel mood was one that I had not previously encountered among ecumenical centrists. What had happened? What had changed?

This study is an attempt to probe at least some parts of the answer to that question. 1966 was the pivot of a shift of ecumenical sensibilities that greatly affected ecumenical social action, research, and public-policy formation. The leaders became increasingly out of touch with church members and eventually took a quantum leap toward a new "fundamentalism of the left."

Geneva left a persimmon-like aftertaste in my consciousness that has never quite gone away. The Western legal corpus was peremptorily drawn and quartered. Socialist rhetoric was simplistically identified with the mission of the church. We from the West were supposed to go through craven gestures of guilt, self-effacement, and embarrassment over our economic sins—the sins of creating wealth, making profits, paying wages, trading goods and services. Those who led the list of Western penitents at Geneva were soon to take increased leadership in ecumenical affairs. They were the ones who got key roles in the next production, the 1968 Detroit Conference, where Geneva was replayed for a press that was able to garner from it a few desperate, hand-wringing media events.

I had long discussions in Geneva with Paul Ramsey, Walter Muelder, Richard Schaull, Paul Abrecht, Harvey Cox, André Dupré, and others, about the new mood, which we all interpreted differently. Paul Ramsey went home and took immediate responsible action by writing an exemplary book, *Who Speaks for the Church?* My own response was much slower. It took me about a decade to recover, to figure out what continental plates had shifted in my consciousness and why Geneva had turned me from a loyal ecumenist to a polite but dogged questioner, and gradually to move from political radicalism toward a more chastened, critical, gradual approach. This book is the result of that long, silent search for some answers. Writing it has allowed me to take a fresh look at what has happened to ecumenical ethics and social-policy formation by examining one small but intense arena of activity, the corporate-responsibility movement.

I had spent at least twenty years of my political life committed to utopian social expectations, first as a pacifist and later as a quasi-socialist and "radical theologian"; the painful process of disillusionment took nearly a decade to mature. Since the mid-seventies I have become a crusty critic of modernity, a proponent of post-modern orthodoxy, a skeptic toward psychotherapeutic social-change assumptions, a miner of ancient Christian texts, and an admirer of classical Christian theology. I remain an avid ecumenical loyalist, but I celebrate the ancient ecumenism of the Seven Ecumenical Councils far more heartily than modern politicized ecumenism.

Long before Geneva my political views had been shaped by a deep populist distrust of big business. At the age of twenty, in 1952, I was a local organizer for the Students for Democratic Action and an ardent admirer of Ho Chi Minh's People's Revolution. This was more than a dozen years before heavy American involvement in Vietnam. I firmly believed that Marxist categories offered a vastly more appropriate view of history and politics than did a hopelessly corrupt and corrupting capitalism. When I thought of myself as a socialist, what I meant by socialism was the consistent preference for political control of economic activities. It was a dream I spent years trying to live out. My perceptions of socialist idealism were not acquired second hand and are not those of an unscathed outsider.

As a pacifist-socialist I was a target of McCarthyism in the early 1950s, when even a hint of pink was considered traitorous by the zealous (and when both Richard Nixon and Robert Kennedy were fervent anti-Communists). Even today I remain extremely sensitive both to the dreadful memory of real McCarthyism and to present-day activists who cheaply invoke defensive charges of a "new McCarthyism" but who never had to face the old one. Some may construe my efforts to sort out benign and malignant types of soft and hard Marxist and quasi-Marxist influences in ecumenical advocacy activism as a kind of McCarthyism. The corporate-responsibility movement has, in fact, an unfortunate record of answering critics with the ploy that efforts to show Marxist influence constitute a "new form of McCarthyism" (cf. T. H. Smith and Leah Margulies, BRE 12 [the list of abbreviations is on page 133]).

If anything I have written seems less than trustful of Marxist analysis, it comes out of a long experience of being enamored by that analysis. I have lived with socialism long enough to know some of its and my own weaknesses. But to categorize my observations as McCarthy-like is to misunderstand both my method and my intention. I have refrained from implying that anyone was giving aid and comfort to socialist revolutions or Marxist dreams without letting him speak for himself through direct quotation or extensive documentation. The extent of Marxist leanings or sympathies of various religious writers is very difficult to determine. I prefer to let them speak for themselves and leave the reader to judge.

Over the last quarter century I have lived happily as a theologian in two professional communities, academic and clerical. I genuinely love both of these communities and have a life-long pattern of friendships in them. In both it is generally expected of me that I be appropriately left-leaning politically, anti-free-market and pro-regulatory in economic affairs, mildly cynical about business, and generally enthusiastic about social revolutionaries whatever hills they happen to be fighting in. Yet I find convincing the hypothesis of Reginald Jones (CTI 130) that the criticisms people make of business activities tend to increase in direct proportion to the distance of those critics from decision-making about actual business operations. Many people in organized labor, government, law, and other professions that interact daily with business seem to have a clearer understanding of how business works than academics and religious moralists who have tended to stand aloof with supposedly cleaner hands. The most intransigent and sometimes hysterical criticism of corporate operations comes not from organized labor but from these two sources with the greatest distance from business realities— tenured academics and liberal bureaucratic church professionals. Something deeply engrained in many leading academics and clerics makes them, with the best of intentions, implacable adversaries of business. The minds of many are closed to the possibility that any sort of business, especially big business, could be less corrupt than they imagine. Both tend to place their hopes in government.

As I proceeded with this controversial study, I increasingly felt a strong sense of vocational commitment to the task. Never before have I been so strongly advised by concerned academic colleagues to take special care in argumentation and to observe the rules of evidence. Some cautioned against entering the arena at all, on the grounds that the subject is not the central area of my expertise, or that the issues are sufficiently complex that to do them full justice could reasonably occupy a lifetime of study, or that I am likely to arouse a hornet's nest of special interests. Taking all caveats into consideration, I came to the conviction that I could not in good conscience step aside from this challenge. In no previous writing have I felt a greater compulsion to tell the truth accurately as I see it and let the chips fall. So I wish to express my gratitude for colleagues who have given me thoughtful admonitions out of their concern for me, and also the gratitude that I feel toward God for enabling me to continue along this path even with its many obstacles.

APPENDIX A

Corporate Responsibility: The Secondary Network

The primary network of Protestant and Catholic organizations involved in corporate-responsibility activism is described in chapter one. The secondary network is more diffuse and extensive. Many church activist, educational, lobbying, and research organizations that seem oriented generally toward the same goals may regard corporate responsibility as only one of many areas of their concern. What follows is hardly a complete list, nor is it wholly current. Some of the organizations named no longer exist. The groups differ in overall outlook, and their views on particular CR issues may differ. What the list does is to suggest the range of movements and agencies that have promoted certain causes or activities of the corporate-responsibility movement, or have provided it with literature, research studies, or resources, or have been involved in education, political action, lobbying, or public communications on issues relating to corporate responsibility.

The Africa Fund, 305 E. 46th St., New York, N.Y. 10017 (receives NCC assistance for publication of *Southern Africa Perspective*). / **Agribusiness Accountability Project,** 1000 Wisconsin Ave. N.W., Washington, D.C. 20007. / **Agribusiness Accountability Project, West,** San Francisco Study Center, P.O. Box 5646, San Francisco, Calif. 94101 (publisher of *AgBiz Tiller*). / **American Baptist Churches in the U.S.A.,** Board of National Ministries, Valley Forge, Pa. 19481. / **American Committee on Africa,** 305 E. 46th St., New York, N.Y. 10017. / **American Friends Service Committee,** 1501 Cherry St., Philadelphia, Pa. 19102. / **Boston Industrial Mission,** 56 Boylston St., Cambridge, Mass. 02138.

Canadian Council of Churches, World Concerns Commission, 20 St. Clair Ave. E., Toronto, Ontario M4T 1M9. / **Center for New Corporate Priorities,** 1516 Westwood Blvd., Los Angeles, Calif. 90024. / **Center for the Study of Development and Social Change,** 1430 Massachusetts Ave., Cambridge, Mass. 02138. / **Chicago Coalition on Southern Africa,** 22 East Van Buren, Chicago, Ill. 60605 (reports on Chicago corporations with South African connections). / **Chicago Religious Task Force on El Salvador,** 407 South Dearborn, Chicago, Ill. 60605. / **Christian Church (Disciples of Christ), Division of Homeland Ministries,** 222 S. Downey Ave., Indianapolis, Ind. 46206. / **Church Committee on Human Rights in Asia,** 5700 Woodlawn Ave., Chicago, Ill. 60637. / **Church of the Brethren,** 110 Maryland Ave. N.E., Washington, D.C. 20002. / **Church Women United in the U.S.A.,** 475 Riverside Dr., New York, N.Y. 10115. / **Citizens' Action Program,** 600 W. Fullerton, Chicago, Ill. 60614. / **Clearinghouse on Corporate Social Responsibility,** 277 Park Ave., New York, N.Y. 10017. / **Clergy and Laity Concerned,** 198 Broadway, New York, N.Y. 10038. / **Coalition for Human Rights in South Africa,** 10 E. 87th St., New York, N.Y. 10028. / **Committee for Economic Development,** 477 Madison Ave., New York, N.Y. 10022. / **Committee to Oppose Bank Loans to South Africa,** 305 E. 16th St., New York, N.Y. 10017. / **Community Action on Latin American (CALA),** 731 State St., Madison, Wisc. 53703. / **Comparable Worth Project,** 488 41st St., Oakland, Calif. 94609. / **Corporate Accountability Research Group,** 1346 Connecticut Ave. N.W., Washington, D.C. 20036. / **Corporate Action Project,** 1500 Farragut St. N.W., Washington, D.C. 20011 (publisher of *Corporate Action Guide*). / **Corporate Data Exchange,** 198 Broadway, New York, N.Y. 10038. / **Corporate Democracy,** 1165 Park Ave., New York, N.Y. 10028. / **Corporate Responsibility Action Group,** 3900 N. Third St., Milwaukee, Wisc. 53212. / **Corporate Responsibility Planning Service,** Human Resources Network, 2010 Chancellor St., Philadelphia, Pa. 19103. / **Council for Corporate Review,** 212 W. Franklin Ave., Minneapolis, Minn. 55404. / **Council on Economic Priorities,** 84 Fifth Ave., New York, N.Y. 10011. / **Cuba Resource Center,** Box 206, Cathedral Station, New York, N.Y. 10025.

Energy Action Committee, 1523 L St. N.W., Washington, D.C. 20005. / **Episcopal Church: Domestic and Foreign Missionary Society,** Episcopal Church Center, 815 Second Ave., New York, N.Y. 10017; **Public Issues Office,** same address; **World Mission in Church and Society,** same address. / **Exploratory Project for Economic Alternatives,** 2000 P St. N.W., Washington, D.C. 20036. / **Farm Labor Organizing Committee (FLOC),** 714½ South St. Clair, Toledo, Ohio 42609. / **Federation of Women Shareholders in American Business,** P.O. Box 190, Grand Central Station, New York, N.Y. 10017. / **Friends United Meetings, Wider Ministries Commission,** 101 Quaker Hill Dr., Richmond, Ind. 47374. / **GATT-Fly,** 11 Madison Ave., Toronto, Ontario M5R 2S2. / **Glide Foundation,** 330 Ellis St., San Francisco, Calif. 94102. / **Howard Schomer Associates,** Consultants on Social Policy, 13 Fairmount Ave., Upper Montclair, N.J. 07043. / **Infant Formula Action Coalition (INFACT),** 1701 University Ave., Minneapolis, Minn. 55414. / **INFORM,** 381 Park Ave. South, New York, N.Y. 10016. / **Institute for Food and Development Policy,** 2588 Mission St., San Francisco, Calif. 94110. / **Institute for Local Self-Reliance,** 2425 18th St. N.W., Washington, D.C. 20009. / **International Council for Equality of Opportunity Principles,** 1501 North Broad St., Philadelphia, Pa. 19122. / **International Documentation on the Contemporary Church (IDOC),** 235 East 49th St., New York, N.Y. 10017. / **Interreligious Taskforce on U.S. Food Policy,** 110 Maryland Ave. N.E., Washington, D.C. 20002. / **Investor Re-**

sponsibility Research Center, 1319 F St. N.W., Washington, D.C. 20004 (publishes *News for Investors* and *Proxy Issues Report*). / **Joint Strategy and Action Committee,** 475 Riverside Dr., New York, N.Y. 10115. / **Leadership Conference of Women Religious,** 8808 Cameron St., Silver Spring, Md. 20910.

National Action Research on the Military Industrial Complex (NAR-MIC), 160 North 15th St., Philadelphia, Pa. 19102 (an American Friends Service Committee project). / **National Catholic Coalition for Responsible Investment,** 3900 N. Third, Milwaukee, Wisc. 53212. / **National Commission on Coping With Interdependence,** P.O. Box 2820, Princeton, N.J. 08540. / **National Farmworker Ministry,** 1430 W. Olympic Blvd., Los Angeles, Calif. 90015. / **National Federation of Priests Councils,** 1307 S. Wabash Ave., Chicago, Ill. 60605. / **National Land for People,** 1759 Fulton, Fresno, Calif. 93721, and 2348 N. Cornelia, Fresno, Calif. 93711. / **New Chicago African Liberation Support Committee,** P.O. Box 87141, Chicago, Ill. 60680. / **New World Resource Center,** and the **Chicago Committee for African Liberation,** 1476 W. Irving Park Rd., Chicago, Ill. 60613. / **North American Anti-Imperialist Coalition,** 2526 North Holsted, Chicago, Ill. 60614. / **North American Congress on Latin America,** 151 West 19th St., New York, N.Y. 10011. / **Northern California ICCR,** 870 Market St., San Francisco, Calif. 94102. / **Office of Political Prisoners in Chile,** 1414 Broadway, New York, N.Y. 10025. / **Pacific Rim Project,** Box 26415, San Francisco, Calif. 94126. / **Project Equality,** 4049 Pennsylvania, Kansas City, Mo. 64111. / **Project on Corporate Responsibility,** 1609 Connecticut Ave. N.W., Washington, D.C. 20009. / **Project Standard Oil,** 6075 E. Alta, Fresno, Calif. 94727. / **Public Citizen,** 2000 P St. N.W., Washington, D.C. 20036. / **Reformed Church in America, Section for World Mission,** 475 Riverside Dr., New York, N.Y. 10115. / **Taskforce on the Churches and Corporate Responsibility,** 129 St. Clair Ave., West Toronto, Ontario M4V 1N5.

Unitarian Universalist Service Committee, 78 Beacon St., Boston, Mass. 02108. / **United Church of Christ: Board for Homeland Ministries,** 132 W. 31st St., New York, N.Y. 10001; **Office for Church in Society,** 110 Maryland Ave. N.E., Washington, D.C. 20002. / **United Methodist Church: Board of Church and Society,** 100 Maryland Ave. N.E., Washington, D.C. 20002; **Board of Global Ministries,** 475 Riverside Dr., New York, N.Y. 10115. / **United Nations Center Against Apartheid,** United Nations, New York, N.Y. 10017. / **United Nations Center on Transnational Corporations,** United Nations, New York, N.Y. 10017. / **United Presbyterian Church, Ministries of Health, Education, and Social Justice,** 475 Riverside Dr., New York, N.Y. 10115. / **United States Catholic Conference (USCC), Secretariat for Social Development and World Peace,** 1312 Massachusetts Ave. N.W., Washington, D.C. 20005. / **Washington Office on Africa,** 110 Maryland Ave. N.E., Washington, D.C. 20002 (publishes *Washington Notes on Africa*). / **Western New York Coalition,** Center for Justice, 2278 Main St., Buffalo, N.Y. 14214.

Corporate Responsibility: The Leaders

The twenty persons listed here were among the most influential leaders during the first decade and a half of the corporate-responsibility movement. The positions and affiliations given are not necessarily current.

Richard Barnet, co-director, Institute for Policy Studies

Diane Bratcher, manager of publications, Interfaith Center on Corporate Responsibility

Ruth E. Busko, former editor, *The Corporate Examiner*

Michael Crosby, O.F.M./Cap., Corporate Responsibility Program of the Justice and Peace Center, Milwaukee

Charles Dahm, O.P., Illinois Coalition for Responsible Investment

Michael Donahue, S.J., New York Province, Society of Jesus

Horace Gale, treasurer, American Baptist Home Mission Societies

Christian T. Iosso, Committee on Mission Responsibility Through Investment, United Presbyterian Church

Florence Little, former treasurer, General Board of Global Ministries, United Methodist Church

Charles P. Lutz, director, Office of Church and Society, American Lutheran Church

Regina Murphy, S.C., Sisters of Charity of St. Vincent de Paul, New York

Robert Nee, S.S.C.C., co-chairman, New England Catholic Coalition for Responsible Investment

Charles W. Powers, formerly executive director of corporate action, Cummings Engine Company; previously at Yale Divinity School

Claire Randall, former general secretary, National Council of Churches

Howard Schomer, Howard Schomer Associates

Timothy H. Smith, executive director, Interfaith Center on Corporate Responsibility

Audrey Smock, World Issues Office, United Church Board for World Ministries

Joyce Soule, treasurer, Women's Division, United Methodist General Board of Global Ministries

Frank White, first director, Corporate Information Center

Patricia Young, National Committee for World Food Day

APPENDIX C

A Question on
NCC Representation

In this excerpt from a June 4, 1965, hearing before the House Committee on Education and Labor on the proposed repeal of a section of the Taft-Hartley Act, two congressmen question an NCC spokesman about whether his statement represents the views of members of NCC member churches.

Rev. Mr. J. Edward Carothers: I am the Reverend J. Edward Carothers, associate general secretary, National Division of the Board of Missions of the Methodist Church. I am also a member of the Program Board of the Division of Christian Life and Mission of the National Council of Churches of Christ in the U.S.A. and secretary of its Commission on the Church and Economic Life. I have been asked to make this statement on behalf of the National Council of Churches. As you know from previous testifiers for the Council, it comprises thirty-one Protestant and Orthodox communions. Obviously, we make no claim to be speaking for each of these member churches individually nor for all the members in any one communion. The viewpoints presented in this statement have been officially endorsed by the National Council of Churches' policy-determining General Board, which is broadly representative of its member church bodies, and whose members are designated by them. . . .

Congressman Robert Griffin: Has the National Council of Churches ever polled the members of the member churches of the National Council of Churches on this issue?

Rev. Carothers: No, we don't proceed in that way. Perhaps I can briefly outline our procedure. The General Board is made up of persons elected or designated by the denominations. The denominations designate or elect these persons—they have different ways of doing it themselves—to the General Board. When a position or policy statement is being prepared, it is with the understanding that the General Board is speaking as the General Board of the National Council of Churches, and the persons who are there to make the decision obviously are representing their own point of view, although they are sent there by their denominations. In that sense, it is a representative body, and it does not, any more than the average state or county or even the federal government, go back to the citizens for a mandate on every issue.

Mr. Griffin: But as a representative board, it would be the intention and purpose of the board to try to reflect the views on the membership that they represent. Wouldn't that be true?

Rev. Carothers: Not necessarily. I think there would be some times when

111

persons after long study—and in this case it was two years—experienced a change of mind and actually knew that their constituency would differ with them. Yet they would vote for it, and this constitutes some problems for the representatives from denominations. . . .

Mr. Griffin: Rev. Carothers, I am a member of a church that is affiliated with the National Council of Churches, and I want to say on the record that I bitterly resent the fact that the National Council of Churches is involving itself in an issue such as this, which is not a moral issue as such, but which is a legislative issue, particularly when you are taking a position which is demonstrably in opposition to the views of a majority of the member churches of the National Council of Churches.

Rev. Carothers: I don't think it is so obvious, Mr. Griffin.

Mr. Griffin: Would you take a poll of your members and see whether that statement is true?

Rev. Carothers: I don't know whether it is. I just say it is not obvious. Something that is obvious must be demonstrable. That is not demonstrable. You know, a minority can be right. Even one person can be right, and I would want to grant you that right without resentment.

Mr. Griffin: Rev. Carothers, the interesting difference, however, in the situation that I find myself in as a member of a church affiliated with the National Council of Churches, resenting the fact that the board, first, has involved itself in a political issue, and secondly, has taken a position with which I disagree—the interesting and crucial difference is that I can withdraw voluntarily from the church of which I am a member, if I wish to do so. I don't have to be forced to contribute to the financing of the National Council of Churches, if I don't want to. You, on the other hand, speaking in behalf of the National Council of Churches, are advocating the repeal of Section 14(b), which would make it possible and legal for people to be forced to join a union or to pay dues in order to hold their jobs. . . .

Congressman Ralph Scott (acting chairman): Just a moment ago I was handed the following telegram addressed to me at this address: "We, the undersigned members of the denominations affiliated with the National Council of Churches, hereby protest the scheduled appearance of a council official before the congressional subcommittee. . . . Any statement or intimation that the National Council's 39 million clergy and lay members favor repeal of Section 14(b) is unsupportable. No person may presume to speak on this issue on behalf of the Council's membership, inasmuch as member congregations have not been polled on the repeal or retention of Section 14(b)." This telegram is signed by more than 100 clergymen and church officials of practically all denominations.

APPENDIX D

Three Denominational Statements

In the brief statements included here, (1) a United Presbyterian presbytery asks the 1970 General Assembly to elicit guidelines for church investment policy, (2) the 1979 General Synod of the United Church of Christ hears about the goal of corporate-responsibility actions, and (3) the 1980 United Methodist General Conference resolves to take action on infant-formula distribution.

1. Overture on Guidelines for Church Investment Policy From the Presbytery of San Francisco to the General Assembly of the United Presbyterian Church, 1970.

Whereas Jesus and the whole biblical teaching is consistent in calling upon believers to make their words and deeds coincide: and *Whereas* the Church has intensified its concern and sense of responsibility for both peace, racial, economic, and social justice; and *Whereas* the environmental or ecological crisis imposes upon the Church heavy responsibilities for witness and mission with respect to man's stewardship of the resources of God's whole created order; and *Whereas* the Church's investment policies have for decades reflected its refusal to invest in tobacco or liquor stocks, thereby indicating a partial recognition of the Church's responsibility to apply ethical criteria to its investment program; and *Whereas* the scope of the Church's vision as to the effect of investment on the faithfulness of its witness was recently broadened to include counsel against support of repressive regimes like those in Southern Africa; and *Whereas* efforts to bring investment policy into line with the ethical and social teaching of the General Assembly and make investment decisions a conscious instrument of mission should be guided by a comprehensive policy rather than fragmented individual decisions,

Now, Therefore the Presbytery of San Francisco, meeting in San Francisco on April 28, 1970, does hereby respectfully overture the 182nd General Assembly (1970) to direct the Council on Church and Society to: (1) conduct a study of the issues in applying ethical and social criteria to church investment policy, involving appropriate staff and Board members of General Assembly agencies as well as technical consultants, (2) prepare comprehensive guidelines by which the process of portfolio analysis and investment decision of all corporate entities related to the United Presbyterian Church in the U.S.A. (including, but not limited to the United Presbyterian Foundation,

113

all Boards, agencies, and judicatories) can best express the whole Church's commitment to its mission in the world and its ethical teachings, (3) report the findings and recommendations growing out of its study and the suggested guidelines to the 183rd General Assembly (1971) and that, until such time as comprehensive guidelines for investment policy are adopted by the General Assembly, the 182nd General Assembly direct the Council on Church and Society to give counsel to United Presbyterian Boards, agencies, and judicatories as they seek to bring their investment portfolios to the support of corporations or governments that take the lead in reducing manufacture of or dealing in weapons, in taking affirmative steps in overcoming racism, economic and social injustice, and/or eliminating the pollution and exploitation of the environment.

2. **Excerpt from "Report to the Twelfth General Synod of the United Church of Christ on 1977-79 Corporate Social Responsibility Actions," 1979.**

The business system as it exists today has evolved in an endeavor to meet the needs and aspirations of humankind. Those needs and aspirations are ever changing. Over the long run, a business corporation or other organization must serve society and meet the changes desired by society; if the organization does not do so, its business will decline and ultimately it will perish. Thus, every business organization is, or should be, under continuing pressure to assure that what it does it useful and provides effective service to people. This involves a continuing appraisal and reappraisal of objectives, methods, and performance.

Such an examination of conscience and action will be thoroughgoing only if it is undertaken in the light shed by religious perspectives on all economic activity. Hopefully, church investors should be able to bring such perspectives to bear on matters that corporate management can influence, and persuade corporate management to pursue socially desirable policies.

3. **Resolution on Infant Formula Distribution, General Conference of the United Methodist Church, 1980.**

Whereas, the problem of infant malnutrition and mortality is a critical aspect of global hunger; and, *Whereas,* an intense international debate is underway concerning the provision of optimum infant nutrition in conditions of chronic poverty, illiteracy, and disease; and, *Whereas,* the issues of this debate are of considerable scientific, economic, psychological, and political complexity; and *Whereas,* Christians from a number of churches and religious organizations have been engaged in the continuing debate and in a variety of actions relating to the issues, including consultation and a selective boycott of one of the major suppliers (the Nestlé Company);

Therefore, Be It Resolved that the 1980 General Conference authorize the General Council on Ministries (GCOM) to establish a representative task force of persons from the council and the church at large, including persons designated by the Board of Global Ministries and the Board of Church and Society and persons of special expertise with instructions to:

(a) Review and update developments in the continuing debate and action relating to the controversy.

(b) Take initiatives with the three major American suppliers of such infant formula products (Bristol-Myers Corporation, American Home Products, and Abbott Laboratories) and with Nestlé, the largest supplier, to establish constructive dialogue, seeking modifications of advertising, promotion, and distribution methods which may contribute to nutritional harm of infants in areas of chronic poverty, illiteracy, and inadequate hygienic conditions.

(c) Convey to the suppliers the sense of utmost urgency felt by United Methodists and other persons for the nutritional protection and development of the infants of the world.

(d) Consult with persons of expertise in the technical fields related to the issues involved.

(e) Report to the GCOM regularly on the progress of the consultation and specific steps taken by the suppliers.

(f) Recommend to the GCOM no later than July 1, 1982, further appropriate actions by that body and other United Methodist agencies. Such actions might include, but not be limited to: (1) Continuation of the dialogues if they have proven fruitful and effective in producing constructive change. (2) Formal participation in a boycott of the company or companies involved, such action to be taken in conjunction with other concerned groups.

(g) Recommend to the 1984 General Conference such further response and actions as may be deemed appropriate at that time to continue the effective involvement of the Church.

Be It Further Resolved that this action become effective immediately upon the adjournment of the 1980 General Conference, and that the GCOM be requested to establish the designated task force as soon thereafter as possible.

Sample Shareowners' Resolution

This 1983 resolution asking Control Data Corporation (CDC) to explain to shareholders the closing of its plant in South Korea was sponsored by Church Women United, an ecumenical organization with offices in the Interchurch Center in New York (2 shares), Maryknoll Fathers and Brothers (22,300 shares), and Sisters of St. Francis, Dubuque, Iowa (1,000 shares).

Whereas: On July 23, 1982, Control Data Corporation announced, without warning, the closing of its South Korea plant, attributing the closure primarily to technological advances but declaring the decision accelerated by "labor unrest."

The predominantly female workforce there was paid low wages and denied rudimentary collective bargaining rights, including the right to strike by the government. The unrest included:

- a breakdown in labor/management relations between the male management and the female assembly workers;
- the summary firing of six women union leaders during contract negotiations, an illegal action under Korean law;
- a July 16th attack on some of the women employees by anti-union employees—while five women were hospitalized, three of whom were pregnant, none of the perpetrators were arrested.

CDC has worked hard at portraying a positive public image in the United States, but actions in South Korea have damaged this image.

Control Data has taken no steps to effectively counter the government-controlled media which attempted to portray falsely the union and the Churches Urban Industrial Mission as culprits causing the plant shutdown.

Resolved: The shareholders request the Board of Directors to authorize a report available to shareholders on Control Data's operation in South Korea. The report is to be prepared at reasonable expense and shall include:

a. the reasons for the plant closing from management's point of view and a summary of the reactions of CDC, their Korean workers, South Korean organizations, and organizations in the United States;

b. any actions by management to keep the plant open and negotiate an agreement with workers;

c. a description of labor/management disputes since the 1967 plant opening and a description of the South Korean laws that affected Control Data's labor relations, compensation, and grievance procedures;

d. a chart of South Korean employees indicating position, sex, wages, and benefits including severance pay.

APPENDIX F

Excerpts From the 'Jessup Report'

The following is a small portion of the "Preliminary Inquiry Regarding Financial Contributions to Outside Political Groups by Boards and Agencies of the United Methodist Church, 1977-79," prepared by David Jessup in April 1980.

Most Methodist churchgoers would react with disbelief, even anger, to be told that a significant portion of their weekly offerings were being siphoned off to groups supporting the Palestine Liberation Organization, the governments of Cuba and Vietnam, the pro-Soviet totalitarian movements of Latin America, Asia, and Africa, and several violence-prone fringe groups in this country.

Before such a claim can be dismissed out of hand, however, some hard questions need to be answered regarding the amount of support, both financial and in-kind, that is flowing to outside political groups from several boards and agencies of the United Methodist Church. . . .

My interest in the political orientation of the Methodist Church began when my wife and I started to attend services at Marvin Memorial Methodist Church in 1977 not long after moving to the Washington, D.C., area from the West Coast. My wife is a family nurse practitioner whose grandfather was a Methodist minister. I am employed by the AFL-CIO. We had been active in the Peace Corps in Peru, and we were interested in becoming involved in church-related projects such as refugee assistance. When my children brought home Sunday-school appeals for wheat shipments to the government of Vietnam, and the controversy over Methodist support for the Patriotic Front in Zimbabwe became public, I was troubled, but not persuaded that these projects represented anything more than minor aberrations from a more consistent tradition of Methodist support for democratic values. After several visits to the Methodist Building near the U.S. Capitol, and several months of research on the political orientation of groups receiving church funds, I am no longer so certain. . . .

In pursuing such explanations, it is perhaps inevitable that charges of witch-hunting and "McCarthyism" will be raised, but that is not the spirit in which this inquiry is made. No one is calling for government investigations to determine the identity of alleged individual "Communists," nor is there any intention of stifling the civil liberties of church staff members, or even of limiting political activity on the part of church boards and agencies. I, for one, hope that at least some official church effort will be expended on questions of human rights, democratic freedoms, and economic and social betterment, over and above the more fundamental church mission of religious persuasion.

117

The fundamental question posed concerns the direction of political activity, and whether the membership has any say in determining that direction at the all-important level of staff and funding decisions. . . . There is no doubt that much good has been wrought by this bureaucracy and that Methodists should continue to support it. Methodists should also continue to scrutinize it, lest their generosity be transformed into the financial underpinning of a political movement that might, in the end, destroy it altogether.

ORGANIZATIONS DEALING WITH CUBA AND LATIN AMERICA

In the struggle against economic oppression and political tyranny that occupies much of Latin America, two forces have long contended for popular support: the democratic left, represented by many Christian and Social Democratic parties, free trade unions, and the democratic governments of Venezuela, Costa Rica, and Colombia, on the one hand, and the totalitarian left, represented by Cuba and the movements it supports, on the other. Judging from their financial contributions, statements, and actions, several agencies of the Methodist Church seem to be favoring the totalitarian option.

The Women's Division and the World Division of the Board of Global Ministries gave $31,651 over a two-year period to five pro-Cuban organizations: the Cuba Resource Center, the Chile Legislative Center, the North American Congress on Latin America, the Washington Office on Latin America (located in the Methodist Building in Washington, D.C.), and the Puerto Rican Solidarity Committee. . . .

Cuba Resource Center (CRC)

The promotion of the virtues of Cuban society and of Castro's attempts to export his revolution to other parts of the world with Soviet backing appears to be the primary purpose of this organization, along with ending the U.S. trade embargo and extending diplomatic recognition. Center coordinator Mary Lou Suhor contrasts the "exploitation" of pre-Castro Cuba with the "new dignity" and "more human existence" of the people under Communism. . . . The Women's Division gave $250/year to the CRC in 1977-78. The World Division provided $16,000 in 1978. . . .

North American Congress on Latin America (NACLA)

Often self-described as the research arm of the movement, NACLA attempts to publicize the futility of democratic reforms in Latin America and the need for revolutionary change. In its manual on "How to Interview the Ruling Class and Its Agents," NACLA claims that "research is a weapon" intended to "change the existing power relations in capitalist society". . . . The Women's Division gave $500 per year to NACLA in 1977 and 1978. The World Division gave $2,000 in 1978 and $6,000 in 1979 to NACLA.

Washington Office on Latin America (WOLA)

In its publication *Latin America Update,* the Washington Office on Latin America regularly condemns human-rights violations in all Latin American dictatorships except Cuba, and blames the United States for most of the difficulties. . . . The Women's Division gave $500 to WOLA in 1978, and the World Division paid $5,101 to WOLA in 1979.

Puerto Rican Solidarity Committee (PRSC)

In spite of repeated popular votes and public opinion polls indicating that the people of Puerto Rico overwhelmingly favor ties with the United States, small groups of Puerto Rican activists continue to press for "decolonization". . . . The PRSC is closely connected with the Castro-backed Puerto Rican Socialist Party (PSP), with which it co-sponsored an October 30, 1977, White House demonstration against a grand jury investigation of the alleged terrorist activities of the Armed Forces of National Liberation (FALN). . . . The Women's Division gave $100 in 1977 and $200 in 1978 to the PRSC. The Board of Church and Society and the National Division of the Board of Global Ministries passed resolutions in support of the Cuba-sponsored U.N. resolutions calling for the "decolonization" of Puerto Rico.

Excerpt From '60 Minutes' Report on NCC and WCC

In this segment of a CBS-TV program broadcast on January 23, 1983, correspondent Morley Safer speaks with parishioners of a United Methodist church in Logansport, Indiana.

Morley Safer: It is near impossible to follow church money in any precise way. When Pastor Lesaux and his parishioners tried to, they found that it was being absorbed into the coffers, committees, and ad hoc committees of the United Methodist Church, National Council of Churches, and the World Council, and then surfacing in some surprising places. They found some of it was being spent on causes that seem more political than religious, on causes that seem closer to the Soviet-Cuban view of the world than Logansport, Indiana's, and they didn't like it.

Parishioner: The World Council in particular, it seems, has become a political organization and not, as they set out to be, a fellowship of Christian organizations who accept Jesus Christ as God and Savior.

Parishioner: We don't feel—that is, the people in our church that have discussed it—that the Methodists belong in an organization which permits the use of money to accomplish political objectives. Why should we support one group rather than another in Africa, any more than we should in the United States?

Parishioner: I think most of our parishioners feel like that—that their outcries of—of total frustration are falling on deaf ears. I think there's a bureaucracy there that—maybe it's so large that we can't get to it.

Safer: The bureaucracy they're concerned about, indeed what many American Protestants are concerned about, is largely headquartered here, 475 Riverside Drive, in New York City. This building is officially known as the Interchurch Center. The people who work in it call it "the God Box." It's the home of the National Council of Churches. It's also the national headquarters for dozens of agencies attached to the United Methodists, the United Presbyterians, and other Protestant churches. It's also the U.S. headquarters of the World Council of Churches, which is headquartered in Geneva, Switzerland.

All these agencies claim a strict independence from each other. But in fact there's a constant exchange of programs and personnel. And although they may be technically independent, they do work in concert and are often hard to distinguish one from the other.

What all the agencies have in common is that they get most of their budgets from the people in the pews, a small percentage of each Sunday's collection plate. The annual budgets are: the United Methodists, $70 million; the United Presbyterians, $35 million; the National Council of Churches, $44 million; and $12 million from American contributions alone to the World Council of Churches. All that money is spent on a very complex maze of programs by groups and organizations in the thousands that touch people's religious and social and their political lives as well. There are bureaucracies within bureaucracies in this building, and often one hand does not know what the other's up to.

Excerpt From Report of Presbyterian Task Force on TNCs

These are the general conclusions of the "Review of Policies, Strategies, and Programs of the United Presbyterian Church Related to Transnational Corporations," a report published in 1983.

Conclusion 1: The church must make clear that affirmation of economic activity and institutions as a part of God's gracious provision for human life is the fundamental basis for its approach to transnational corporations and similar entities. Vocation and service within them are in response to our calling to serve God's intention for the welfare of the human community.

Conclusion 2: The church must uphold the Reformed Church's double vocation of affirmation and criticism. The church's witness in economic affairs has frequently suffered from an overemphasis on the negative aspects of corporate and governmental policy.

Conclusion 3: The church must be willing to examine its own character and behavior as a transnational corporation by the same rigorous criteria it applies to the economic transnational corporation.

Conclusion 4: The Presbyterian Church must take its engagement with transnational corporations more seriously than it has in the past.

Conclusion 5: The Presbyterian Church must acknowledge and address the submerged tension in its own life over transnational corporations and related issues if there is to be vigorous and effective witness by Presbyterians.

Conclusion 6: The sizeable number of Presbyterians whose vocation is within transnational corporations or related entities constitute a potentially significant but largely neglected mission resource.

Conclusion 7: Presbyterians and the church must hear and reflect on the perspectives and critiques of third world Christians with regard to transnational corporations.

Conclusion 8: The strategies and programs developed by the agencies of the Presbyterian Church to implement General Assembly policies related to transnational corporations have been consistent with the direction and authority defined by General Assemblies and with the church's historic mission policies and goals. Their effectiveness, however, has been lessened by a lack of coordination and balance; and occasionally by unclear priorities, ineffective communication, and inadequate research.

Conclusion 9: The Presbyterian Church must broaden its strategic options and shift its strategic focus, if its approach to transnational corporations is to have effective impact in the 1980s and 1990s.

Corporate Responsibility Challenges, 1984

The Spring 1984 issue of "The Corporate Examiner" summarized the proxy resolutions that church groups had submitted to companies for action at their 1984 annual meetings. There were 82 resolutions, to 70 companies; the previous year there had been 119 resolutions, to 86 companies. The information in this appendix is in three parts: first, a list of companies, general topics of the resolutions submitted to them, and the resolution sponsors; next, a topical listing of the resolutions and a summary of their contents; and third, from the following issue of "The Corporate Examiner," an explanation of why a number of the resolutions on the 1984 list had been withdrawn by late March. These pages are reproduced by permission of the Interfaith Center on Corporate Responsibility from "The Corporate Examiner," volume 13, numbers 1 and 2.

CORPORATE SOCIAL RESPONSIBILITY CHALLENGES
Spring 1984

ABC . . . . *Media images of women and minorities*
Friars of the Atonement; National Council of Churches, USA; Sisters of St. Joseph of Peace.

ALLIED . . . . *Disclosure of nuclear involvement*
American Baptist Home Mission Society; Loretto Literary and Benevolent Institution; Society of Catholic Medical Missionaries.

ALLIS-CHALMERS . . . . *Sign Sullivan Principles*
Board of Pensions, United Methodist Church.

AMERICAN ELECTRIC POWER . . . .
. . . . *Nuclear power review committee*
Corporation of Roman Catholic Clergymen (Jesuits of Maryland); United Christian Missionary Society.

AMERICAN HOME PRODUCTS . . . . *Drug lobbying in Third World*
Catholic Foreign Missionary Society of America (Maryknoll); Marianist Society; Sisters of Charity of St. Elizabeth.

AMERICAN HOME PRODUCTS . . . .
. . . . *Third World marketing of dangerous drugs*
Marianist Society; Mercy Consolidated Assets Management Program (Sisters of Mercy); Sisters of Charity of St. Vincent De Paul, NY; Sisters of the Divine Savior.

AMERICAN HOSPITAL SUPPLY . . . . . *Employment of Mexican women*
National Division, General Board of Global Ministries, United Methodist Church.

AMERICAN TELEPHONE AND TELEGRAPH . . . .
. . . . *Criteria for military contracts*
Brothers of the Christian Schools, St. Louis District; Congregation of Sisters of St. Joseph, Buffalo; Corporation of New Melleray; Episcopal Church Publishing Co.; Marianist Society; Nazareth Literary and Benevolent Institution; Sisters of Charity of St. Elizabeth; Sisters of Charity of St. Vincent De Paul, NY; Sisters of Mercy, Rochester, NY; Sisters of St. Joseph of Carondelet, St. Louis Province; Sisters of St. Joseph, Nazareth, Michigan; Sisters of St. Joseph, Third Order of St. Francis; United Christian Missionary Society.

AMERICAN TELEPHONE AND TELEGRAPH . . . . *Plant closings*
Lutheran Church in America.

AMERICAN TELEPHONE AND TELEGRAPH . . . .
. . . . *Termination of nuclear weapons contract*
American Baptist Home Mission Society; Archdiocese of Cincinnati; Church Women United; Community of the Sisters of St. Anne; Convent of Mary Reparatrix; Corporation of Roman Catholic Clergymen (Jesuits of Maryland); Detroit Province; Domestic and Foreign Mission Society, Episcopal Church; Dominican Sisters of the Sick Poor; Franco-American Oblate Fathers (Oblates of Mary Immaculate); Judson Memorial Church; Mercy Consolidated Assets Management Program (Sisters of Mercy); Missionary Society of St. Paul the Apostle (Paulist Fathers) New England Province, Society of Jesus; New Orleans Province, Society of Jesus; New World Foundation; Order of Friars Minor (Franciscans), Holy Name Province, NY; Oregon Province, Society of Jesus; Reformed Church in America; Servants of Mary; Sisters of the Blessed Sacrament; Sisters of Charity of Cincinnati; Sisters of Mercy, St. Louis Province; Sisters of Notre Dame de Namur, Boston Province; Sisters of

St. Dominic, Blauvelt, NY; Sisters of St. Francis, Dubuque, Iowa; Society of Catholic Medical Missionaries; Society of Jesus, Province of Missouri.

BANK OF MONTREAL . . . . *Report on Loans to South Africa*
Jesuit Fathers of Upper Canada; United Church of Canada; White Fathers of Montreal.

BANK OF NOVA SCOTIA . . . . . . *No loans to South African government*
Anglican Church of Canada; Jesuits of Upper Canada; Sisters of Charity, Halifax; Sisters of the Sacred Heart, Montreal; United Church of Canada.

BANKERS TRUST . . . . *World debt crisis*
Catholic Foreign Missionary Society of America (Maryknoll).

BAXTER-TRAVENOL LABORATORIES . . . . *Sign Sullivan Principles*
Board of Pensions, United Methodist Church.

CANADIAN IMPERIAL BANK OF COMMERCE . . . . *Secret ballot*
Jesuit Fathers of Upper Canada; Sisters of St. Martha, Antigonish; United Church of Canada; White Fathers of Montreal.

CATERPILLAR . . . . *Plant closings*
Adrian Dominican Sisters; Loretto Literary and Benevolent Institution.

CBS . . . . *Media images of women and minorities*
Sisters of the Blessed Sacrament; Unitarian Universalist Association.

CHASE MANHATTAN . . . . *World debt crisis*
Unitarian Universalist Association.

CHEMICAL BANK . . . . *World debt crisis*
Catholic Foreign Mission Society of America (Maryknoll); Sisters of Charity of St. Elizabeth.

CIGNA . . . . *No loans to South African government*
Domestic and Foreign Missionary Society of the Episcopal Church; Lutheran Church in America.

CINCINNATI GAS AND ELECTRIC . . . .
. . . . *Stop construction of nuclear power plant*
Catholic Foreign Mission Society of America (Maryknoll); United Christian Missionary Society.

CITICORP . . . . *Report on loans to South Africa*
Presbyterian Church (USA).

CITICORP . . . . *World debt crisis*
Catholic Foreign Mission Society of America (Maryknoll).

COMMONWEALTH EDISON . . . . *Nuclear power lobbying*
Dominican Fathers, Province of St. Albert the Great; Dominicans, Province of St. Albert the Great; School Sisters of St. Francis, Patrimony Fund; School Sisters of St. Francis, Mount St. Francis Province.

CONSOLIDATED EDISON . . . . *Evacuation plans*
Presbyterian Church (USA).

CONSOLIDATED EDISON . . . . *Lifeline rates*
Sisters of St. Joseph, Brentwood, NY.

CONSOLIDATED EDISON . . . . *Nuclear power lobbying*
Sisters of Charity of St. Vincent de Paul.

CONSUMERS POWER..... *Stop construction of nuclear power plant*
Province of St. Joseph of the Capuchin Order.

CONTINENTAL ILLINOIS........................ *World debt crisis*
Clergy and Laity Concerned; Dominicans, Province of St. Albert the Great;
School Sisters of Notre Dame, Chicago Province.

CONTROL DATA.................. *Computer sales in South Africa*
Catholic Foreign Mission Society of America (Maryknoll).

CONTROL DATA.......... *Employment of women in South Korea*
Church Women United; Sisters of St. Francis of Dubuque, Iowa; Jean Dorsett.

DART AND KRAFT............................. *EEO reporting*
Reformed Church in America; Society of Catholic Medical Missionaries.

DAYTON POWER AND LIGHT....... **Nuclear power review committee*
Catholic Foreign Mission Society of America (Maryknoll).

DRESSER............................. *Sign Sullivan Principles*
Domestic and Foreign Missionary Society of the Episcopal Church.

DUN AND BRADSTREET.................. *Sign Sullivan Principles*
Board of Pensions, United Methodist Church.

EASTMAN KODAK......... *Involvement in militarization of space*
Corporation of Roman Catholic Clergymen (Jesuits of Maryland); Franciscan
Sisters of Allegany; Franciscan Sisters, Little Falls, Minnesota; Friars of the
Atonement; Marianist Society; Reformed Chruch in America; Servants of
Mary; Sisters of the Blessed Sacrament; Sisters of Mercy, Rochester; Sisters
of St. Francis, Philadelphia; Society of Catholic Medical Missionaries; Unitar-
ian Universalist Association.

EATON........................... *No expansion in South Africa*
American Baptist Home Missionary Society.

EMERSON ELECTRIC................ *Criteria for military contract*
Loretto Literary and Benevolent Institution; Nazareth Literary and Benevolent
Institution.

EXXON........... **No sales to South African police and military*
Lutheran Theological Seminary at Philadelphia.

EXXON.. *Pollution control*
Sacred Heart Center for Christian Formation; St. Clara College (Sinsinawa Dominicans).

FOSTER WHEELER..................... **Sign Sullivan Principles*
Board of Pensions, United Methodist Church.

GENERAL DYNAMICS............................. *Secret ballot*
Holy Cross Fathers; Loretto Literary and Benevolent Institution; Sisters of St.
Joseph of Peace.

GENERAL ELECTRIC................. *Criteria for military contract*
Adrian Dominican Sisters; American Baptist Home Mission Society; Commu-
nity of the Sisters of St. Dominic, Caldwell, NJ; Congregation of the Sisters of
St. Joseph, Buffalo; Franciscan Sisters, Little Falls, Minnesota; Friars of the
Atonement; Grey Nuns of the Sacred Heart; Holy Cross Fathers; Literary Soci-
ety of St. Catharine of Siena (Dominican Sisters); Marianist Society; National
Council of Churches of Christ, USA; Nazareth Literary and Benevolent Institu-
tion; Order of Friars Minor (Franciscans), Holy Name Province, NY; Reformed
Church in America; St. Clara College (Sinsinawa Dominicans); Servants of
Mary; Sisters of the Blessed Sacrament; Sisters of Charity of St. Vincent De
Paul, NY; Sisters of Mercy, Province of Detroit; Sisters of St. Francis, Du-
buque, Iowa; Sisters of St. Francis, Philadelphia; Sisters of St. Joseph, Naza-
reth, Michigan; Sisters of St. Joseph, Rochester, NY; Sisters of St. Joseph,
Third Order of St. Francis; Society of Catholic Medical Missionaries; Society of
the Holy Child Jesus; Unitarian Universalist Association; Ursulines of the
Eastern Province, USA; John V. Surr; William T. Whistler.

GENERAL FOODS .. *Coffee imports from El Salvador and Guatemala*
Adrian Dominican Sisters; Sisters of Charity of the Blessed Virgin Mary.

GENERAL MOTORS... *No sales to South African police and military*
Council of Churches, City of NY; Presbyterian Church (USA); Sisters of
Mercy, Rochester; Sisters of St. Francis, Dubuque, Iowa; Union Theological
Seminary.

GTE.............................. *Criteria for military contract*
Catholic Foreign Mission Society of America (Maryknoll); Congregation of the

Sisters of St. Joseph, Boston; Detroit Province of the Society of Jesus; Franco-
American Oblate Fathers; Holy Cross Fathers; Marianist Society; Mercy Consolidated Assets Management Program (Sisters of Mercy); Servants of Jesus;
Sisters of Divine Providence, Kentucky; Sisters of Notre Dame de Namur, Boston Province; Sisters of St. Francis, Philadelphia; Sisters of St. Joseph, Nazareth, Michigan; Sisters of St. Joseph of Peace; Sisters of St. Joseph of Peace
(St. Michael Provincial House); Ursuline Sisters of Tildonk.

HONEYWELL...................... *Criteria for military contract*
Clergy and Laity Concerned; Marianist Society; Pension Boards, United
Church of Christ; Sisters of St. Francis, Holy Name Province; United Church
Board for Homeland Ministries; United Church Foundation.

HOUSTON INDUSTRIES........................... *Conservation*
American Baptist Home Mission Society.

HOUSTON INDUSTRIES... **Stop construction of nuclear power plant*
Brothers of the Christian Schools, St. Louis District; Sisters of the Sorrowful
Mother, Wisconsin.

IBM (International Business Machines)................. *Human rights*
Board of Pensions, Lutheran Church in America; Community of the Sisters of
St. Dominic, Caldwell, NJ; Dominican Sisters of the Sick Poor; Dominican Sis-
ters, Sparkill, NY; Lutheran Theological Seminary, Gettysburg; Marianist So-
ciety; Sisters of St. Francis, Dubuque, Iowa; Sisters of St. Ursula of the
Blessed Virgin, NY; Society of Catholic Medical Missionaries; Society of the
Sisters of St. Joseph of Carondelet, Albany Province; Unitarian Universalist
Association; United Church Board of World Ministries.

INGERSOLL RAND..
.... *No expansion in South Africa; sign Sullivan Principles*
American Baptist Home Mission Society.

INTERNATIONAL FLAVORS AND FRAGRANCES......................
.... *Sign Sullivan Principles*
Board of Pensions, United Methodist Church.

K-MART...................... *Minority economic development*
Adrian Dominican Sisters; Sisters, Servants of the Immaculate Heart of Mary;
United Christian Missionary Society.

MCDONNELL DOUGLAS.............. *Criteria for military contract*
Brothers of the Christian Schools, St. Louis District; Loretto Literary and Bene-
volent Institution; St. Mary's Institute (Sisters of the Most Precious Blood,
O'Fallon); Senior Adorers Corporation; Sisters of St. Mary, Third Order of St.
Francis; Society of Mary, Province of St. Louis; C.J. Guenther.

MARTIN MARIETTA........ *Involvement in militarization of space*
Loretto Literary and Benevolent Institution.

MOBIL.... *Adopt Tutu's condition or withdraw from South Africa*
American Baptist Home Mission Society; Literary Society of St. Catharine of
Siena (Dominican Sisters); Society of Catholic Medical Missionaries; United
Church Board for World Ministries.

J.P. MORGAN................ **No loans to South African government*
American Baptist Home Missionary Society; Domestic and Foreign Missionary
Society of the Episcopal Church.

J.P. MORGAN................................. *World debt crisis*
Catholic Foreign Missionary Society of America (Maryknoll).

MOTOROLA............... *Employment practices in South Korea*
Presbyterian Church (USA).

MOTOROLA......... *No sales to South African police and military*
Catholic Foreign Missionary Society of America (Maryknoll); Domestic and
Foreign Missionary Society of the Episcopal Church; Dominican Sisters of the
Sick Poor; Pension Boards, United Church of Christ; United Church Board for
Homeland Ministries; United Church Foundation.

NEWMONT MINING................ *No expansion in South Africa*
Catholic Foreign Missionary Society of America (Maryknoll).

NL INDUSTRIES..................... **Radioactive contamination*
American Baptist Home Mission Society.

NORTH CAROLINA NATIONAL BANK............................
.... *No loans to South African government*
American Baptist Home Mission Society.

PEPSICO . . . . *Sign Sullivan Principles*
Board of Pensions, United Methodist Church.

PHILADELPHIA ELECTRIC . . . . *Conservation*
Society of Catholic Medical Missionaries.

PHILADELPHIA ELECTRIC . . . . *Cancel nuclear power plant*
American Baptist Home Mission Society.

RAYTHEON . . . . *Criteria for military contract*
Domestic and Foreign Missionary Society of the Episcopal Church; Sisters of
St. Dominic, Blauvelt.

RCA/NBC . . . . *Media images of women and minorities*
Catholic Foreign Missionary Society of America (Maryknoll); Convent of the
Sisters of Mercy, Brooklyn; Dominican Sisters of the Sick Poor; Sisters of the
Order of St. Dominic, Amityville, NY; National Council of Churches of Christ,
USA.

ROCKWELL INTERNATIONAL . . . . . . *Manufacture of nuclear weapons*
Dominicans, Province of St. Albert the Great; Fellowship of Reconciliation;
Ladies of Bethany/Bethany Community; Loretto Literary and Benevolent Insti-
tution; Sisters of Mercy, Allegheny County.

SCHLUMBERGER . . . . *Sales to the Soviet Union*
Domestic and Foreign Missionary Society of the Episcopal Church; Marianist
Society.

SINGER . . . . *Criteria for military contract*
Sisters of St. Joseph of Peace.

STANDARD OIL OF CALIFORNIA . . . .
. . . . *Adopt Tutu's conditions or withdraw from South Africa*
American Baptist Home Mission Society; General Board of Global Ministries,
United Methodist Church; Sisters of St. Dominic, Congregation of the Most
Holy Name; Society of Catholic Medical Missionaries; United Church Board for
World Ministries; Women's Division, General Board of Global Ministries,
United Methodist Church.

STERLING DRUG . . . . *Review committee on dipyrone*
Catholic Foreign Mission Society of America (Maryknoll); Marianist Society;

Province of St. Joseph of the Capuchin Order; Society of Catholic Medical Missionaries.

TEXACO . . . .
. . . . *Adopt Tutu's condition or withdraw from South Africa*
Congregation of Divine Providence; Society of Catholic Medical Missionaries;
United Church Board for World Ministries; United Church Board for World Min-
istries.

UNION ELECTRIC . . . . . . *Cancel construction of nuclear power plant*
Loretto Literary and Benevolent Institution; St. Mary's Institute (Sisters of the
Most Precious Blood, O'Fallon); School Sisters of Notre Dame, St. Louis; Sis-
ters of St. Joseph of Carondelet, St. Louis Province; Sisters of St. Mary, Third
Order of St. Francis.

UNITED TECHNOLOGIES . . . . *Plant closings*
Episcopal Church Publishing Co.; Sisters of Charity of St. Vincent De Paul,
NY.

US STEEL . . . . *Plant closings*
Province of St. Joseph of the Capuchin Order; Sisters of St. Francis, Millvale.

UPJOHN . . . . *Report on Depo-Provera*
Catholic Foreign Mission Society of America (Maryknoll); Presbyterian Church
(USA).

WELLS FARGO . . . . *World debt crisis*
Sisters of the Presentation.

WESTINGHOUSE . . . . *Employment practices*
Missionary Society of St. Paul the Apostle (Paulist Fathers); Sisters of the
Blessed Sacrament.

WESTINGHOUSE . . . . *No nuclear contract with South Africa*
Presbyterian Church (USA); Sisters of the Presentation.

XEROX . . . *Adopt Tutu's conditions or withdraw from South Africa*
American Baptist Home Mission Society; St. Clara College (Sinsinawa Dominicans); United Church Board for World Ministers.

*Resolution withdrawn.

CORPORATE SOCIAL RESPONSIBILITY CHALLENGES
Spring 1984

Introduction

The proxy resolution is the legal means by which institutional
and individual investors may submit proposals to corporations on
issues that have a potential impact on their business. It is an important mechanism for voicing social concerns about corporate activities. In coordination with ICCR, church groups have submitted
82 resolutions to 70 companies this year, 119 resolutions to 86 companies in 1983, 95 resolutions to 75 companies in 1982, 111 resolutions to 80 companies in 1981 and 104 resolutions to 77 companies
in 1980. This year as in other years, several concerned individual
shareholders and institutional investors have joined the more than
100 church agencies sponsoring the resolutions. Among the institutional investors sponsoring resolutions with the churches are the
New World Foundation, the Lutheran Theological Seminary at
Philadelphia, the Lutheran Theological Seminary at Gettysburg,
Union Theological Seminary and the Fellowship of Reconciliation.
A local congregation, the Judson Memorial Church in New York
City, joined in sponsoring the resolution to American Telephone
and Telegraph which calls for termination of its nuclear weapons
production contract. Also in 1984 Canadian church shareholders
are sponsoring resolutions to three Canadian banks — Bank of
Montreal, Bank of Nova Scotia and Canadian Imperial Bank of
Commerce. Lists of their sponsors and explanations of their requests are included in this issue of the newsletter.

Prior to their being voted on at 1984 annual meetings, a number
of the proposals will have been negotiated with company manage-

ment and withdrawn (They will be marked with an *.); a few may
be excluded from company proxy statements by the Securities and
Exchange Commission. The list presented here is accurate as of
January 30, 1984. The status of resolutions will be reported in
future issues of this newsletter along with information about
resolutions from groups or individuals other than churches. Social
issues under consideration include, in order of appearance: 1)
community reinvestment, 2) domestic equality, 3) energy and the
environment, 4) international health, 5) international justice and 6)
militarism.

For more information about church-sponsored proposals, contact the sponsoring group or the Interfaith Center on Corporate
Responsibility. Additional copies of this special issue of "The Corporate Examiner" are available from ICCR for $.75. Complete
copies of church sponsored shareholder resolutions are printed in
Church Proxy Resolutions 1984. $4 plus postage and handling,
available also from ICCR.

I. COMMUNITY REINVESTMENT

—**Plant closings policy report.** AMERICAN TELEPHONE & TELE-
GRAPH.

AT & T is asked to report its policies and procedures on a variety of issues related to plant closings, including advance notice of
closings, severance pay, extension of health benefits, transfer op-

portunities, retraining, retirement opportunities, family counseling, employee purchase of facilities and compensation to local communities.

—**Plant closings diversification study.** CATERPILLAR TRACTOR.

Observing that the company has suffered some economic losses due to the world debt crisis and world recession, sponsors ask the company to consider "vastly diversifying its product lines to help ameliorate the effects of the business cycle on both profitability and employment." The resolution suggests the use of outside consultants to help with the study and specifically recommends that plants which the corporation plans to close or may close, be studied to determine if alternative product lines are possible.

—**Plant closings policy.** UNITED TECHNOLOGIES.

UNITED TECHNOLOGIES began reducing the workforce at its Yonkers, New York OTIS ELEVATOR plant after acquiring OTIS in 1976 and eventually closed the plant in 1983. The company is asked "to develop a written policy on plant closings describing measures it will take to reduce the impact of future plant closings on employees and communities." The resolution suggests the company consider advance notice, severance pay, health benefits, early retirement, transfer rights, job retraining, employee purchase and gradual phasing out of local taxes when developing the policy.

—**Plant closings report and policy.** U.S. STEEL.

U.S. STEEL, America's largest steel manufacturer, recently announced plans to close all or part of twenty-three mills and mines, permanently terminating over 15,000 workers. The resolution asks the company to prepare a special report on projected plans to modernize existing facilities between 1983 and 1988, expected closings during that same period and a statement of its policy on plant closings including steps to be taken to minimize the impact of future closings.

II. DOMESTIC EQUALITY

—**Employment practices.** WESTINGHOUSE.

The directors of this company are asked to establish an independent review committee with access to relevant data on employment practices in order to review the company's practices and policy related to training, compensation, promotion, performance evaluation to ensure that "compensation incorporates the principle of equal pay for comparable work and that there are no sex or race segregated departments." The committee is to make recommendations for changes and report to shareholders by October 1984.

—**Equal employment opportunity reporting.** DART & KRAFT.

Prior to its merger with DART, KRAFTCO regularly reported to shareholders, in its post-annual meeting report, data on its performance on employment opportunity. DART & KRAFT, however, discontinued such reporting and sponsors are renewing their request to the company to resume the practice.

—**Employment of Mexican women.** AMERICAN HOSPITAL SUPPLY.

U.S. corporations participating in the Mexican Border Industrialization Program employ high percentages of women in plants known as maquiladoras (literally translated "grist mills"). Citing complaints from the women of problems such as inadequate wages, lack of maternity leave and child care benefits, lack of occupational mobility, job instability and insecurity, sexual harassment by supervisors and exposure to eyestrain, toxic substances and other health hazards, shareholders ask the company to review the employment circumstances and conditions of its Mexican workforce and apprise shareholders by April 1, 1984 of the conclusions and actions resulting from the review.

—**Media images of women and minorities.** ABC, CBS, NBC/RCA.

Concerned about the impact of the media on employment and character portrayals of racial minorities and women, shareholders have suggested four ways by which the three major networks could review their impact as media organizations: First, the networks are asked to enhance educational, training and other programs designed to overcome underutilization of minority and women managers and behind-the-scenes professionals. Second, the networks are asked to describe measures initiated which address the concerns of the Third World nations regarding their portrayal in the television media, particularly those identified in the New World Information and Communications Order. Third, the networks are asked to report the criteria regarding the utilization of racial minorities and women in acting roles and production crews when developing and funding series. Finally, the networks are asked to reaffirm quality programming for children and entertainment programming which enhances the images of racial minorities, women, the elderly, the disabled and working people.

—**Minority economic development.** K-MART.

This proposal asks the company to report on its minority economic development practices including how its minority economic development program is administered, data on the number of suppliers with the total dollar amount, special features of the minority economic development program, advertising and promotion of the program, along with the provision of a copy of the corporate-wide policy.

III. ENERGY AND ENVIRONMENT

Conservation:

—**Lifeline rates.** CONSOLIDATED EDISON.

The company is asked to investigate the feasibility of establishing a conservation rate for minimum-use residential customers (lifeline rate) and to report to shareholders.

—**Conservation.** HOUSTON INDUSTRIES.

This utility is asked to "develop a comprehensive policy favoring renewable energy, conservation and decentralization" and to implement and/or increase a wide range of measures designed to conserve energy which are outlined in the resolution.

—**Conservation.** PHILADELPHIA ELECTRIC.

The resolution notes a 1982 recommendation from the Pennsylvania Public Utility Commission that "it would be in the public interest for the company to pursue aggressive conservation programs" and requests the company immediately increase measures designed to accomplish this. Some objectives are to reduce electrical heating and cooling needs through improved efficiency, cogeneration, passive solar and other renewable energy technologies; implement commercial and industrial load management and provide additional customer financing programs for energy saving efforts. The company is also asked to publicize the programs to customers, develop a consumer advisory council for the programs and report to shareholders.

Nuclear power

—**Evacuation plans.** CONSOLIDATED EDISON.

CON ED is asked to issue a report, available to shareholders, which would summarize the company's evacuation plans for the Indian Point Nuclear Power Station and the Nuclear Regulatory Commission's response and recommendations; list fines or penalties the company has received due to the inadequacy of past plans and describe management's beliefs about the adequacy of the plans and critics' points in disagreement.

—**Nuclear power lobbying.** COMMONWEALTH EDISON, CONSOLIDATED EDISON.

These resolutions ask the companies to cease all contributions to the U.S. Committee on Energy Awareness, a pronuclear energy, industry-sponsored group involved in massive spending on nuclear advertising and promotion. The resolutions ask the companies to stop contributing to the CEA, withdraw their representatives from the CEA's board of directors and guarantee that already contributed to the CEA will not be passed on in charges to their customers. The resolutions also ask the companies to disclose other pronuclear energy promotional expenditures and lobbying activities and their plans for radioactive waste disposal and evacuation plans for areas surrounding their nuclear plants.

—**Nuclear power review committee.** AMERICAN ELECTRIC POWER, DAYTON POWER & LIGHT.

These two of the three partners in the trouble-plagued Zimmer nuclear power plant, located to the east of Cincinnati, Ohio, are asked to establish a review committee with representatives of management, stockholders and consumers, to assess the comparative feasibility of cancelling and abandoning the Zimmer plant, converting the plant to a coal or natural gas facility and divesting the companies' various financial interests in the facility.

—**Stop construction of nuclear power plant.** CINCINNATI GAS & ELECTRIC.

CG&E, the third partner in the problem-plagued Zimmer nuclear plant, located east of Cincinnati, Ohio, is asked to halt immediately all further construction on Zimmer as a nuclear facility and investigate converting it to a coal or natural gas facility.

—**Stop construction of nuclear power plant.** CONSUMER'S POWER.

Delays and quality-control problems in construction of a CONSUMER'S POWER nuclear power plant in Midland, Michigan have led to loss of business and downgrading of CONSUMER'S POWER debt and securities ratings. The company is asked to halt construction of the Midland plant pending review of completion costs by an independent financial analyst and until problems of nuclear waste disposal have been resolved. The results of this independent financial analysis "should be made available to all shareholders for a final determination at the 1985 annual stockholders meeting," according to the request.

—**Stop construction of nuclear power plant.** HOUSTON INDUSTRIES.

Citing numerous problems with construction defects and scheduling, disagreements among partners in the project and disputes with construction contractors, sponsors ask the company to support cancellation of the South Texas Nuclear Project and to "approach the partnership with a request to cancel" the project.

—**Cancel nuclear power plant.** PHILADELPHIA ELECTRIC.

Directors of this utility are asked to "cancel plans for completion of Limerick Unit II," the company's current nuclear power plant under construction and to develop "alternative methods of power generation and an aggressive program of conservation."

—**Cancel nuclear power plant.** UNION ELECTRIC.

Outlining their extensive reasoning and supporting facts, sponsors of this resolution state: "We believe cancellation of the Callaway plant [Missouri] is merited because of dangers and financial uncertainty associated with nuclear power and radioactive waste disposal," and ask the directors to cancel the Callaway Nuclear Power Plant project.

Environment:

—**Pollution control.** EXXON.

Concerned that the subsistence economy and culture of the neighboring Sokaogon Chippewa Indian community will be disrupted by seepage of toxic metals from the EXXON-owned Crandon copper-zinc sulfide deposit in northern Wisconsin, sponsors ask the company to invest in the most modern pollution control technology to separate out highly toxic pyrite tailings from waste storage ponds to reduce the heavy metal content and acid generating potential of tailings in the tailings pond.

—**Radioactive contamination.** NL INDUSTRIES.

This resolution asks company directors to begin immediate cleanup of on-site and off-site contamination at its Colonie, New York plant where the company used spent uranium in manufacturing armor-piercing bullets and counterweights for airplanes.

The directors were also asked to conduct health studies of present and former employees and nearby residents and to conform with demands of a suit brought by the New York State attorney general's office which seeks clean-up.

IV. INTERNATIONAL HEALTH

—**Drug lobbying in the Third World.** AMERICAN HOME PRODUCTS.

Directors of the company are asked to "adopt a policy forbidding lobbying to oppose developing country governments introducing and implementing new legislation to ban dangerous or therapeutically ineffective drugs" and to issue a statement outlining the types of drug reform legislation the company would support in developing countries.

—**Third World marketing of dangerous drug.** AMERICAN HOME PRODUCTS.

The resolution requests that the company set up a committee to study the risks and benefits of clioquinol, an antidiarrheal drug responsible for a crippling disease of the nervous system which has affected thousands of people. The committee should review relevant information and results of recent studies and report a detailed statement of what ongoing mechanism the company has for therapeutic evaluation of all its drug products. If the committee finds inadequate evidence to justify clioquinol, AMERICAN HOME PRODUCTS is asked to stop manufacturing the drug and withdraw all clioquinol products from the market worldwide.

—**Review committee on dipyrone.** STERLING DRUG.

Use of the drug, dipyrone, has been banned or severely restricted in several European nations, the U.S., Japan, Australia and the Philippines because of high risks and widespread concern over safety. The resolution requests that a review committee examine literature on dipyrone, the company's dipyrone marketing practices and consider reformulating dipyrone products by substituting another analgesic, recognized to be safer than dipyrone. The panel should also review the company's mechanism for ongoing therapeutic evaluation of all STERLING's drug products.

Report on Depo-Provera. UPJOHN.

UPJOHN manufactures Depo-Provera, an injectable hormonal contraceptive widely available elsewhere, but not licensed in Japan, India or the United States. In 1978 the U.S. government refused to license the drug for use as a contraceptive because animal tests had shown a variety of side effects and potential risks. The resolution asks the company to report to shareholders a list of side effects including description of the scientific debate over each and continuing studies of efforts to improve the product; a description of efforts to have Depo-Provera licensed in the U.S.; UPJOHN's criteria for assessing Depo-Provera's risks and benefits worldwide and its policies for obtaining the informed consent of recipients and the company's policy for overseas sale of drugs banned or not licensed in the U.S.

V. INTERNATIONAL JUSTICE

Central America:

—**Coffee imports from El Salvador and Guatemala.** GENERAL FOODS.

Explaining that coffee sales are a major source of revenue for the governments of El Salvador and Guatemala, notorious for their role in gross violations of human rights, the corporation is asked to discontinue buying coffee from El Salvador and Guatemala until these governments halt their gross violations of the U.N. Universal Declaration of Human Rights.

Human Rights:

—**Human rights.** IBM.

According to the resolution, IBM's chairman stated that the company would not knowingly sell equipment which could be used for repressive purposes or to abridge human rights. The resolution asks the directors to report its policy on marketing computer equipment which could be used by repressive governments to abridge human rights; report its definition of "repressive purposes" and "abridge human rights"; provide a list of occasions when IBM declined to do business because of its policy and a projection of any future changes in its policy.

South Africa:

—Adopt Tutu's conditions or withdraw from South Africa. MOBIL, STANDARD OIL OF CALIFORNIA, TEXACO, XEROX.

Bishop Desmond Tutu, general secretary of the South African Council of Churches, recently outlined several conditions of investment which would enable U.S. companies to make a positive contribution to change in South Africa. They concern housing of the black workforce, recognition of black trade unions, labor mobility and South Africa's influx control laws, fair labor practices and investment in black education and training. The resolutions ask the companies to implement Bishop Tutu's principles, which are specifically stated in the resolution, and to report how the company's presence in South Africa is a positive influence for improving the quality of life for blacks and for leading to the end of apartheid. If the corporations do not endorse the principles, they are asked to withdraw from South Africa.

—Computer sales in South Africa. CONTROL DATA.

The company is asked to update its 1983 report on South Africa, including the criteria used by the company to assess whether sales are used to support the system of apartheid, a list of occasions when the company refrained from sales based on these criteria and a description of CONTROL DATA's sales in 1983 to the South African government's Electricity Commission and the Iron and Steel Corporation and how these sales could be used to further apartheid.

—No expansion in South Africa. EATON, NEWMONT MINING.

Directors of these companies are asked to adopt policy that the companies will not invest foreign capital or expand in South Africa until the government commits itself to ending apartheid and takes meaningful steps in that direction.

—No loans to the government of South Africa. BANK OF NOVA SCOTIA, CIGNA, NORTH CAROLINA NATIONAL BANK (NCNB), J.P. MORGAN.

Directors of these banking corporations are asked to adopt policy that the banks will not make or underwrite any loan to the South African government or any of its agencies until the government commits itself to ending apartheid and takes meaningful steps in that direction. NCNB and MORGAN have been further requested to disclose criteria used to determine whether a loan is beneficial to the well-being of blacks or supports the system of apartheid.

—No nuclear contract with South Africa. WESTINGHOUSE.

According to the resolution WESTINGHOUSE has obtained a ten-year, $50 million dollar contract to service and train personnel for South Africa's two Koeburg nuclear plants. South Africa has not signed the nuclear nonproliferation treaty and is widely believed to be developing nuclear weapons. The company and all its subsidiaries and affiliates are asked to terminate all present contracts and refuse all future contracts in South Africa until the government commits itself to ending apartheid and takes meaningful steps in that direction.

—No sales to the South African police and military. EXXON, MOTOROLA, GENERAL MOTORS.

These resolutions request the boards of director to make no sales to the police or military in South Africa until apartheid is abolished. GM is also asked to monitor all bulk sales to insure that the police or military are not the end destination of these sales and to report its status vis-a-vis the South African Key Points legislation and its position on possible government takeover in the event of civil unrest. The EXXON resolution also commends the company for positive steps it has taken to advance the social and economic status of its nonwhite employees and urges extension of these efforts.

—Report on loans to South Africa. BANK OF MONTREAL, CITICORP.

These banking corporations are asked to report on their current commitments in South Africa, including a list of all loans to the government, state-owned corporations and private companies over the past ten years, criteria for such loan decisions, a description of rejected loan requests, the companies' policies on future loans and an evaluation of how each loan contributed to the political, social and economic well-being of blacks.

—No expansion in South Africa; sign the Sullivan Principles. INGERSOLL-RAND.

The company is asked to not infuse foreign capital or expand its product line in South Africa until the government takes steps to bring full political, economic and social rights to black South Africans. The company is also asked to sign the Sullivan Principles for employment in South Africa.

—Sign the Sullivan Principles. DRESSER.

DRESSER is asked to sign the Sullivan Principles, which "establish minimum desegregation and fair employment standards for their South African operations."

—Sign the Sullivan Principles. ALLIS CHALMERS, BAXTER TRAVENOL LABORATORIES, DUN & BRADSTREET, FOSTER WHEELER, INTERNATIONAL FLAVORS AND FRAGRANCES, PEPSICO.

These companies are asked to sign the Sullivan Principles.

South Korea:

—Employment practices in South Korea. MOTOROLA.

Directors are asked to report to shareholders on the company's Korean subsidiary, describing all Korean employees by age, sex, position, seniority wage and benefit levels; how the South Korean government affects labor relations, compensation and grievance procedures and describing the roles of union organizing. The directors are also asked to present the company's policy on workers' rights to free speech and assembly in countries where democracy and human rights are restricted and to assess the company's Korean employment practices in light of stated commitments to equal employment opportunity.

—Employment of women in South Korea. CONTROL DATA.

The corporation is asked to increase efforts to provide retraining opportunities or $1,200 for alternative training to all former women employees; take public steps to counter government harassment and blacklisting; develop training for the corporation's overseas managers so that corporate actions do not reinforce local repressive or antilabor policies; review the adequacy of CONTROL DATA's present plant closing policy and report to shareholders.

U.S.S.R.:

—Report on sales to the Soviet Union. SCHLUMBERGER.

The directors of this company are asked to report to shareholders on the extent and nature of its sales to the government of the Soviet Union, including gross revenue from such sales for 1979-1983; the amount of such revenue which came from sales of products for use by the police or military or of any of its allies and a description of these products; a description of products for which the company sought a U.S. license for export to the U.S.S.R.; and a description of company products sold to the U.S.S.R., which require licensing to be shipped from the U.S. but were shipped from somewhere else.

Third World:

—World debt crisis. BANKERS TRUST, CHASE MANHATTAN, CHEMICAL, CITICORP, CONTINENTAL ILLINOIS, J.P. MORGAN, WELLS FARGO.

Resolutions to these banking corporations request management to prepare a report on the world debt crisis and how it affects the corporation including a list of the banks' loans to developing countries, specifying problem loans and descriptions of how social, economic, political and human rights factors were considered in making the loans. The reports should also contain an assessment of the impact on the company of a default by a major Latin American borrower and the impact of rescheduling fees. The resolutions ask for an assessment of International Monetary Fund austerity programs on those countries' ability to repay and on the poor of those countries. CITICORP, BANKERS TRUST, CHEMICAL, CONTINENTAL ILLINOIS and MORGAN are also asked to include a comparison of prime interest rates charged from 1979-1984 and to describe their in-state lending for single-unit dwelling, small business and agricultural loans. CHASE MANHATTAN is also asked to comment on the likelihood that the IMF repayment plans will result in a debt moratorium.

VI. MILITARISM

—**Secret ballot.** CANADIAN IMPERIAL BANK OF COMMERCE, GENERAL DYNAMICS.

GENERAL DYNAMICS, 1982's largest Department of Defense contractor with $5.891 billion in military production—95.7 percent of the company's 1982 revenues, is asked to implement a secret ballot for shareholder voting. In 1983 the company management "actively resolicited votes of many shareholders" who voted in opposition to management on a church-sponsored resolution on the cruise missile. The bank is also asked to institute a secret ballot procedure.

Military contracts:

—**Criteria for military contracts.** AMERICAN TELEPHONE & TELEGRAPH, HONEYWELL.

Directors of these companies are asked to "define and articulate" the principles—ethical, economic and social—used in evaluating prospective contracts with the Departments of Energy or Defense for involvement in research, development or production of weapons or components of weapons of mass destruction and to explain how these principles are developed within the company.

—**Criteria for military contracts.** EMERSON ELECTRIC, GENERAL ELECTRIC, MC DONNELL DOUGLAS.

These corporations, among the top 100 Department of Defense contractors, are asked to formulate social, economic and ethical criteria for management to apply to prospective military-related contracts to determine whether the corporations should accept the contracts. The criteria suggested address the following areas: basic canons of ethical business practice; long term environmental impact; stability of employment; lobbying practices and costs; company involvement in military contracts as percent of total sales or business; competitive bidding; sales to foreign governments and contracts for nuclear, biological or chemical weapons. MC DONNELL DOUGLAS is asked in the resolution simply to develop such criteria and the specific criteria are recommended as part of the "Statement of Support" to the resolution. The resolution to GENERAL ELECTRIC recommends that the criteria adopted address the above-outlined areas. EMERSON ELECTRIC, however, is asked to adopt a specific set of criteria which encompass the above-described issue areas and also include a

commitment to negotiate contracts with the Department of Defense that support peace research and economic conversion planning and to promote regular public discussion of the criteria as they apply to the company's contract decisions.

Criteria for military contracts. GTE CORPORATION.

GTE is asked to begin the process of adopting criteria for military contracts which "are based upon economic, social and ethical considerations such as the dignity of persons, respect for life and promotion of peaceful coexistence"; which give priority to government contracts which enhance the company's positive image and which recognize the company's responsibility for manufacturing products that could result in death or environmental destruction.

Criteria for military contracts: RAYTHEON, SINGER.

These companies, which are among the top 100 contractors to the Department of Defense, are asked to formulate social, economic and ethical criteria for management to apply to prospective military-related contracts to determine whether the company should bid on them and report the criteria to shareholders.

Nuclear weapons production:

—**Termination of nuclear weapons contract.** AMERICAN TELEPHONE & TELEGRAPH.

The resolution requests that the company not renew its Department of Energy contract to manage the Sandia National Laboratories in Albuquerque, New Mexico for research and development of nuclear weapons technology and effectiveness.

—**Disclosure of nuclear involvement.** ALLIED CORPORATION.

ALLIED CORPORATION, which took control of BENDIX's nuclear weapons activities with their 1982 merger, is asked to report to all shareholders a description of its nuclear-related work and an assessment of the advisability of renewing its current nuclear weapons contract when it expires.

—**Manufacture of nuclear weapons.** ROCKWELL INTERNATIONAL.

ROCKWELL INTERNATIONAL, the eighth largest defense contractor in 1982, manufactures nuclear explosive components for all U.S. nuclear weapons and is asked to report to all shareholders a description of its nuclear-related work and an assessment of the advisability of renewing its current nuclear weapons contract when it expires.

Space weapons:

—**Involvement in the militarization of space.** EASTMAN KODAK, MARTIN MARIETTA.

Concerned about escalation of the arms race into outer space and corporate dependency on defense contracts, sponsors ask these companies to issue reports about their involvement in the development of weapons for outer space. The resolutions define space weapons to include "satellites with military function, directed energy weapons and other antisatellite and ballistic missile defense technology." The resolutions ask the companies to report the current value of the companies' space weapons contracts; how much of the companies' own money and how much government funding is involved in the research; whether the companies are involved in materials-processing-in-space experiments and whether the companies have corporate policy on commercial development of space or development of space as a battlefield.

Shareholder Resolutions Withdrawn

While a number of resolutions were noted as withdrawn in the previous issue of the "Corporate Examiner", there was insufficient space to include explanations. As of late,March, the following resolutions were withdrawn and the reasons for those actions are described below:

—ALLIED. *Disclosure of nuclear involvement.*

Sponsors withdrew the resolution when the company agreed that after shareholder representatives asked the questions contained in the resolution at the annual meeting, the company would answer the questions in a report available to all shareholders.

—ABC, CBS, RCA/NBC. *Media images of women and minorities.*

During a day-long meeting in late 1983 officials of the television networks explained their companies' programs for addressing the concerns raised in the resolutions, some with printed materials, others with written reports. Representatives of church investors were satisfied that the networks were trying to be socially responsible in their business practices.

—CHEMICAL BANK. *World debt crisis.*

The resolution, filed late, will not appear on the ballot.

—AMERICAN ELECTRIC POWER, CINCINNATI GAS & ELECTRIC, DAYTON POWER & LIGHT. *Stop construction of nuclear power plant.*

The three partners in the Zimmer nuclear power plant announced a halt in construction of the trouble-plagued plant and will investigate converting the plant to coal.

—AMERICAN HOME PRODUCTS. *Third World marketing of dangerous drugs.*

Filers withdrew the resolution following the company's agreement to withdraw clioquinol, an anti-diarrheal drug known to have dangerous side effects, from the worldwide market by the end of 1984.

—AMERICAN HOSPITAL SUPPLY. *Employment of Mexican women.*

Company officials agreed to provide a narrative and statistical report on the employment conditions of its Mexican workforce, 60 percent of whom are women, and the sponsor withdrew the resolution.

—AMERICAN TELEPHONE & TELEGRAPH. *Plant closings.*

AT&T has agreed to make available to all shareholders a report requested in the resolution, preparing a brochure that outlines its plant closings policies and notifying shareholders of its availability in its second quarter report.

—CIGNA. *No loans to the South African government.*

Company officials informed sponsors that it is required to keep a certain amount of funds in South African government bonds and that the company attempts to choose bonds related to health and welfare interests, for example. The company stated:

CIGNA has no operations which engage in underwriting loans. Neither CIGNA nor any of its subsidiaries not based in South Africa makes loans to the South African government or any of its agencies or instrumentalities.

—CITICORP. *Report on loans to South Africa.*
Sponsors withdrew the resolution.

—CITICORP. *World debt crisis.*

The resolution was withdrawn and plans are underway to continue pursuing shareholder concerns.

—COMMONWEALTH EDISON. *Nuclear power lobbying.*

The resolution was withdrawn after the company announced it will not pass on to customers the costs of contributions to the Committee on Energy Awareness.

—DART & KRAFT. *EEO reporting.*
Sponsors withdrew the resolution when the company agreed to report employment data on the status of racial minorities and women in the company's nine employment categories.

—EXXON. *No sales to the South African police and military.*

The sponsor withdrew the resolution in light of the company's continued support of a non-expansion in South Africa policy and its report that it does not solicit contracts to supply the South African police or military and its promise to report to shareholders its analysis of the proposed Orderly Movement and Settlement of Black Persons bill and the Sullivan Principles.

—FOSTER WHEELER. *Sign the Sullivan Principles.*
The company agreed to sign the principles.

—HOUSTON INDUSTRIES. *Conservation.*

The resolution was withdrawn after the company outlined to sponsors its efforts on conservation which have made it an industry leader in some areas of energy conservation and cogeneration.

—K-MART. *Minority economic development.*

The resolution was withdrawn after the company agreed to provide a written report on its business relationships with minority or women-owned businesses.

—MARTIN MARIETTA. *Involvement in militarization of space.*

The resolution was withdrawn after the company agreed to make available to shareholders the information requested in the resolution.

—J.P. MORGAN. *No loans to the South African government.*

The company agreed to make the following response to annual meeting questions about its South African lending policies:

Our policy in deciding whether to extend credit to a prospective borrower, either governmental or private, in South Africa is both to consider the creditworthiness of that borrower and to ascertain that the credit sought is not inconsistent with the improvement of conditions for blacks and non-whites. We are particularly sensitive to the extension of credit to the South African government or its agencies. In considering loans to the South African government and its agencies, we make every effort to assure ourselves that any loans will have a demonstrable positive effect on the improvement of conditions for blacks and other non-whites. . . .

—NL INDUSTRIES. *Radioactive contamination.*

The company is making progress in the clean up of on-site and off-site locations which have been contaminated by low-level radioactivity. The company has agreed to make a report to shareholders on this progress at the 1984 annual meeting.

—WESTINGHOUSE. *Employment practices.*

The resolution was withdrawn after the company agreed to provide employment data to the proponents and to publish a booklet on its employment programs.

—WESTINGHOUSE. *No nuclear contract with South Africa.*

The sponsors withdrew the resolution after the company did not receive the first part of the contract to provide services and train personnel for South Africa's two Koeburg nuclear plants. The remaining parts of the contract will not be allocated for a year or more.

Resolutions Excluded by the SEC

The SEC has ruled that the following resolutions could be excluded from company proxy statements:

—AMERICAN HOME PRODUCTS. Drug lobbying in the Third World.

—AMERICAN TELEPHONE & TELEGRAPH. Criteria for military contracts.

—AMERICAN TELEPHONE & TELEGRAPH. Termination of nuclear weapons contract.

—CONTROL DATA. Computer sales in South Africa.

—EXXON. Pollution control.

—PHILADELPHIA ELECTRIC. Conservation.

—SINGER. Criteria for military contract.

—UNITED TECHNOLOGIES. Plant closings.

'Our Credo':
Johnson and Johnson

This statement by a large pharmaceutical firm is an example of reflections on corporate responsibility made by multinational corporations.

We believe our first responsibility is to the doctors, nurses, and patients, to mothers and all others who use our products and services. In meeting their needs, everything we do must be of high quality. We must constantly strive to reduce our costs in order to maintain reasonable prices. Customers' orders must be serviced promptly and accurately. Our suppliers and distributors must have an opportunity to make a fair profit.

We are responsible to our employees, the men and women who work with us throughout the world. Everyone must be considered as an individual. We must respect their dignity and recognize their merit. They must have a sense of security in their jobs. Compensation must be fair and adequate, and working conditions clean, orderly, and safe. Employees must feel free to make suggestions and complaints. There must be equal opportunity for employment, development, and advancement for those qualified. We must provide competent management, and their actions must be just and ethical.

We are responsible to the communities in which we live and work and to the world community as well. We must be good citizens—support good works and charities and bear our fair share of taxes. We must encourage civic improvements and better health and education. We must maintain in good order the property we are privileged to use, protecting the environment and natural resources.

Our final responsibility is to our stockholders. Business must make a sound profit. We must experiment with new ideas. Research must be carried on, innovative programs developed, and mistakes paid for. New equipment must be purchased, new facilities provided, and new products launched. Reserves must be created to provide for adverse times. When we operate according to these principles, the stockholders should realize a fair return.

Notes

ABBREVIATIONS

Some sources that are cited repeatedly in the notes are designated by the following abbreviations:

ANF   *The Ante-Nicene Fathers.* Edited by A. Roberts and J. Donaldson. 10 vols., 1885-96. Reprint edition, Grand Rapids, Mich.: Eerdmans, 1979.

BRE   *Business, Religion, and Ethics: Inquiry and Encounter.* Edited by Donald G. Jones. Cambridge, Mass.: Oelgeschlager, Gunn, and Hain, 1982.

CCPD   Commission on the Churches' Participation in Development, World Council of Churches, Geneva.

CDCT   *Christianity, Democracy, and the Churches Today.* Washington: Institute on Religion and Democracy, 1982.

CE   *The Corporate Examiner.* New York: Corporate Information Center, National Council of Churches, 1971-73; New York: Interfaith Center on Corporate Responsibility, 1974ff.

CIC   Corporate Information Center, National Council of Churches, New York. In 1974 became part of Interfaith Center on Corporate Responsibility, which continued to publish *CIC Briefs*—later called *ICCR Briefs*.

CICSA   *Church Investments, Corporations, and Southern Africa.* New York: Corporate Information Center, National Council of Churches, 1973.

CRRI   *Corporate Responsibility and Religious Institutions.* New York: Corporate Information Center, National Council of Churches, 1971.

CSC   *Church, State, and Corporation: A Report on the Impact of Religious Organizations on Corporate Policy.* New York: Burson-Marsteller, 1982.

CSRA   *Corporate Social Responsibility Actions,* 1977-79, 1979-81, 1981-83. Reports to General Synods of the United Church of Christ. New York: Social Responsibility in Investments, United Church Boards for Homeland and World Ministries, Pension Boards, and United Church Foundation.

CTI   *The Corporation: A Theological Inquiry.* Edited by Michael Novak and John W. Cooper. Washington: American Enterprise Institute, 1981.

EP   *Economic Primer.* Edited by Annette Hutchins-Felder. New York: United Methodist General Board of Global Ministries, 1980.

IAM   *ICCR Agribusiness Manual.* New York: Interfaith Center on Corporate Responsibility, 1978.

ICCR   Interfaith Center on Corporate Responsibility, New York.

ICF   *Investing Church Funds for Maximum Social Impact,* Report of the Committee on Financial Investments. New York: United Church of Christ, 1970.

IRRC   Investor Responsibility Research Center, Washington, D.C.

LC   *Lobbying the Corporation: Citizen Challenges to Business Authority.* By David Vogel. New York: Basic Books, 1978.

MMPT   *Multinational Managers and Poverty in the Third World.* Edited by Lee A. Tavis. Notre Dame: University of Notre Dame Press, 1982.

NACLA   North American Congress on Latin America, New York.

NPNF   *A Select Library of Nicene and Post-Nicene Fathers of the Christian Church.* Edited by H. Wace and P. Schaff. 1st series, 14 vols.; 2nd series, 14 vols. Reprint edition, Grand Rapids, Mich.: Eerdmans, 1966.

NV   *News & Views,* Special Edition on Corporate Responsibility. Wheaton, Ill., June 1978.

PC   *Politicizing Christianity: Focus on South Africa.* By Edward Norman. Washington: Ethics and Public Policy Center, 1979. (Reprinted from *Christianity and the World Order.* New York: Oxford University Press, 1979.)

PTF   Presbyterian Task Force: *Review of Policies, Strategies, and Programs of the United Presbyterian Church Related to Transnational Corporations,* Narrative Summary. New York: General Assembly Mission Council, United Presbyterian Church, 1983. (Page numbers marked CC.) See also PTFA.

PTFA   Presbyterian Task Force: *Background Report and Appendices to the Report of the Transnational Review Task Force.* See PTF, above.

PVP   *Prophesy vs. Profits.* By D. J. Kirby. Maryknoll, N.Y.: Orbis, 1980.

RD   *Religion and Democracy,* Newsletter. Washington: Institute on Religion and Democracy.

RTB   *The Role of Transnational Business in Mass Economic Development*. New York: United Church Board for Homeland Ministries, 1975.

SM   *A Shareowners' Manual: For Church Committees on Social Responsibility in Investments*. By Eleanor Craig, S.L., for the Interfaith Center on Corporate Responsibility. New York: ICCR, 1977.

SRI   *Social Responsibility and Investments*. By Charles W. Powers. Nashville: Abingdon Press, 1971.

TCCEM   *Transnational Corporations, the Churches, and the Ecumenical Movement*. Report of the WCC International Consultation on TNCs, Bad Boll, West Germany, 1981. Geneva: World Council of Churches, 1982.

TW   *Time to Withdraw*. Geneva: World Council of Churches, Programme to Combat Racism, 1973.

YACC   *Yearbook of American and Canadian Churches*, 1982. Edited by Constant H. Jacquet, Jr. Nashville: Abingdon Press, 1982.

PREFACE

1. Cf. CSC, pp. 2 ff.
2. Reinhold Niebuhr, *The Nature and Destiny of Man* (New York: Scribner's, 1941), vol. I, pp. 1ff.
3. Cf. Neil H. Jacoby, *Corporate Power and Social Responsibility* (New York: Macmillan, 1973).
4. PTF, p. 137.

INTRODUCTION

1. Isaiah Frank, *Foreign Enterprise in Developing Countries* (Baltimore: Johns Hopkins University, 1980), chap. 2.
2. TCCEM, p. 1.
3. Walter Owensby, "Multinationals: Impact and Accountability," *Church and Society*, Jan.-Feb. 1976, p. 24. See also *Multinational Corporations in World Development* (New York: United Nations, 1973), pp. 4-5.
4. Michael Z. Brooke and H. Lee Remmers, *The Strategy of Multinational Enterprise, Organization and Finance* (New York: American Elsevier Press, 1978), p. 5.
5. RTB, p. 6.
6. *Statistical Yearbook* (New York: United Nations, 1973), pp. 709ff.
7. John Hein, "The World's Multinationals: A Global Challenge," Conference Board Information Bulletin #84, 1981; included in PTFA, A-4ff.
8. Owensby, "Multinationals: Impact and Accountability," p. 24.
9. EP, p. 23.
10. According to EP, the simple reason for direct investment of international capital abroad is as "a strategic move to eliminate competition from other firms" (M. Nkosi, p. 23). Yet there is little evidence that the absolute elimination of competition is a principal or constant purpose of MNC investment abroad.
11. Ibid., p. 24.
12. Ibid., p. 22.
13. Gustavo Gutiérrez, "Praxis of Liberation and the Christian Faith," p. 8, in *CCPD Documents* 6 (February 1975).
14. MMPT, p. 97.
15. Ibid., pp. 98-99.

CHAPTER ONE

1. Michael J. Francis and Cecilia G. Manrique, "Clarifying the Debate: Multinational Managers and Poverty in the Third World," MMPT, pp. 68-69.
2. Donald G. Jones, Preface, BRE, p. ix. Vogel, LC, had used an earlier figure of $160 billion (p. 162).
3. *Fortune* magazine, April 30, 1984, p. 276.
4. LC, p. 162.
5. Schomer, BRE, p. 32.
6. Ibid.
7. Ibid., using 1975 figures.
8. Vogel, LC, p. 218, using 1972 figures, and Schomer, BRE, p. 32.

9. LC, p. 162.

10. General Board of Pensions of the United Methodist Church, Annual Report, 1983; Cf. T. Smith, CTI, p. 63.

11. See T. Smith, CTI, p. 63, using the earlier figure of $6 billion. See also 1983 letter from Paul M. Neuhaus, ICCR attorney, to Securities and Exchange Commission, March 31, 1983.

12. *Fortune* magazine, April 30, 1984, p. 276.

13. Joel Fajardo, "Corporate Crime Against Nations," *Church and Society,* 67 (March-April 1977), p. 55, using 1972 figures.

14. MMPT, p. 97.

15. PTFA, V1.

16. Ibid., B3-3.

17. Ibid., B3-4,5.

18. Ibid., B3-4.

19. Ibid., B3-5.

20. PTF, CC-108.

21. PTFA, V6.

22. PTF, CC-109.

23. PTFA, V5.

24. Ibid.

25. PTF, CC-109.

26. PTFA, V5.

27. Ibid.

28. Ibid., V9.

29. Ibid.

30. Ibid., V11.

31. Ibid.

32. PTF, CC-110.

33. Ibid., CC-109.

34. PTFA, V10.

35. Ibid., V11.

36. Ibid.

37. Ibid., V12.

38. Ibid., V13.

39. PTF, CC-110.

40. PTFA, V6.

41. Ibid., V7.

42. Ibid., V19.

43. Ibid.

44. PTF, CC-143. Jan Van Meter, vice-president of Hill and Knowlton, a leading public-relations firm, stated that although public-opinion polls clearly show that the public believes that "big business ought to be watched," "the good news is that 80 percent of the public believes large corporations are essential for the nation's growth and expansion" (CE, Aug./Sept. 1983, p. 5).

45. Cf. *Public Opinion,* published monthly, Princeton, N.J.; D. W. Brogan, *The American Character* (New York: Knopf, 1944), pp. 25, 29; Louis Harris, "The Public Credibility of American Business," *Conference Board Record,* March 1973, pp. 3-38.

46. ICCR Annual Report, June 30, 1982. For a brief overview of the work of ICCR, see CSC, p. 7.

47. PTF, CC-124.

48. ICCR promotional brochure, n.d., p. 1.

49. Ibid., p. 2.

50. PTF, CC-124.

51. ICCR Annual Report, June 30, 1982.

52. PTF, CC-124.

53. Ibid.

54. Ibid., CC-127.

55. See "The National Council of Churches," CSC, p. 12.

56. For official United Church of Christ statements on corporate responsibility, see: Minutes of the General Synod, 1965-79; "The Social Impact of United Church of Christ Invested Funds, 1971-73" (Board for World Ministries, 1973), p. 13; "Church as Shareholder" (World Issues Office); "The Role of Transnational Business in Mass Economic Development" (Board for Homeland Ministries, 1975), p. 70; "Corporate Social Responsibility Actions, 1977-79," Report to the 12th General Synod (Board for World Ministries, 1979).

57. For official United Presbyterian statements on corporate responsibility, see: Minutes of the General Assembly, 1969 ff.; "Manual of the Committee on Mission Responsibility Through Investment" (General Assembly Mission Council, 1979).

58. For official United Methodist statements on corporate responsibility, see: "Statement of Investment Policy" (General Council on Finance and Administration, 1973, 1980); "Guidelines for the Subcommittee on Investments of the Committee on Finance" (National Division, Board of Missions, 1971); "Recommendation by Special Investment Committee to Finance Committee—Proposed Program for Coordinating Social Consciousness Considerations With Investment and Proxy Voting Matters" (World Division, Board of Missions, 1971); "Investment Guidelines" (Women's Division, Board of Global Ministries, 1974); "Understanding Investments as a Missional Thrust" (Women's Division, Board of Missions, 1972); "Guidelines Concerning Investments" (Women's Division, Board of Missions, 1973); "Journal of the General Conference," 1972, 1976, 1980, 1984; and "Book of Discipline," 1972, 1976, 1980, 1984.

59. General Assembly of the Christian Church, *Ethical Guidelines for Investment Policies*, February 1973.

60. IRRC, *News for Investors*, vol. X, no. 9, p. 1.

61. PTF, CC-130.

62. Cf. CSRA, 1981-83, pp. 12ff.; ICF, chap. 1; "Cooperation Among Church Shareowners," SM, p. 14; "Interest of Church People," RTB, pp. 4ff.; "The Churches and the Challenge of the TNCs," TCCEM, chap. 2.

63. See "The National Catholic Coalition for Responsible Investment," CSC, pp. 14, 20.

64. CSC, pp. 14ff. See Michael Crosby, *Catholic Church Investments for Corporate Social Responsibility* (Milwaukee: Justice and Peace Center, 1973).

65. For further discussions of the Catholic side of the corporate-responsibility movement, see PVP and MMPT.

CHAPTER TWO

1. For the story of how the American tradition of social perfectionism affected the society prior to the development of the social gospel, see the superb analysis by T. L.

Smith, *Revivalism and Social Reform: American Protestantism on the Eve of the Civil War* (New York: Harper and Row, 1957). I am deeply indebted to Dr. Smith, a professor at Johns Hopkins University, for the light his work has thrown on the development of the social consciousness of American Protestantism.

2. CSC, pp. 2ff.

3. Methodist Discipline, 1952, para. 735.7.

4. Methodist Discipline, 1964, para. 1612.4. In saying that the 1968 NCC statement "The Church as Purchaser of Goods and Services" contained the "first specific reference to church investments" (LC, p. 162), David Vogel apparently overlooked these earlier statements.

5. CSC, p. 7; LC, p. 162.

6. Corporate Information Center, Agenda Item no. 13 for Presentation to the NCC General Board, Feb. 11-15, 1972, p. 6.

7. CSC, p. 7; LC, p. 162.

8. See "The Roots of Advocacy," CSC, pp. 5-6.

9. F. S. Sheridan, "FIGHT and Eastman Kodak," no. 9-373-207 (Boston: Inter-Collegiate Case Clearinghouse, 1973), p. 2.

10. Ibid., p. 6.

11. LC, p. 34.

12. Alinsky, *Rules for Radicals* (New York: Vintage, 1971), pp. 169, 173.

13. CSC, p. 2.

14. Cf. General Board of the NCC, "Christian Concern and Responsibility for Economic Life," Feb. 24, 1966.

15. TW, p. 2.

16. Ibid., p. 3.

17. Henry J. Pratt, *The Liberalization of American Protestantism: A Case Study in Complex Organizations* (Detroit: Wayne State University, 1972).

18. Ibid., p. 260.

19. Ibid., p. 264.

20. Ibid., p. 262.

21. Ibid., p. 263.

22. Ibid., p. 259.

23. Ibid., p. 239.

24. Ibid., p. 259.

25. NV, pp. 30-31; cf. LC, pp. 161ff.

26. YACC, 1982, p. 11.

27. Quoted in NV, p. 1.

28. NV, p. 11.

29. Pratt, op. cit., pp. 141ff.

30. Ibid., pp. 141-280.

31. Gustavo Gutiérrez, "Praxis of Liberation and the Christian Faith," p. 5, in *CCPD Documents* 6 (February 1975).

32. CSC, p. 6.

33. ICF, pp. 3ff.

34. United Methodist Church, Book of Resolutions, 1972, p. 21.

35. ICF, pp. 47ff.

36. Cf. "Guidelines Concerning Investments," Committee on Investments, Women's Division, United Methodist Board of Global Ministries, 1970. For a view of the growing militancy of theology and social-policy formation during this period see

Gustavo Gutiérrez, "Notes for a Theology of Liberation," *Theological Studies* 31 (1970), pp. 243-61; and "Racism," *International Review of Mission,* vol. LIX, no. 235 (1970).

37. *Corporate Action Guide* (New York: NCC, 1973).

38. *Grapevine,* Joint Strategy and Action Committee (JSAC), February 1971.

39. PTF, p. 122.

40. Ibid.

41. For a significant theological interpretation during this period, see J. B. Metz, *Theology of the World* (New York: Herder and Herder, 1971).

42. For accounts of increasing activism, see: "Churches Getting More Active as Company Stockholders," *Industry Week,* Feb. 15, 1971, pp. 14-16; "Corporate Critics Gain New Allies," *Business Week,* Feb. 13, 1971, p. 29; William J. Horvath, "Investments: The Church's Secret Weapon," *Social Action* 37 (January 1971), pp. 3-29; "Should Churches Use Their Funds to Force Social Change?," *U.S. News and World Report,* Sept. 20, 1971, pp. 71-72; Horace E. Gale, "Why Are the Churches Getting Involved in Investments?," CRRI, p. 34.

43. CRRI, passim.

44. LC, p. 164.

45. CSC, p. 7.

46. Religious News Service, May 24, 1971, p. 9.

47. Among persons who were ejected from the meeting for unruly behavior were T. H. Smith, then an assistant for African affairs of the United Church of Christ's Council for Christian Social Action, and Dr. Carlton Goodlett, whose World Peace Council was described by a U.S. congressional committee as "a Soviet-controlled international 'peace' front" (1970 staff study of the Committee on Internal Security, U.S. House of Representatives). Critics of Goodlett had repeatedly called attention to the fact that he was refused entry into Britain on the grounds that his visit would be "inimical to the interests of the free world" (NV, p. 2).

48. *Grapevine,* Joint Strategy and Action Committee (JSAC), February 1971.

49. Religious News Service, April 29, 1971.

50. Claire Cox, Copley News Service, *Wheaton Journal,* Feb. 7, 1971.

51. Religious News Service, April 29, 1971.

52. David Jessup, "Preliminary Inquiry Regarding Financial Contributions to Outside Political Groups by Boards and Agencies of the United Methodist Church, 1977-79," mimeographed, April 7, 1980; excerpts appear in appendix F.

53. For evidence in commercial mass media that this research network was beginning to have some effect, see "Companies Feel the Wrath of the Clergy," *Business Week,* March 18, 1972, pp. 84-86.

54. Religious News Service, Sept. 14, 1972.

55. J. Gajardo, in *Church and Society,* March-April 1977, p. 66.

56. Dusseldorf conference on International Organization for Investment, 1973.

57. Louis Escobar, *Worldview,* February 1974, p. 26.

58. Chief among them were Goodyear, Mobil, and Gulf; NV, p. 5.

59. LC, pp. 177ff. Cf NV, p. 5.

60. Religious News Service, July 6, 1972. At about the same time, a study guide issued by the Lutheran Church in America, *Social Criteria for Investments,* cited the familiar cluster of issues that "focus attention on investments": "war, preserving the environment, and racism and social and economic justice at home and abroad." Later we will explore the question of issue selectivity and the curious homogeneity that has pervaded issue definition in the CR movement from its beginnings.

61. TW, p. 11.

62. Ibid., p. 1.

63. *New York Times,* March 26, 1972.

64. CSC, pp. 5ff.

65. LC, pp. 170ff.

66. NV, p. 55.

67. *Daily World,* April 27, 1972.

68. See *CIC Briefs,* 1973 (New York: Corporate Information Center), passim.

69. Ibid. Cf. Michael Crosby, O.F.M./Cap., "Catholic Church Investments for Corporate Responsibility" (Milwaukee: Justice and Peace Center, 1973).

70. SM, chap. 3.

71. General Council on Finance and Administration, United Methodist Church; quoted in mission brochure, Board of Global Ministries, 1974.

72. Ignored was the fact that the autonomous human capacity for "humanizing the world" was hardly a conspicuous theme of the New Testament.

73. *Esquire,* November 1973. For wider reporting of CR activism during this period, see "Churches Lose Bid on G.E. Disclosure," *New York Times,* April 26, 1973.

74. Editorial, *Fortune,* November 1973; see NV, p. 41.

75. *Gulf Boycott Coalition Newsletter,* March 1973.

76. Cf. *CRC Newsletter,* April 1973, p. 11; October 1973, p. 30.

77. Religious News Service, August 7, 1973.

78. SM, pp. 14-15.

79. It is a depressing point that church advocacy and action groups have often found ways to eliminate moderating internal opposition. Even though the word *dialogue* occurs frequently in their rhetoric, most apparently do not want it, and react defensively when it occurs. They have found ways of putting off potential inquirers who might disturb the prevailing internal consensus with embarrassing questions. In 1974 the mandate of Church World Service, an NCC agency, included service to refugees. However, when CWS assisted Cuban refugees in the early seventies, the executive director was severely criticized and eventually lost his job, in part because it was said that CWS had "permitted and encouraged exiles to tell their side of the story in local churches, in the press, and so forth. This one-sided education of the American people provided a base of public opinion which the government needed in order to initiate and maintain its official state of hostility toward Cuba" (D. Hostetter and M. McIntyre, "The Politics of Charity," *The Christian Century,* Sept. 18, 1974, pp. 845, 850).

80. For the chronicle of these actions, see *CIC Briefs,* 1974.

81. For reports of Catholic CR actions of 1975, see Capuchin Fathers, "Financial Policy of the Province of St. Joseph" (Detroit, 1975); Regina Williams and Michael Crosby, O.F.M./Cap., "Procter and Gamble: Image-Maker?," *Catholic Church Investments for Corporate Responsibility,* vol. 2, no. 11 (Milwaukee: Justice and Peace Center, 1975).

82. RTB, chap. 4; see *ICCR Briefs,* 1975.

83. Michael Crosby, O.F.M./Cap., "A Primer for Shareholder Responsibility at the IBM Annual Meeting," *Catholic Church Investments for Corporate Responsibility,* vol. 2 (Milwaukee: Justice and Peace Center, 1975).

84. See *ICCR Briefs,* 1975.

85. T. E. Scheetz, *ICCR Brief,* October 1975, p. 3B.

86. Ibid.

87. "Stockholder Proposal Relating to a Report to Stockholders on Activities in the

Dominican Republic," G + W Annual Shareowners' Meeting, 1975.

88. TW, p. 4.
89. Ibid., p. 6.
90. Ibid., p. 8.
91. Ibid., p. 12.
92. Ibid., pp. 12-13.
93. PTF, CC-136.
94. TW, pp. 7ff.
95. *ICCR Briefs,* 1973ff.
96. Richard E. Sincere, *The Politics of Sentiment: Churches and Foreign Investment in South Africa* (Washington: Ethics and Public Policy Center, 1984), chap. 5.
97. PC, p. 10.
98. The literature on the South African question is extensive. For supplementary reading see the bibliography. For brief reviews see Sincere, op. cit.; LC, pp. 169ff.; "South Africa: Continuing Target," CSC, p. 21; and T. H. Smith, "South Africa: The Churches vs. the Corporations," *Business and Society Review,* Winter 1974, pp. 54-64.
99. IAM, pp. 1-3; cf. p. 162.
100. *San Francisco Chronicle,* Sept. 28, 1977.
101. Among the Catholic members of this ICCR taskforce at that time were Sister Mary Jean Audette, Sister Regina Murphy, the Rev. Michael Crosby, O.F.M./Cap., and the Rev. Charles Dahm, O.P. Protestant members included Robin Jurs, Robert Nee, Palmera Peralta (LCA), Mary Ellen Summerville (UCC), Patricia Young (UP), Walter Owensby (UP), and Kim Jefferson (UM). Ruth E. Bushko, then ICCR associate director, helped in preparing the manual.
102. IAM, p. 4.
103. Ibid., pp. 2ff.
104. Ibid.
105. Ibid.
106. Ibid.
107. Ibid.
108. Roger Burbach and Patricia Flynn, *Agribusiness in the Americas* (New York: NACLA, 1981), p. 11.
109. IAM, p. 4.
110. Ibid.
111. IAM, inside cover. Regrettably, it hardly seems plausible to reply that these dealings with NACLA are confined to an era long passed, for NACLA was still receiving money from Presbyterian Hunger Program sources in 1980 ($10,500) and from the NCC in 1981 ($300). "Money from the Presbyterian hunger program helped NACLA publish this book, *Agribusiness in the Americas,* an indictment of capitalism and American agricultural corporations" (Morley Safer, CBS "60 Minutes," Jan. 23, 1983). NACLA also appeared as a recipient on the 1981 Financial Disclosure Report of the Women's Division of the United Methodist Board of Global Ministries.
112. See Erving Goffman, *The Presentation of the Self in Everyday Life* (New York: Doubleday, 1959), on impression management.
113. Helen Shapiro narrated an oral history of NACLA—*NACLA Report to the Americas* (New York: NACLA, 1981)—in which the group's philosophy of "research" was straightforwardly articulated. The two-fold purpose of NACLA from the beginning was (1) the study of Latin American revolutionary potentialities, and (2) "the political

use of information." The research done by the SDS activists who founded NACLA was thought of as "demystifying research" that included an "emphasis of developing expertise on the Left." As early as 1967, SDS leaders, aware that certain highly placed persons in American Protestantism "knew what Marxism was all about," set about to utilize soft, idealistic church structures wherever possible to further their political aims. Although the extent of their own commitment to the church has remained extremely questionable, they recognized in liberal ecumenism an enticing opportunity to gain support from a respected constituency. The Interchurch Center provided just the bureaucratic structure they needed. As early as 1968 "NACLA-type research was introduced" (Shapiro). This NACLA model of so-called research, "the political use of information," grasped the imagination of some liberal church bureaucrats who had little constituency other than their paid staffs at the Interchurch Center. The Joint Strategy and Action Committee and various mission boards have helped to fund NACLA for almost a decade, and apparently trusted NACLA's information sources about Del Monte and other multinationals.

CHAPTER THREE

1. PTF, CC-152.

2. See also Howard Schomer, address at Conference on Investor Responsibility and Corporate Accountability, IRRC, Washington, D.C., Sept. 28, 1977, mimeographed.

3. One signal in one denomination of this centrist reassessment was an embattled call for relocation of the United Methodist Board of Global Ministries. The call began as early as 1966 but was hotly debated in Portland at the 1976 General Conference, which ordered that it be studied during the following quadrennium. Its effect would have been to end the proximity of the Board to the NCC and WCC offfices at 475 Riverside Drive. The strength of the opposition to the Board's trajectory at that time indicated a deep skepticism, not about the Board's intentions, but about the prudence of its staff in some of their ecumenical activist connections. (In 1980 the decision was made not to move for financial reasons—it would have cost $3 million.) Another interesting test question came before the 1976 General Conference: Should bureaucratic political activists who have no religious beliefs be allowed to continue on the church payroll? Gloria Perez, an employee of the National Division of the Board of Global Ministries, said she "dropped out of church at seventeen because religion didn't grab me. I am not a Christian, and I don't believe in God" (*Tulsa Daily World,* May 1, 1976). She was allowed to retain her position.

4. CSC, pp. 9ff.

5. Religious News Service, May 24, 1976.

6. Cf. "Fifth Anniversary Issue," *The Corporate Examiner,* vol. 5, no. 8-9, September 1976, p. 1; Thomas H. Stahel, "More Action Than They Called For: The Detroit Meeting," *America,* Nov. 6, 1976, pp. 292-96; and Thomas Stevenson, "Churches Wield Stock as Instrument for Challenging Corporate Practices," *National Catholic Reporter,* Nov. 5, 1976.

7. Cf. *ICCR Briefs* on infant formula, 1975ff.

8. *ICCR Briefs,* 1976-77.

9. Although the November 1976 *ICCR Brief* on Gulf + Western admitted that "the

influence of a transnational firm on a government" was "generally difficult to trace," it did not hesitate to make public some charges about which it had assembled inconclusive evidence. "Many Dominicans also believe that G + W had a hand in digging the enormous loopholes in the 1972 law restricting extension of sugar acreage," it reported. It spoke diffusely about "widely held suspicions in the Dominican Republic about the company's conduct there," and alleged "that G + W and other large landowners are using their political muscle to undermine the recently instituted land reform measures." The report admitted a high rate of Dominican economic growth in the past decade but complained that "it is growth measured only in terms of the value of increased production ... definitely not in terms of 'a general reduction of mass poverty, unemployment and inequality' " (A. Howard, *ICCR Brief,* November 1976, p. 3D).

10. *A.D.* magazine, November 1976.

11. *ICCR Brief,* November 1976.

12. Christian Conference on Asia, "People Toiling Under Pharoah," *Japan Christian Quarterly,* 43 (Winter 1977), p. 23. Cf. Donald K. White, "Pre-meeting Media Hype," *San Francisco Chronicle,* April 22, 1977, p. 2; and "Publicizing an Issue Through the Media," SM, chap. V, sec. B, p. 128.

13. *ICCR Briefs,* 1976-77.

14. Howard Schomer, "South Africa: Beyond Fair Employment," *Harvard Business Review,* May-June 1983, pp. 145ff; cf. LC, pp. 169ff.

15. Schomer, op. cit.: "By 1982, 146 of the 400 American companies with subsidiaries or affiliates in South Africa" had become signatories. Cf. LC, pp. 179f.

16. LC, p. 179.

17. See *The Oil Conspiracy,* UCC Center for Social Action, June 21, 1976; this was based on information from OKHELA, described as "a clandestine organization of white South African patriots who, as militants, are engaged in providing invisible support to the National Liberation struggle, headed by the African National Congress of South Africa."

18. *ICCR Brief,* June 1978.

19. See *ICCR Briefs,* 1977.

20. IAM, p. 162.

21. *ICCR Briefs,* 1977.

22. Ibid.

23. Sister Helen Volkomener of the Sisters of Providence testified in glowing terms about the successes of the Cuban Revolution to a subcommittee of the House Committee on International Relations, July 9, 1975: "People speak of the 'Revolution' as a continuing event, as 'new life,' much as persons talk about a biblical 'liberation' or 'salvation'" (*Cuba Review,* New York: Cuba Resource Center, September 1975).

24. J. Armstrong and R. Dilley, "A Report From Cuba," United Methodist Church of the Dakotas Area, June 1977, p. 9.

25. NCC Response to *Reader's Digest,* January 1983.

26. SM, p. 134.

27. Ibid.

28. Ibid., p. 130.

29. Cf. Bill Toohey, "Religious 'Davids' Tackle Corporate 'Goliaths' in Responsibility Fray," *National Catholic Reporter,* Feb. 24, 1978, p. 3.

30. Religious News Service, May 12, 1978.

31. This support is discussed in Ernest W. Lefever, *Amsterdam to Nairobi: The World Council of Churches and the Third World* (Washington: Ethics and Public Policy Center, 1979).

32. The efforts of Robert Mugabe, now prime minister, were regarded as qualified on humanitarian grounds by the WCC Special Fund, while Methodist bishop Muzorewa did not qualify on humanitarian grounds, nor was it thought that his efforts fit into the Fund's primary framework of objectives. Muzorewa's relief programs were in time aided by Church World Service and other humanitarian agencies but not by the WCC Special Fund.

33. Anon., "A Note to the Conference Treasurer," Oct. 2, 1978, mimeographed, pp. 1-4; cf. Dow Kirkpatrick, "Two Sundays in May: Castro and Wesley," *United Methodist Reporter*, July 22, 1977.

34. CSRA, 1977-79.

35. United Methodist *Newscope*, vol. 11, no. 5 (Feb. 4, 1983).

36. Ad Hoc Lay Study Committee on General Conference, April 1979, pp. 1-9.

37. Henry J. Frundt, *Gulf + Western in the Dominican Republic: An Evaluation* (New York: ICCR, 1979).

38. Cf. William Stemper, "A Theological-Ethical Appraisal of Corporate Social Responsibility Today," *CR Forum*, Summer-Fall 1979, pp. 12-16.

39. CSC, p. 3.

40. Ibid., p. 26.

41. Ibid., pp. 26ff.

42. For further clarification of the role of the Christian Right, see CSC: "The Christian Right," pp. 26ff; "The Coalition for Better Television," pp. 34ff; "Opposition Voice: People For the American Way," p. 36.

43. CDCT, p. 12.

44. Cf. D. J. Kirchhoff, "Corporate Missionary: Those Who Believe in Capitalism Must Fight Back," *Barron's*, Feb. 19, 1979, and "Antibusiness Radicals in Clerical Garb," *Business and Society Review* 32 (Winter 1979-80), pp. 55-58; Michael Novak, "God and Man in the Corporation," *Policy Review* 9 (Summer 1980), p. 32; Herman Nickel, "The Corporation Haters," *Fortune*, June 16, 1980, pp. 126-36 (reprinted as Essay 24, *Crusade Against the Corporation*, Washington: Ethics and Public Policy Center, 1980).

45. EP, p. 27. See also "Looking Toward General Conference: Mission Issues 5, Corporate Responsibility," *New World Outlook*, March 1980, p. 45; and "Corporate Responsibility Challenges, Spring 1980," CE, February 1980.

46. EP, p. 28. Under NCC auspices it was written that "the revolutionary Cuban government which took power January 1, 1959, established a socialist society that focused national priorities on the needs of the people instead of those of the multinational corporations" (quoted in CDCT, p. 48).

47. EP, pp. 27f. At the Women's Division conference on Theology in the Americas in Detroit in 1980, the rhetoric climaxed when Renee Pearson concluded: "My resolve is to bring back to middle-class, politically naïve people what I learned about the capitalist system and its exploitation of peoples and nations overseas" (United Methodist Communications Office, Oct. 11, 1980, p. 2). A stated goal of the conference was open exploration of "a creative socialist alternative in a faith context" (ibid.). BGM funds that same year also went to the National Film Institute of Nicaragua (INCINE) to make a film to "promote the revolution through programs of education

and documentation and analyze in depth the historical condition which oppressed the people" (Briefs, BGM, May 15, 1980). In the light of this it is hardly surprising to learn that when Cuba sent twelve Cuban teachers to Nicaragua to assist in a literacy campaign in 1980, their living expenses were in part funded by the World Division of the Board of Global Ministries (Briefs, BGM, May 15, 1980). Cuba, however, refused to allow any representatives from the U.S.A. to join the delegation.

48. EP, p. 27.

49. CSC, pp. 35ff.

50. Ibid.

51. "Response to Emerging Political Patterns," NCC, Commission on Regional and Local Ecumenism (CORLE), April 22, 1981.

52. Ibid., p. 2. Meanwhile outrageous caricatures continued to bubble up in the ecumenical cauldron from time to time. For example, in the Summer 1981 issue of *Common Ground,* a newsletter of the United Methodist Voluntary Service, Cuba was idealized in terms that few American Protestants could affirm: "Cuba represents a vision of the future shared by many poor and working people in the United States today" (p. 14). "As community activists from the United States, we share Cubans' faith in the future, although ours seems a long way off, at times" (p. 15).

53. CDCT, pp. 2ff.

54. Howard Schomer, "South Africa: Beyond Fair Employment," *Harvard Business Review,* May-June 1983, p. 154.

55. Ibid.

56. Ibid., p. 147. See excerpts from speeches at a "Symposium on Current Issues Facing American Corporations in South Africa," *ICCR Brief,* February 1982; "Economic Dislocation: Community or Chaos?," *ICCR Brief,* March 1982; "Apartheid's Bankers," *ICCR Brief,* April 1982.

57. *Time,* March 28, 1983, p. 58.

58. *United Methodist Reporter,* April 1983.

59. World Council of Churches, Program on the Churches and the Transnational Corporations, Resolution Approved by the Central Committee, August 1983.

60. Vancouver Assembly, Resolution on Justice and Human Dignity, August 1983.

61. Vancouver Assembly, Resolution on International Food Disorder, August 1983.

62. Vancouver Assembly, Resolution on the Pacific, August 1983.

63. "World Council of Churches Moves Left on World Economy," RD, August 1983.

64. PTF, CC-135: "The perception that the church is always negative or critical toward corporations was a prominent theme of task force discussion. Though sometimes exaggerated it is basically accurate and reveals a serious imbalance in the church's missional activity."

65. Ibid.

66. *Wall Street Journal,* Aug. 17, 1983.

67. CE, August/September 1983.

68. PTF, CC-155.

69. Ibid.

70. Ibid., CC-156.

71. Ibid.

72. Ibid.

CHAPTER FOUR

1. "The New International Economic Order: History and Perspectives," *ICCR Brief,* June 1980.

2. *Japan Christian Quarterly* 43 (Winter 1977), pp. 21-23.

3. CTI, pp. 72ff.

4. Ibid.

5. Ibid., p. 135.

6. Ibid., p. 137.

7. George H. Gallup, "What Mankind Thinks About Itself," *Reader's Digest,* October 1976, pp. 132ff.

8. Letter from Paul M. Neuhaus, ICCR attorney, to Securities and Exchange Commission, March 31, 1983; CTI, p. 63.

9. See the ICCR response to criticism in a *Fortune* article of June 16, 1980, in CTI, p. 72. Cf. BRE, pp. 3-20.

10. The most obvious case is the WCC's grants to guerrilla groups in southern Africa, but there apparently are many others that are harder to ferret out. It may be years before the full story is made public.

11. That truth-telling and care in public representation of one's case are presumed values of Christian social action hardly needs to be said. Critics of the CR movement argue that it has not always held itself to the same standards it rigorously applies to MNCs. For one example, see NV, pp. 34-37.

12. NV, p. 32.

13. LC, p. 188.

14. Gulf is not on the 1983 or 1984 ICCR lists of church proxy resolutions. (For the 1984 list, see appendix I). Cf. LC, pp. 110ff., 185ff.; and CICSA, pp. 87ff.

15. Herman Nickel, in BRE, pp. 9-10.

16. PTF, CC-138.

17. CE, December 1982, p. 5.

18. Ibid. Problems of agency authorization are to some degree dealt with in "Establishing a Committee on Financial Investments," ICF, pp. 53ff.

19. CE, December 1981, p. 1.

20. CE, July 1981, p. 4.

21. In *Fortune* magazine; see BRE, p. 15.

22. IRRC *News for Investors,* vol. X, no. 9, p. 1.

23. Letter from Paul M. Neuhaus, ICCR attorney, to Securities and Exchange Commission, March 31, 1983.

24. ICCR, *Church Proxy Resolutions, 1982,* Introduction.

25. Ibid.

26. Ibid.

27. See Smith's article in CTI, pp. 62ff. Smith predicted that we will continue to hear "the voice of the church" speaking through corporate-responsibility activities (p. 63).

28. Ibid., p. 76.

29. John Stuart Mill, *On Liberty* (Indianapolis: Bobbs-Merrill, 1956), pp. 43ff.

30. Happily, I was courteously received by most of the boards and agencies that I visited. Only in the Interfaith Center on Corporate Responsibility did staff members

attempt to find out in advance what political "point of view" I was writing from before releasing any information to me. I resisted the implication that the perceived orientation of my writing should be a determining factor in whether I had a right to receive information that was supposedly available to all church persons. I indicated that I could not draw any conclusions until I had first made the investigation, and that to do this I had to have the ICCR data. Moreover, as a scholar I would not enter into an agreement that curbed my ability to make fair and reasonable judgments. After some initial awkwardness the ICCR director did consent to provide me with full information, cordially and politely, and in fact was extremely helpful.

31. PTF, CC-134.

32. Ibid.

33. *Time,* March 28, 1983, p. 59.

34. Ibid. Cf. James A. Waters, "Of Saints, Sinners and Socially Responsible Executives," *Business and Society Review,* Winter 1980, pp. 67-73.

35. *Time,* March 28, 1983, p. 59.

36. Peter Riesenberg, "Profit and the Church: A Gradual Accommodation," *MBA* 11 (November 1977), pp. 46ff. See "Trade with Communist Countries of Eastern Europe," CSRA 1979-81, p. 22.

37. For examples of this rhetoric, see Richard Barnet and Ronald Mueller, *Global Reach: The Power of Multinational Corporations* (New York: Simon and Schuster, 1974); and "Do Cash Crops Benefit Third World Nations?," *ICCR Brief,* February 1977. For a different view see James V. Schall, "Religion and Development—A Minority View," *Worldview* 16 (July 1973), pp. 35-40.

38. For a critique of these assumptions, see Reinhold Niebuhr, *Moral Man and Immoral Society* (New York: Scribner, 1932), chaps. 2 and 3.

39. See Reinhold Niebuhr, *The Nature and Destiny of Man* (New York: Scribner, 1941), vol, I, pp. 83ff., 284; vol. II, p. 165.

40. Cf. "U.S. Bank Loans to Chile," *ICCR Brief,* December 1978, pp. 7-12; and Thomas Scheetz, "GM and Chile: A Case Study," *America,* Nov. 6, 1976, pp. 297-300.

41. Cf. *CCPD Documents* 6 (February 1975).

42. Cf. Gustavo Gutiérrez, "Notes for a Theology of Liberation," *Theological Studies* 31 (1970), pp. 243-61. One can almost hear the wheels whirring and the gears shifting in the mind of Philip Potter, general secretary of the World Council of Churches, when asked by CBS's Morley Safer whether he agreed with the statement (by Madame Adler) that "Marxist analysis should be used to examine Australian racism":

Safer: "But I should think the phrase 'Marxist analysis' would be anathema to anyone representing the World Council of Churches." *Dr. Potter:* "Miss Adler spoke for herself, but I would say that Marxist analysis—Marxist analysis of—of—of the causes of—of—of poverty and of oppression have—has been a very useful analysis; but Christians use that analysis on—with—very critically, in terms of our own faith" (transcript, CBS "60 Minutes," Jan. 23, 1983, p. 11).

43. See Francisco Catao, "An Alternative to TNCs," *CCPD Documents* 21 (1982), and Catao, "A 'New Society.' " TCCEM, chap. I.

44. "TNCs as Mechanism of Oppression: Building Countervailing Powers," TCCEM, chap. IV.

45. In 1977, the WCC's CCPD distributed a revealing statement by Jens Harms on "Bourgeois Idealism and Capitalistic Production" that concludes: "The equalization

of wages seems to me to be the most viable way of achieving greater justice in our economic system, even though large income differences between wage earners appears to be a basic element in the ideology of the bourgeois state. An unequal distribution of income concretizes social inequality and solidifies a person's status in society. A redistribution of income therefore means a complete change in the social structure" (p. 16, *CCPD Documents* 11, August 1977).

46. WCC, Nairobi Assembly, Statement on Transnational Corporations, 1975.

47. For Jens Harms, in an article distributed by the WCC: "The goal of sound economic management meant insisting on the fulfillment of the laws of commercial production which led inevitably to the alienation of the human being." The reader is directed to Karl Marx's *Das Kapital* for an explication of the laws of commercial production that are thought to be inevitably alienating ("Bourgeois Idealism and Capitalistic Production," p. 1, *CCPD Documents* 11, August 1977).

48. Richard S. Juma, "Ujamaa Development in Tanzania," CCPD Bossey Workshop, April 1973.

49. RD, May 1983, p. 4.

50. BRE, pp. 5-6.

51. Apostolic Constitutions, ANF, vol. 7, book VI, p. 434.

52. Mandates, sec. 27.5, *Apostolic Fathers,* ed. J. Sparks (New York: Thomas Nelson, 1978), p. 184.

53. Apostolic Constitutions, ANF, vol. 7, book VI, p. 435.

54. Ibid. ICCR thinks of its efforts as theologically mature. Writes T. H. Smith: "As churches motivated and informed by Roman Catholic or Protestant theology, ICCR's members spend much time reflecting theologically upon the actions of corporate America" (CTI, p. 60). Yet where is the evidence of all this theological reflection? It is extremely rare to find references to Scripture or classic Christian tradition anywhere in the ever-increasing Protestant anti-corporate literature.

55. The bibliography is enormous here, but one could note especially Clement, ANF, vol. 2; Augustine, *The City of God,* NPNF, 1st series, vol. 2; Chrysostom, NPNF, 1st series, vols. 9-14; Thomas Aquinas, *Summa Theologica,* 3 vols. (New York: Benziger, 1947-48), vol. 2, passim; John Calvin, *Theological Treatises,* Library of Christian Classics (Philadelphia: Westminster Press, 1958); Richard Baxter, *Practical Works,* 23 vols. (London: James Duncan, 1830), volumes on Christian economics; John Wesley, *Works,* 14 vols. (London: Wesleyan Conference Office, 1877), vols. 5-6.

56. CTI, pp. 81f.

57. Cf. my *Agenda for Theology* (San Francisco: Harper and Row, 1979), chaps. 1-2.

58. For a brilliant clarification of the political dynamics of this guilt, see P. T. Bauer, "Western Guilt and Third World Poverty," *Commentary,* January 1976 (reprinted as Essay 3, Washington: Ethics and Public Policy Center, 1977).

59. For a preliminary clarification of how guilt and antinomianism may collude, see my previous discussions of: *Radical Obedience* (Philadelphia: Westminster Press, 1967), conclusion; *The Structure of Awareness* (Nashville: Abingdon Press, 1969), part I; *Game Free* (New York: Harper and Row, 1974), chap. 3; and *TAG: The Transactional Awareness Game* (San Francisco: Harper and Row, 1977), chaps. 1-4.

60. This alliance I spelled out in a preliminary way in my book *Guilt Free* (Nashville: Abingdon Press, 1970), chap. 1.

61. SRI, p. 87.

62. For a widely read Protestant statement of this point, see Emil Brunner, *The Divine Imperative* (London: Lutterworth, 1937), pp. 198ff.

63. CTI, p. 67.

64. PTF, CC-127.

65. *ICCR Brief,* December 1982, p. 3B.

66. PTF, CC-127ff.

67. Ibid., CC-130.

68. CTI, p. 80.

69. T. H. Smith stated that "U.S. companies are a mirror of the racist South African society in almost every way" (Religious News Service, June 3, 1971, p. 2). According to the NCC's *Corporate Action Guide* (1973), "reform" can bring about only "cosmetic" changes, not substantive changes, which would have to address systemically the whole order of capitalistic economy.

70. PTFA, V11. For reflections on values assumed in participation in stockholders meetings, see ICF, pp. 38ff. Cf. "Priorities for Shareholder Action During the Biennium," CSRA 1977-79, chap. 3, and 1979-81, pp. 5ff.

71. PTFA, V11.

72. BRE, p. 52.

73. ICCR, *Church Proxy Resolutions, 1981.*

74. BRE, p. 9.

75. *United Methodist Reporter,* Nov. 18, 1983, p. 3.

76. *ICCR Brief,* April 1983, p. 3A. Cf. PTF, CC-126.

77. BRE, pp. 41f.

78. *ICCR Brief,* April 1983, p. 3C.

79. Ibid., p. 3A.

80. Ibid., p. 3B.

81. Ibid., p. 3A.

82. BRE, pp. 41f.

83. Letter from Paul Neuhaus, ICCR attorney, to Securities and Exchange Commission, March 31, 1983.

84. PTF, CC-126.

85. BRE, p. 43.

86. Conservation Foundation News Release, Oct. 19, 1983.

87. *ICCR Brief,* April 1983, p. 3A.

88. Cf. Patrick Kerans, *Sinful Social Structures* (New York: Paulist Press, 1974); Robert L. Heilbroner, ed., *In the Name of Profit* (Garden City, N.Y.: Doubleday, 1972).

89. CTI, p. 129.

Bibliography

The books, articles, and journals listed here are grouped under the sections of the book to which they are most pertinent, from the preface through chapter 4. Within these sections there are some broad topical divisions. A few titles appear more than once.

PREFACE

General perspectives on corporate social ethics:

Anshen, Melvin. *Corporate Strategies for Social Performance.* New York: Macmillan, 1980.

Bell, Daniel, et al. "Corporations and Conscience: The Issues." *Sloan Management Review* 13 (Fall 1971), pp. 1-24.

Chamberlain, Neil. *The Limits of Corporate Responsibility.* New York: Basic Books, 1973.

Jones, Donald G., ed. *Doing Ethics in Business.* Cambridge, Mass.: Oelgeschlager, Gunn, and Hain, 1982.

Powers, Charles W., and Vogel, David. *Ethics in the Education of Business Managers.* Hastings-on-Hudson, N.Y.: Institute of Society, Ethics, and the Life Sciences, 1980.

Sethi, Prakash, and Votaw, Dow. *The Corporate Dilemma.* Englewood Cliffs, N.J.: Prentice-Hall, 1973.

Stone, Christopher D. *Where the Law Ends: The Social Control of Corporate Behavior.* New York: Harper and Row, 1975.

The nature of corporate activity:

Barber, Richard J. *The American Corporation: Its Power, Its Money, Its Politics.* New York: E. P. Dutton, 1970.

Berle, Adolf A., Jr. *The Twentieth Century Capitalist Revolution.* New York: Harcourt, 1954.

Council on Economic Priorities. *Guide to Corporations: A Social Perspective.* Chicago: Swallow Press, 1974.

Drucker, Peter. *Concept of the Corporation.* New York: John Day, 1972.

151

The extent to which corporate power is capable of moral response:

Andrews, Kenneth R. "Can the Best Corporations Be Made Moral?" *Harvard Business Review*, May-June 1973, pp. 57-64.

Cohn, Jules. *The Conscience of the Corporations: Business and Urban Affairs, 1967-1970*. Baltimore: Johns Hopkins Press, 1971.

French, Peter A. "The Corporation as a Moral Person." *American Philosophical Quarterly* 16 (July 1979), pp. 207-15.

_____. "Institutional and Moral Obligations." *Journal of Philosophy* 74 (1977), pp. 575-87.

Manne, Henry G., and Wallich, Henry C. *The Modern Corporation and Social Responsibility*. Washington: American Enterprise Institute, 1972.

Moore, Wilbert E. *The Conduct of the Corporation*. New York: Random House, 1962.

Interpretations of corporate power that have been widely used by church advocacy groups:

Barnet, Richard, and Muller, Ronald. *Global Reach*. New York: Simon and Schuster, 1974.

Galbraith, John Kenneth. *The New Industrial State*. Boston: Houghton Mifflin, 1967.

_____. *Economics and the Public Purpose*. New York: New American Library, 1975.

Hunt, E. K. *Property and Prophets: The Evolution of Economic Institutions and Ideologies*. 2d ed. New York: Harper and Row, 1975.

Nader, Ralph; Green, Mark; and Seligman, Joel. *Taming the Giant Corporation*. New York: W. W. Norton, n.d.

Zeitlin, Maurice, ed. *American Society, Inc*. Chicago: Markham, 1970.

Background resources evaluating the moral assumptions of corporate life:

Acton, Harry Burrows. *The Ethics of Capitalism*. London: Foundation for Business Responsibilities, 1972.

Beauchamp, Tom L., and Bowie, Norman E., eds. *Ethical Theory and Business*. Englewood Cliffs, N.J.: Prentice-Hall, 1979.

DeGeorge, Richard. *Business Ethics*. New York: Macmillan, 1981.

_____, and Pichler, Joseph A., eds. *Ethics, Free Enterprise, and Public Policy: Original Essays on Moral Issues in Business*. New York: Oxford University Press, 1978.

Donaldson, Thomas. *Corporations and Morality.* Englewood Cliffs, N.J.: Prentice-Hall, 1982.

Heilbroner, Robert L., et al. *In the Name of Profit: Profiles in Corporate Responsibility.* Garden City, N.Y.: Doubleday, 1972.

Jacoby, Neil H. *Corporate Power and Responsibility.* New York: Macmillan, 1973.

Jones, Donald G., ed. *Doing Ethics in Business.* Cambridge, Mass.: Oelgeschlager, Gunn, and Hain, 1982.

Litschert, Robert J., et al. *The Corporate Role and Ethical Behavior: Concepts and Cases.* New York: Van Nostrand Reinhold, 1977.

Sethi, S. Prakash, ed. *Up Against the Corporate Wall: Modern Corporations and Social Issues of the Seventies.* 2d ed. Englewood Cliffs, N.J.: Prentice-Hall, 1973.

Velasquez, Manuel. *Business Ethics: Concepts and Cases.* Englewood Cliffs, N.J.: Prentice-Hall, 1981.

Walton, Clarence. *The Ethics of Corporate Conduct.* Englewood Cliffs, N.J.: Prentice-Hall, 1977.

Moral evaluations of corporations from a variety of religious viewpoints:

Armbruster, Wally. *It's Still Lion vs. Christian in the Corporate Arena.* St. Louis: Concordia, 1979.

Camara, Dom Helder. "Principalities and Corporations." *Worldview* 15 (March 1972), pp. 42-44.

Forell, George W., et al., eds. *Corporation Ethics: The Quest for Moral Authority.* Philadelphia: Fortress Press, 1980.

Murray, Robert B. "A Christian's View of the Marketplace." *America* 142 (May 31, 1980), pp. 460ff.

Vogel, David. *Lobbying the Corporation.* New York: Basic Books, 1978.

Williams, Oliver F., and Houck, John W. *Full Value: Cases in Christian Business Ethics.* New York: Harper and Row, 1978.

Wright, J. Patrick. *On a Clear Day You Can See General Motors.* Grosse Pointe, Mich.: Wright Enterprises, 1979.

INTRODUCTION

Analyses of the corporate-church encounter:

Schomer, Howard. "Little Church and Big Business: Confrontation or Consultation?" *Forum for Correspondence and Contact,* January 1979, pp. 50-56.

Silk, Leonard, and Vogel, David. *Ethics and Profits: The Crisis of Confidence in American Business*. New York: Simon and Schuster, 1976.

Vogel, David. *Lobbying the Corporation*. New York: Basic Books, 1978.

CHAPTER ONE

Church responses to multinational corporations, and a moral assessment of multinational corporations:

Craig, Eleanor, S.L. *A Shareowners' Manual: For Church Committees on Social Responsibility in Investments*. New York: Interfaith Center on Corporate Responsibility, 1977.

Ells, Richard. *Global Corporations: The Emerging System of World Economic Power*. New York: Interbook, 1972.

Owensby, Walter. "Corporate Accountability in a Global Context." *CCPD Documents* 21 (1982). Geneva: World Council of Churches, Commission on the Churches' Participation in Development.

Reuss, Carl F., ed. *Conscience and Action: Social Statements of the American Lutheran Churches*. Minneapolis: Augsburg, 1971.

Santa Ana, Julio de. "The TNCs from the Point of View of the Churches." *CCPD Documents* 21 (1982). Geneva: World Council of Churches, Commission on the Churches' Participation in Development.

Schomer, Howard. "The Church and the Transnational Corporation: How and Why the Churches Are Intervening in the Worldwide Business Affairs of American Corporations." *A.D.*, February 1975, pp. 15-25.

Sethi, Prakash. "Corporations and the Church," in Sethi, ed., *Up Against the Corporate Wall*. Rev. ed. Englewood Cliffs, N.J.: Prentice-Hall, 1977.

United Church of Christ. "Many Levels of Responsibility." In *Corporate Social Responsibility Actions, 1979-1981*. New York: United Church of Christ.

Vernon, Raymond. *Sovereignty at Bay: The Multinational Spread of U.S. Enterprises*. New York: Basic Books, 1971.

World Council of Churches. "Transnationality of Business and the Ecumenical Movement." In *Transnational Corporations, the Churches, and the Ecumenical Movement*, 1982.

Views from within the corporate-responsibility network:

Arruda, Marcos. "The WCC Programme on TNCs: Some Lessons and Challenges." *CCPD Documents* 21 (1982). Geneva: World Council of Churches, Commission on the Churches' Participation in Development.

Bennett, John C. "Capitalism and Ethics." *The Catholic Mind*, May 1967, pp. 42-51.

Buffalo, Audreen. "Christian Witness in the Board Room." *The Interpreter*, February 1980, pp. 5-8.

Exploitation or Liberation: Ethics for Investors. Minneapolis: Province of St. Paul–Minneapolis in conjunction with the National Federation of Priests Councils, 1973.

Powers, Charles W., ed. *Social Responsibility and Investments*. Nashville: Abingdon Press, 1971.

_____, ed. *People, Profits: The Ethics of Investment*. New York: Council on Religion and International Affairs, 1972.

Schomer, Howard. "Church Tolls Bells for Investors' Interests." *Directorship: The Forum for the Corporate Director* 3 (September 1978), pp. 5-6.

_____. "Church Investors and Corporate Governance." *Forum for Correspondence and Contact* 9 (July 1976), pp. 24-26.

Smith, Timothy H. "Churches vs. Corporations." *Business and Society Review* 15 (Fall 1975).

Williams, Oliver F., and Houck, John W., eds. *The Judeo-Christian Vision and the Modern Corporation*. Notre Dame, Ind.: University of Notre Dame Press, 1982.

CHAPTER TWO

Carter, Paul A. *The Decline and Revival of the Social Gospel, 1920-1940*. Ithaca, N.Y.: Cornell University Press, 1956.

Cavert, Samuel McCrea. *Church Cooperation and Unity in America: A Historical Review, 1900-1970*. New York: Association Press, 1970.

Darrow, R. Morton. "The Church and Techniques of Political Action." In James W. Smith and A. Leland Jamison, eds., *Religious Perspectives in American Life*, vol. 2. Princeton, N.J.: Princeton University Press, 1961.

Ebersole, Luke E. *Church Lobbying in the Nation's Capital*. New York: Macmillan, 1951.

Hopkins, Charles H. *The Rise of the Social Gospel in American Protestantism, 1865-1915*. New Haven, Conn.: Yale University Press, 1940.

Hutchinson, John A. *We Are Not Divided: A Critical and Historical Study of the Federal Council of the Churches of Christ in America*. New York: Round Table Press, 1941.

Key, V. O. *Politics, Parties, and Pressure Groups*. 5th ed. New York: Cromwell, 1964.

Meyer, Donald B. *The Protestant Search for Political Realism*, 1919-1940. New York: Doubleday.

Oldham, J. H., ed. *The Churches Survey Their Task*. London: Allen and Unwin, 1937.

Pew, J. Howard. *The Chairman's Final Report to the National Lay Committee*. New York: National Council of Churches, 1955.

Other discussions of this period of ecumenical policy formation:

Segundo, Juan Luis. "Has Latin America a Choice?" *America*, Feb. 22, 1969, pp. 213-16.

_____. "Social Justice and Revolution." *America*, April 27, 1968, pp. 574-78.

United Church of Christ. *Minutes of the Sixth General Synod*. 1967.

Further historical reviews of CR activism during this period:

ANC—*African National Congress (South Africa), and Namibia (South West Africa): The Struggle for Liberation*. Geneva: World Council of Churches, 1971.

"Companies Feel the Wrath of Clergy." *Business Week*, March 18, 1972.

Copock, R.; Dierkes, M.; Snowball, H.; and Thomas, J. *Social Pressure and Business Actions: An Empirical Study of Corporate Social Responsibility in the U.S., 1965-1971*. Seattle, Wash.: Battelle Seattle Research Center, November 1972.

Craig, Eleanor, S.L. "Issues and Actions—A Survey of Church-Related Shareowner Actions, 1972-1977." In *A Shareowners' Manual*. New York: Interfaith Center on Corporate Responsibility, 1977.

"Discovering Proxy Power." *Together*, July 1972.

Halsey, Peggy. "Corporate Responsibility, A Brief History of Women's Division Involvement." *Response*, April 1977.

Joint Strategy and Action Committee. "A New Area for Mission—Investment Policies." *Grapevine* 2 (February 1971).

Schomer, Howard. "The Church and the Transnational Corporation." *A.D.* vol. 4, no. 2 (1975).

Sethi, S. Prakash, ed. *Up Against the Corporate Wall*. Englewood Cliffs, N.J.: Prentice-Hall, 1971.

United Church of Christ, Committee on Financial Investments. *Investing Church Funds for Maximum Social Impact*. 1970.

United Church of Christ. *Minutes of the Eighth General Synod*. 1971.

United Methodist Church, Board of Missions, National Division. *Guidelines for the Subcommittee on Investments of the Committee on Finance*. 1971.

United Methodist Church, Board of Missions, World Division. *Proposed Program for Coordinating Social Consciousness Considerations with Investment and Proxy Voting Matters*. 1971.

White, Frank. "The Church and Corporate Responsibility—Three Tasks."In *Corporate Responsibility and Religious Institutions*. New York: Corporate Information Center, 1971.

A developing mode of ethical analysis of investments:

"Churches Mount First Joint Campaign Against U.S. Firms in Southern Africa." *Wall Street Journal*, Feb. 15, 1972.

Corporate Information Center. *Church Investment, Corporations, and Southern Africa*. New York: Friendship Press, 1973.

"Crow Indian Tribe Sues to Void Coal Contracts Let by U.S. in Montana." *Wall Street Journal*, September 23, 1975.

Crow Indians of Montana, Tribal Council. "Funding Proposal to Support Litigation." Submitted to Capuchin Fathers, June 24, 1975.

Franciscan Friars of the Atonement. "A Statement Concerning Individual and Corporate Social Awareness and Responsibility." 1973.

Gutiérrez, Gustavo. *A Theology of Liberation: History, Politics, and Salvation*. Maryknoll, N.Y.: Orbis Books, 1973.

Powers, Charles W. *Social Responsibility and Investments*. New York: Abingdon Press, 1972.

Sethi, S. Prakash. "The Corporation and the Church: Institutional Conflict and Social Responsibility." *California Management Review* 15 (Fall 1972).

Simon, John G.; Powers, Charles W.; and Gunneman, John P. *The Ethical Investor*. New Haven: Yale University Press, 1972.

United Church of Christ. *Minutes of the Ninth General Synod*. 1973.

United Church of Christ, Board for World Ministries. *The Social Impact of United Church of Christ Invested Funds, 1971-73*. 1973.

U.S. Catholic Conference. "The Economy: Human Dimensions." *Origins* 5 (1975), p. 389.

The South African question:

Biersteker, Henk. "A Multinational Company as Agent for Change in Southern Africa?" *Study Encounter*, vol. XI, no. 4 (1975). See also vol. 8, no. 1 (1972); vol. 10, no. 3 (1974).

Boesak, Allan A. *Farewell to Innocence; A Socio-Ethical Study on Black Theology and Power*. Maryknoll, N.Y.: Orbis Books, 1977.

Center for Social Action. *The Oil Conspiracy*. New York: United Church of Christ, 1976.

Christian Concern for South Africa, *Corporate Responsibility and the Institutional Investor.* London: CCSA, February 1974.

Colon, Dominique, and Dunn, Truman. *South Africa: Taking Stock of Divestment.* New York: American Committee on Africa, October 1979.

Commission on Faith and Order and the Program to Combat Racism. *Racism in Theology: Theology Against Racism.* Geneva: World Council of Churches, 1975.

Corporate Information Center. *Church Investments, Corporations, and Southern Africa.* New York: Friendship Press, 1973.

Corporate Information Center. "Gulf Oil: Portuguese Ally in Angola." *CIC Brief,* March 1972, updated December 1972. See also other *CIC Briefs* on African issues (published after 1973 by the Interfaith Church on Corporate Responsibility): June 1973, April 1974, April 1976, October 1976; and *The Corporate Examiner,* February 1975, May 1977, October 1977, May 1979, May 1980.

Jackson, Richard A., ed. *The Multinational Corporation and Social Policy: Special Reference to General Motors in South Africa.* New York: Praeger, 1974.

Norman, Edward. *Politicizing Christianity: Focus on South Africa.* Washington: Ethics and Public Policy Center, 1979. (Reprinted from *Christianity and the World Order,* New York: Oxford University Press, 1979.)

Powers, Charles W. "Ethics and IBM in South Africa." In *The Role of IBM in South Africa,* Transcript of a Hearing Sponsored by the National Council of Churches, November 20-21, 1974. New York: Interfaith Center for Corporate Responsibility, 1974.

Rogers, Barbara. *White Wealth and Black Poverty: American Investments in Southern Africa.* Westport, Conn.: Greenwood Press, 1976.

Sincere, Richard E., Jr. *The Politics of Sentiment: Churches and Foreign Investment in South Africa.* Washington: Ethics and Public Policy Center, 1984.

CHAPTER THREE

Boland, John C. "Saints and Sinners? Church-Sponsored Critics of Private Enterprise Gain a Following." *Barron's* 60 (May 5, 1980), pp. 11ff.

"Corporations and Human Economic Rights." *The Corporate Examiner,* October 1979.

Craig, Eleanor, S.L. "A Case Study: A Step by Step Review of Church Shareowner Activities with One Company, 1975-1977." In *A Shareowners' Manual.* New York: Interfaith Center on Corporate Responsibility, 1977.

Davies, C. "The Church vs. Multinationals." *Executive* 19 (October 1977), pp. 66-68.

Engler, Robert. *The Brotherhood of Oil*. Chicago: University of Chicago Press, 1977.

Gollin, James. "There's an Unholy Mess in the Churchly Economy." *Fortune*, May 1976, p. 222.

Haines, Aubrey B. "Buying Christian." *The Christian Century*, Sept. 21, 1977, pp. 804-5.

Kenkelin, Bill. "Apply Ethics from Inside, Says Sister." *National Catholic Reporter* 16 (Nov. 23, 1979), pp. 6ff.

McGovern, Arthur, S.J. *Marxism: An American Christian Perspective*. Maryknoll, N.Y.: Orbis Books, 1980.

Neal, Marie Augusta. *A Socio-Theology of Letting Go: The Role of a First World Church Facing Third World Peoples*. New York: Paulist Press, 1977.

Purcell, Theodore V., S.J. "Electing an 'Angel's Advocate' to the Board." *Management Review*, May 1976, pp. 4-11.

"Revolution by Proxy? The Church vs. the Corporation." *San Francisco Bay Guardian*, Feb. 17, 1977.

Segundo, Juan Luis. *The Liberation of Theology*. Maryknoll, N.Y.: Orbis Books, 1976.

Silk, L., and Vogel, D. *Ethics and Profits*. New York: Simon and Schuster, 1976.

"Study of the Impact of Foreign Economic Aid and Assistance on Respect for Human Rights in Chile." *The Corporate Examiner*, September 1979.

"Third World Perspective on the International Economic Order and the Role of Transnationals, A." *The Corporate Examiner*, January 1979.

United Church of Christ, Board for World Ministries, World Issues Office. *Church as Shareholder*. 1976-77.

United Methodist Church. *Journal of the General Conference*. 1976.

Reports on agribusiness issues of this period:

Berg, Alan. *The Nutrition Factor*. Washington: Brookings Institution, 1973.

Burbach, Roger, and Flynn, Patricia. *Agribusiness in the Americas*. Oakland, Calif.: North American Congress on Latin America, 1978.

Frundt, Henry J. *Gulf + Western in the Dominican Republic: An Evaluation*. New York: Interfaith Center on Corporate Responsibility, 1979.

Gulf + Western Industries, Inc. *Annual Reports, 1974-77*.

Gussow, Joan. *The Feeding Web: Reader on Nutrition Issues*. Palo Alto, Calif.: Bell Publishing Co., 1978.

Interfaith Center on Corporate Responsibility. "Agribusiness and the Food Crisis." *CIC Brief,* November 1974.

Ledogar, Robert J. *Hungry for Profits: U.S. Food and Drug Multinationals in Latin America.* New York: International Documentation on the Contemporary Church (IDOC), 1975.

Discussions of key proxy actions of the CR movement during this period:

"Church Proxy Resolutions in 1981." In *Church, State, and Corporation.* New York: Burson-Marsteller, 1982.

Heymann, Philippe. "Interviews of Business Leaders on Transnational Social Ethics." *CCPD Documents* 21 (1982). Geneva: World Council of Churches Commission on the Churches' Participation in Development.

Interfaith Center on Corporate Responsibility. *ICCR Briefs:* "Church Proxy Resolutions," January 1981; "The 'Code of Marketing for Breastmilk Substitutes' Is Born," September 1981; "Corporate Political Influence and Government Relations Practices," February 1981; "Corporate Responsibility Challenges," Spring 1981 and January 1982; "Excerpts from the 'Petition to Alleviate Domestic Infant Formula Misuse and Provide Informed Infant Feeding Choice,' " July 1981; "Food for All the Children: Profitability and Sustainability in the Food Supply," December 1981.

United Church of Christ. *Corporate Social Responsibility Actions,* 1979-81, 1981-83. "Shareholder Activities in 1981," 1979-81, p. 12. "Other Shareholder Activities," 1981-83, p. 15. "Overview of Social Responsibility in Investment," 1981-83, p. 22.

World Council of Churches. "Power, Accountability, and Social Responsibility" and "Unemployment, Technology, and Organized Labour." In *Transnational Corporations, the Churches, and the Ecumenical Movement.* 1982.

CHAPTER FOUR

Adams, Gordon, and Rosenthal, Sherri Zann. *The Invisible Hand: Questionable Corporate Payments Overseas.* New York: Council on Economic Priorities, 1976.

Best, Michael, and Connolly, William E. *The Politicized Economy.* Lexington, Mass.: Heath, 1976.

Bruyn, Severyn T., et al. *An Ethical Primer on the Multinational Corporation.* New York: International Documentation on the Contemporary Church (IDOC), 1973.

Bruyn, Severyn T.; Farramelli, Norman; and Yates, Dennis A. "An Ethical Primer on the Multinational Corporation." *IDOC/North America* 56 (October 1973).

Drotning, Philip T. "Why Nobody Takes Corporate Social Responsibility Seriously." *Business and Society Review,* Autumn 1972.

Drucker, Peter. "The Future of the Corporation." *Harper's* Magazine, November 1942.

Fuoss, Robert. "Churches Versus Corporations: The Coming Struggle for Power." *A.D.,* February 1973.

Gall, Norman. "When Capitalism and Christianity Clash." *Forbes* 126 (Sept. 1, 1980).

Harrington, Michael. *Socialism.* New York: Simon and Schuster, 1970.

_____. *The Twilight of Capitalism.* New York: Simon and Schuster, 1972.

Hayek, Friedrich. *The Constitution of Liberty.* Chicago: University of Chicago Press, 1972.

_____. *Law, Legislation, and Liberty: A New Statement of the Principles of Justice and Political Economy.* Chicago: University of Chicago Press, 1973-1976.

Hunt, E. K. *Property and Prophets: The Evolution of Economic Institutions and Ideologies.* 2d ed. New York: Harper and Row, 1975.

Interfaith Center on Corporate Responsibility. "Armageddon Inc.: The Manufacturers of the U.S. Nuclear Arsenal. *ICCR Brief,* April 1978.

_____. "Does Military Spending Create Jobs?" *ICCR Brief,* July 1977.

_____. "The Economic Possibilities of Peace." *ICCR Brief,* July 1978.

McGovern, Arthur F. "Should a Christian Be a Marxist?" *Proceedings of the American Catholic Philosophical Association* 51 (1977).

Schomer, Howard. "The Church and the Transnational Corporation." *A.D.,* February 1975.

Steckmest, Francis, et al. *Corporate Performance: The Key to Public Trust.* New York: McGraw-Hill, 1982.

Vernon, R. *Storm Over the Multinationals: The Real Issues.* Cambridge, Mass.: Harvard University Press, 1977.

Discussions of the way the Judeo-Christian tradition may impinge upon current interpretations of corporate responsibility:

Hengel, Martin. *Property and Riches in the Early Church: Aspects of a Social History of Early Christianity.* Philadelphia: Fortress Press, 1974.

Hollenbach, David, S.J. "Corporate Investments, Ethics, and Evangelical

Poverty: A Challenge to American Religious Orders." *Theological Studies* 34 (1973), pp. 265-74.

McDonald, William J. *The Social Value of Property According to St. Thomas Aquinas: A Study in Social Philosophy.* Catholic University of America Philosophical Studies, vol. XLVIII. Washington: Catholic University of America Press, 1939.

Novak, Michael. *Toward a Theology of the Corporation.* Washington: American Enterprise Institute, 1981.

Preliminary attempts to review the theological issues surrounding corporate responsibility and similar initiatives:

Craig, Eleanor, S.L. "Response of Church Shareowners—A Review of the Theological Arguments and Shareowner Actions of Church-Related Institutions." In *A Shareowners' Manual.* New York: Interfaith Center on Corporate Responsibility, 1977.

Lefever, Ernest W. *Amsterdam to Nairobi: The World Council of Churches and the Third World.* Washington: Ethics and Public Policy Center, 1979.

Norman, Edward. *Christianity and the World Order.* New York: Oxford University Press, 1979.

Novak, Michael. "Liberation Theology and the Pope." *Commentary* vol. 67, no. 6 (June 1979). Also in Quentin L. Quade, ed., *The Pope and Revolution.* Washington: Ethics and Public Policy Center, 1982.

————. "The Politics of John Paul II." *Commentary* vol. 68, no. 6 (December 1979).

Stackhouse, Max L. "Theological and Ethical Considerations for Business Decision-Making." *New Catholic World* 223 (November-December 1980).

Stringfellow, William. "Justification, the Consumption Ethic, and Vocational Poverty." *Christianity and Crisis* 80 (April 12, 1976).

Stott, John R. W. "Economic Equality Among Nations: A Christian Concern?" *Christianity Today,* May 2, 1980.

Index of Names

CENTER ESSAYS

Essays are $2 each unless otherwise marked. Postpaid if payment accompanies order. Order of $25 or more, 10 per cent discount.

DATE DUE

			Printed in USA

HIGHSMITH #45230